Coordination
Madeleine Choquette-Delvaux

Editor
Charis Wahl

Production
Donald Matheson
James MacLeod

Design
Jacques Charette and Associates Ltd

Typesetting
Nancy Poirier Typesetting

Printing
Metropole Litho Inc.

Military Uniforms in Canada
1665-1970

Jack L. Summers
René Chartrand

Illustrated by R.J. Marrion

Canadian War Museum
Historical Publication No. 16

National Museum of Man
National Museums of Canada

©National Museums of Canada 1981
National Museum of Man
National Museums of Canada
Ottawa, Canada K1A 0M8

Catalogue No. NM95-16/16E
Printed in Canada
ISBN 0-660-10346-X

Édition française
L'uniforme militaire au Canada   1665-1970
ISBN 0-660-90260-5

For information on previous titles
in the Canadian War Museum Historical
Publications Series and on other works of
military history write to: Publishing
Division, National Museums of Canada,
Ottawa, Ontario, Canada K1A 0M8.

Table of Contents

Foreword

I am greatly honoured to have been given the opportunity to contribute the foreword to this magnificent volume, and delighted that the research of my friend Jack Summers and René Chartrand is being presented as part of the centennial of the Canadian War Museum.

The text, together with the illustrations by Robert Marrion, makes available to us new facts about forty uniforms and the units in Canada that wore them. Whether they were British, French or Canadian, these units contributed greatly to the development of our country and have left their mark upon it. I was particularly pleased to find among the uniforms selected that of the Royal 22^e Regiment, of which I was a part.

No doubt this book will spark in many readers an interest in Canada's rich military heritage. For without the efforts of the armed forces, which defended her at critical moments in her history, Canada would not have been able so vigorously to assert her nationhood.

General J. A. Dextraze, CC, CBE, CMM, DSO, CD, LL.D.

Editor's Note

It would not be appropriate to express in the metric system all the measures that appear in this book. Specific lengths of material, braid, etc., set out in historical descriptions, should remain in the system of measurement in which they were originally established. Similarly, it was considered unwise to convert descriptions of calibre and length of firearms from original measures to their metric equivalents.

The reader may wish to note that the French foot (*pied*), in use before the Conquest, was equal to 32.48 cm, while the British foot is 30.48 cm in length.

Preface

Although Canadians are not a war-like people, our entire history has been marked by armed conflict. Force was required to maintain the existence of the original colony of New France. Subsequently, the country became a peripheral battleground of the French and English wars of the eighteenth century as soldiers trained for European warfare battled not only the enemy, but the demanding climate and topography of the Canadian wilderness. Canada has remained a separate political entity on this continent because on two occasions she was defended by her inhabitants and British regulars from American invasion. In later years Canadian soldiers served abroad in four major overseas conflicts and, in the process, carried the country into nationhood.

The aim of this volume is to depict the dress of some of the soldiers who played a significant role in Canada's development during the past three hundred years. They were French, British, and Canadians; and all made their contribution to the character of this country. Some were regular soldiers, and some were volunteers, the citizens who for so many years made up Canada's meagre defence force.

The book evolved from a research project, commissioned by the Canadian War Museum to determine the dress of some of Canada's soldiers. The project was not to be a definitive study of Canadian uniform, but an examination of select units highlighting examples of dress that were typical of a particular period, or unusual, or characteristically Canadian. Few will agree completely with the choice of units, for many distinguished regiments and corps have been omitted. Few should disagree that it would take many more volumes to give a complete account of military uniforms worn in Canada.

Particular mention must be made of Robert J. Marrion, the artist, whose talent was matched only by his tolerance. Working between Saskatoon, Ottawa, and London, England, was an outstanding feat in communication; and no authors could expect more from their illustrator.

So many persons were helpful in the preparation of this book that it is quite impossible to mention them all by name. Helpful suggestions on uniforms were given by W.Y. Carman, the leading authority on the dress of the British army, by Colonel Dugué MacCarthy of the Musée de l'Armée in Paris and by Eugène Lelièpvre, official artist of the French Army. George F.G. Stanley's sound advice reflected his eminent knowledge of Canada's military history. David Ross, Director of the New Brunswick Museum, provided outstanding research material from his work on Canadian Dress Regulations.

Special thanks are due the curators of Canada's military museums. Lieutenant-Colonel Lucien Turcotte, Major Wynne van der Schee, and Captains Vern Cole, Ray Britton and John Chown, in particular, were the recipients of a steady stream of enquiries over a ten-year period. Invaluable assistance was given by the Public Archives of Canada, the Historic Parks and Sites Branch of Parks Canada, and the libraries of the Department of National Defence, the Canadian War Museum, the Department of Indian and Northern Affairs, and the Ministère de la Défense in Paris.

We would also like to acknowledge the tangible encouragement of President R.W. Begg of the University of Saskatchewan, in the form of a grant from the President's Humanities and Social Sciences Fund.

The late John Swettenham, assisted by Fred Gaffen, of the Canadian War Museum, and Charis Wahl provided editorial expertise. Madeleine Choquette-Delvaux of the National Museums of Canada supervised the publishing process. We are grateful to Mary Le Blanc and Diane Ouellette for typing and retyping the text.

To our families, thank you for your tolerance, particularly during those periods when we were not fit company for other humans. You suffered our strange moods and work habits with better grace than we had any right to expect.

The Authors

History

After a fifty-year struggle for survival against the elements and the Indians, New France attracted the personal interest of Louis XIV, and what had been a commercial venture became a royal colony in 1663. The young king was advised that the relentless attacks of the Iroquois prevented the expansion of his colony, which needed substantial military assistance to counter these fierce Indian warriors. The energetic Marquis de Tracy was appointed the king's Lieutenant-General for America. He landed in Canada during the summer of 1665 with four companies of French regulars from the West Indies and twenty companies of the régiment de Carignan-Salières. The first regular regiment to serve in Canada had arrived.[1]

The régiment de Carignan-Salières was created by amalgamating two older units. The first, an infantry regiment commanded by and named after Johan de Balthasar, a German officer brought to France by the Marquis de Salières, fought in Italy in 1636.[2] When Salières subsequently took command, the unit was renamed the régiment de Salières. The second unit, the régiment de Carignan, was raised in 1644 by Thomas François of Savoy, Prince of Carignan. He was mortally wounded at the siege of Pavia in 1656, and command of the regiment passed to his son and heir, Emmanuel-Philibert-Amédée of Savoy.[3] In January 1659, the Carignan and Salières regiments were combined to form a single unit of fifteen companies named the régiment de Carignan, commanded by Sieur de Salières.[4] By 1665 the regiment had dwindled to eight companies, but drafts from other units brought the strength of the regiment (by this time titled the Carignan-Salières) to the twenty companies that set out for Canada.[5]

The troops were put to work without delay constructing a chain of forts along the Richelieu River, the natural highway of the Iroquois.[6] Courcelle, who was named Governor of New France in 1665, was not content to wait until the following summer, and launched a winter expedition against the Mohawks, a tribe of the Iroquois nation. A force of 300 regulars and 200 Canadien militia set out in January 1666 to invade Iroquois territory. The French were unable to engage the Indians in a full-scale battle and, after destroying some villages and grain stores, they returned in March, having lost 100 men to cold and disease.

In September 1666, de Tracy led a force of 1,200 men – half regulars and half militiamen – against the Mohawks in the Lake Champlain region. Again the Indians avoided pitched battle. The French destroyed some abandoned villages and returned to their base before the onset of winter.[7]

Though not defeated, the Iroquois were sufficiently impressed by the strength and determination of the French to negotiate a truce, which lasted for almost twenty years and ended the immediate threat to the survival of Canada as a French colony. The régiment de Carignan-Salières had achieved its purpose in New France. Four companies of the regiment returned to France with de Tracy in 1667, and by 1668 only four companies remained to garrison the newly established forts along the Richelieu.[8]

Soldiers were offered every inducement to take up land in the colony, and some 400 officers and men took their discharge in Canada.[9] The names of many seigneuries granted to the officers have come down to the present day: Berthier, Sorel, Verchères, and others. The settlers of the régiment de Carignan-Salières provided a corps of trained soldiers that was to stand the new colony in good stead in the turbulent years ahead.

1665-1668

Uniform

The Carignan-Salières was not only the first regiment of regulars to serve in Canada, but also one of the first line regiments of the French army to be dressed in uniform. At the time, French regulations required only that the soldier be well clothed and shod. Only the arms and accoutrements of the soldier distinguished him from a civilian.

The basic item of the soldier's dress was his coat. That of the régiment de Carignan-Salières was of serviceable chestnut brown frieze lined with coarse white and/or grey cloth. The coat was long and collarless, with pocket flaps set low on the hip on each side. Its full skirt reached to just above the knee. The sleeves ended about mid-forearm, and turned back into broad grey and/or white cuffs, which could be turned down to protect the wrists and hands in inclement weather.

Brown cloth-covered buttons ran the full length of the coat. The sleeve buttons were grey or white. The only embellishment of this sombre garment was loops of buff and black ribbon gathered on the point of the shoulders.

The regiment wore a low-crowned black felt hat with a plain wide brim, similar to the hat worn by the French peasants of the period. The brim was turned up in the front, and sometimes also in the back. A black and buff ribbon was worn around the base of the crown; a knot at each end was allowed to fall over the edge of the brim. Originally this ribbon served the practical purpose of adjusting the hat to the soldier's head size.

A long-sleeved vest or waistcoat was worn under the coat or as an outer garment in various orders of undress and in fighting order during hot weather.

Breeches were of brown material similar to that of the coat. Stockings were of brown serge, and were frequently cut from fabric and sewn together rather than knitted, as they would be today. They were held in place by garters fastened just below the knee, where the breeches overlapped the stockings. Garters ended in loops of black and buff ribbons, similar to those on the coat.

A white neckcloth and a white shirt with the cuffs showing beyond the edge of the coat sleeves completed the soldier's dress. The square-toed shoes of the period were not designed for left or right feet. Both shoes of a pair were made to the same pattern, and soldiers were encouraged to switch them frequently from one foot to the other so they would wear evenly. Clothing shipments for the Carignan-Salières included *aiguillettes* for shoes, which were probably woven cords used as laces.[1]

Drummers of line regiments were dressed in coats of the colonel's livery; the Prince of Carignan's livery was a red coat lined with blue and decorated with white and blue livery lace.[2] The tall wooden drums were painted red and emblazoned with the colonel's arms, a white cross on a red shield.[3]

Although it was difficult to get officers of the French army to dress in any uniform fashion at this time, those of the régiment de Carignan-Salières wore a uniform similar to that of the men. Officers' garments were made of finer material, and some individual touches of style were permitted. Some officers wore coats with silver buttons and buttonholes trimmed with silver thread; others wore grey hats rather than black. Officers' swords had silver hilts and grips, and their sword-belts were white with a silk fringe.[4] The illustration depicts a junior officer in his regimentals. The grey hat is a departure from the prescribed dress of the soldiers.

This fine regiment was neither trained nor equipped for North American warfare. We have no records of the clothing worn by the Carignan-Salières regulars during the winter campaign of 1666, but the basic uniform would have been quite inadequate for winter conditions. A hooded *capot* or overcoat was worn by the Canadien militiamen,[5] and it is highly probable that the regular soldiers adopted it, as well as mitts, moccasins, tuques, leggings, and other local items of winter dress.

The soldiers' equipment consisted of a natural leather crossbelt supporting a short sword and plug bayonet. A strap over the left shoulder was attached to a ball bag and brass powderhorn hanging on the right side.

Regiments on European service had a number of pikemen in each company, but it is generally accepted that all soldiers of the Carignan-Salières in New France carried muskets. Some 200 flintlock muskets were sent out for use by the regiment; the other regulars probably used the matchlock musket common in European armies of the period.[6]

History

Frontenac succeeded Courcelle as Governor of New France in 1672. When Joseph-Antoine Le Febvre de La Barre took over the position in 1682, the new Governor found the colony on the brink of war with the Iroquois, but without military resources. In response to La Barre's urgent request for troops, the Ministry of the Navy, which was responsible for the administration of France's North American colonies, was assigned the task of raising a force for service in Canada. Three companies of "Navy Troops" (*Troupes de la marine*), comprising some 156 all ranks, were recruited in France and transported to Quebec in 1683.[1] By 1684, the hastily raised force had been transformed into a permanent body of colonial regulars with a separate establishment of its own, independent of both regular army units and the companies on the naval establishment based in France for seaport protection.[2]

The troops' strength continued to grow during the following years.[3] Between 1689 and 1750, the garrison of Canada consisted of twenty-eight companies of colonial regulars known as the *Companies franches de la marine* (Independent Companies of the Navy). This number was increased to thirty in 1750, and raised again in 1757 to some forty companies. As their title suggests, the colonial regulars consisted of a number of independent companies with a variable establishment. By 1757, a company was ordered to consist of one captain, one lieutenant, two ensigns, three sergeants, four corporals, two cadets, two drummers, and fifty-four soldiers.[4] In fact, the companies were chronically under strength, and Governor Vaudreuil's complaint in 1757 that the colonials were 250 men short was all too typical.

Some of the companies were formed into a battalion in 1757 for service with Montcalm's regular army battalions.[5] Twenty-four companies of colonial regulars were stationed at Louisbourg during the 1750s, although Louisbourg was not then considered part of New France, but a separate colony of "Isle Royale" with its own establishment.[6]

The assignments of colonial regulars varied greatly. Some were posted to garrison the major fortified cities of Quebec and Montreal, while others were subdivided into garrisons for the small fortified outposts guarding the frontiers and supply routes. Small detachments were sent to protect the advance trading posts, which supplied the profitable fur trade of New France.[7]

Officers from the *Compagnies franches de la marine* were selected to organize and command war-parties of Canadien militia and their unpredictable Indian allies, for swift raids across the New England borders. These war-parties usually included at least one company of colonial regulars to provide a dependable, disciplined nucleus for the improvised units.

Away from the endless ceremonial duties and formalized tactical manoeuvres of European armies, the colonial regulars were somewhat lax in matters of drill and dress. But if their deportment and discipline were more casual than those of the line regiments, their skill in moving and fighting over the rugged Canadian terrain was far superior to that of the regular army units. They became experienced bush fighters and a match for the Indians in their own hit-and-run style of fighting.[8]

The *Compagnies franches de la marine* provided regular infantry troop support for the colony until line infantry regiments of the French army (*Troupes de terre*) arrived in 1755. The colonial regulars formed the backbone of the French push down the Ohio valley, which began in 1752 to limit the westward expansion of the New England colonies. In July 1755, the operation culminated in the defeat of Major-General Edward Braddock's column of British regulars on the Monongahela River by a mixed force of colonial regulars, militiamen, and Indians.[9]

During periods of relative peace the soldiers received additional pay for constructing forts and roads. Because of a chronic labour shortage, the regulars were also permitted to augment their meagre pay by working on local farms. As a result, the regular troops became closely identified with the colony.[10]

As the years passed, the *Compagnies franches de la marine* assumed a distinctly Canadien character. The colonial force offered little opportunity for promotion beyond the rank of captain and thus was not particularly attractive to the French career officer. However, it did offer an opportunity for members of prominent Canadien families to enter the service, and an increasing number of officer vacancies were filled locally. To accommodate the demand for these popular appointments, a number of officer cadet positions were created, which were occupied by Canadiens.[11]

The other ranks were recruited in France, and were expected to remain in the colonies when discharged. The enlistment of Canadiens was discouraged because it reduced the work-force available for the essential farming industry.[12]

Although only the officers were native born, the *Compagnies franches de la marine* were the first truly Canadian regular soldiers, and can be considered the forerunners of the Canadian Permanent Force.

Uniform

Clothing and equipment for the troops of New France were purchased in France and shipped out to Canada. Some of the clothing contracts and bills of lading have been preserved and provide considerable detailed information about the dress of colonial regulars. They also provide insight into the inevitable changes in details of dress and equipment that the *Compagnies franches de la marine* underwent during their seventy-five-year history.

In the 1750s, the private soldier was issued a long collarless single-breasted coat or *justaucorps* of greyish white, with lining and deep cuffs of blue. Pockets with horizontal flaps were set low on the hips, and the skirt corners could be hooked back to facilitate movement. The long-sleeved waistcoat, breeches, and stockings were blue.

A black felt tricorn, decorated with a cockade and button, was worn very low over the eyes; its brim was edged with false-gold lace. The buckled shoes were black. Gaiters of white duck, reaching just to the thigh, were fastened below the knee with a black strap. A white cravat and shirt completed the soldier's dress.

Corporals wore a yellow stripe of woollen lace around the top of the coat cuffs. Sergeants' uniforms were of similar pattern, but of better quality material; an inch-wide stripe of gold lace edged the cuffs and pocket flaps. Sergeant-majors wore two gold lace stripes on the cuffs and pocket flaps.[1]

Drummers wore the King's small livery. The blue coat had brass buttons and red cuffs and lining. It was heavily ornamented along the seams and buttonholes with the King's livery lace – white chain on a crimson ground. Waistcoat, breeches, and stockings were red. Otherwise the uniform was similar to that of the private soldier. The drummers' buff sword-belts and drum slings were bordered with livery lace. The blue drum shells were sprinkled with *fleurs-de-lis*.

Drum majors wore the King's great livery, which differed from that of the drummers only in the red triangles on white ground that appeared between the strips of livery lace.[2]

Officers' uniforms were of the same pattern and colour as those of the men, but of better quality cloth. The waistcoat was frequently embellished with gold lace, but the coat was left unadorned. Buttons were gilt, and hats were braided with fine gold lace. Officers wore a gilt gorget on duty, and were armed with a gilt-hilted sword and an espontoon, which was exchanged for a fusil when in the field.[3]

Cadets served in the ranks and wore the same uniform as the men; they were distinguished only by an *aiguillette* of blue and white silk with brass tips.[4]

A buff leather waist-belt with brass buckles was attached to a double frog holding brown leather, brass-tipped scabbards for sword and bayonet. The brass-hilted sword had a straight blade. A red-brown leather cartridge-box was attached to the waist-belt; later, it was suspended on the right hip from a buff leather cross-belt. As descriptions of several patterns of cartridge-box have been found, one can assume that this item went through a number of variations. The standard French *cartouchière* of the mid-eighteenth century held thirty musket cartridges. The older cartridge pouch held only nine cartridges, and the flap was engraved with the King's arms or a white anchor and border. A small brass-mounted powder-horn completed the equipment.[5]

On campaign or when stationed in western outposts, the colonial regulars adopted a casual, serviceable dress modelled on that of the woodsmen: buckskin or cloth leggings, moccasins, and breeches of Indian design. In some cases, soldiers dressed entirely in the Indian fashion.[6]

For winter dress, the Canadian hooded *capot*, woollen tuque and leggings, moccasins, and mittens were issued. The men moved across the deep drifts of the countryside on snowshoes.[7]

While the precise designs of the muskets carried by the *Compagnies franches de la marine* have not survived, it is known that all were of the flintlock type, although many soldiers in Europe were still armed with matchlock muskets as late as the 1690s. As the colonial regulars were the responsibility of the navy, they carried navy-model muskets made at Tulle. In the 1740s, the navy began to purchase muskets from St-Etienne that probably resembled the army's 1728 model. By 1752, the royal magazines at Montreal and Quebec housed a considerable variety of muskets and bayonets. The French steel-mounted .69-calibre musket was somewhat lighter than the British "Brown Bess."[8]

The soldier of the *Compagnies franches de la marine* in the illustration is dressed for a summer campaign. He has discarded his heavy grey-white *justaucorps*, and wears his long-sleeved blue waistcoat as an outer garment. His buckskin *mitasses* (Indian leggings) and moccasins are better suited to the rough conditions than are shoes and white gaiters; the hatchet in his frog is much handier than a brass-hilted sword. A cloth fatigue cap has replaced the cocked hat.

1755-1760
History

Late in 1754, Britain dispatched two battalions of regulars, under the command of Major-General Edward Braddock, to North America. When news of the British plans reached Paris, six battalions of French line infantry were ordered to proceed to New France to counter the British move. The battalions were from the regiments of Artois, Bourgogne, Béarn, Guyenne, La Reine, and Languedoc.[1]

The French troops sailed for Canada early in May 1755, accompanied by their commander, Baron Dieskau, and the Marquis de Vaudreuil, who was to replace the ailing Duquesne as Governor of New France. During the voyage, eight companies of regulars were lost when the vessels *Alcide* and *Lys* were captured by the British and four companies of both the Languedoc and La Reine battalions were taken prisoner. The Artois and Bourgogne regiments disembarked at the fortress of Louisbourg, and the remaining four battalions proceeded to Quebec.[2]

A full-strength French regular battalion of the period numbered thirty-one officers and 525 soldiers, divided into one grenadier and twelve fusilier companies. As the four companies lost to the Royal Navy were not replaced until late 1757, the régiment de Languedoc began its service in Canada badly under strength.[3]

By the time Dieskau and his regulars had recovered from the voyage, Braddock's British regiments had been shattered on the Monongahela River. Warned that a force of provincials under Sir William Johnson was advancing to sieze Crown Point, Dieskau assembled his regulars, militia, and Indians, and raced down Lake Champlain. Leaving most of his force at Ticonderoga, Dieskau moved south on Lake George with 1,500 men, including four companies of regulars, two from both the Languedoc and La Reine regiments, to find Sir William Johnson.

Johnson had established a fortified base 22 km (14 mi.) south of Lake George; he then cut a road north through the forest and camped with the bulk of his force where the road ended at the lake-shore. Moving overland, Dieskau's small force cut the road between the fortified base and the lake-side camp, and planned to attack the base. When a British force of about 1,000 provincials was sighted moving down the road from the advance camp to the base, Dieskau stationed his four companies of regulars on the road, and sent the Canadiens and Indians forward on the flanks. Johnson's provincials walked into the trap: fire caught them from both sides and a steady line of French regulars drove at them from the front. The provincials initially panicked, but recovered and fought a respectable withdrawal to the lake-side camp, which had been barricaded as well as it could be with boats, wagons, and fallen trees. This brisk encounter came to be known as "The Bloody Morning Scout."

That same afternoon, Dieskau's force stormed Johnson's hastily fortified camp, and for four hours the Battle of Lake George raged across the frail barricade of boats. A steady advance against a prepared position supported by guns was neither the Canadiens' nor the Indians' idea of fighting a war, and the brunt of this heavy fighting fell upon the companies of the Languedoc and La Reine. The barricade held; and the battered French regulars withdrew, leaving behind about half their number, including the badly wounded Baron Dieskau.[4] This confused little battle among the lakes and forests was the regiment's first action in North America, the beginning of six years of continuous campaigning for the men of Languedoc.

The Marquis de Montcalm arrived early in the summer of 1756 to replace the unfortunate Dieskau. Under the leadership of this able commander the régiment de Languedoc took part in the capture of Fort William Henry in 1757, and in the successful defence of Ticonderoga in 1758.[5]

When Montcalm drew up his army on the Plains of Abraham to face Wolfe's regulars on 13 September 1759, the Languedoc battalion stood third from the right in the French line of battle. The regiment also formed part of the French force that returned to Quebec in the spring of 1760 to defeat the British at the Battle of Sainte-Foy. The arrival of the British fleet broke the siege of Quebec, and Lévis withdrew his troops to Montreal to carry on the unequal struggle. On September 8, the French capitulated; six days later, the Languedoc battalion embarked for France.[6]

1755-1760

Uniform

The adoption of a uniform dress by French infantry regiments of the line was a gradual process. It began around 1670, and colonels were given great latitude in selecting colours and patterns of clothing and equipment.

The first known general order on dress for French infantry appeared on 10 March 1729. Its primary purpose was to reduce expenses by standardizing the pattern and quality of equipment. The instructions were very general and left most details to the discretion of the colonels.[1] The basic grey-white cloth adopted by most regiments (probably because it was less costly than coloured material) remained the traditional colour for French infantry uniforms until the Revolution.

In 1755, soldiers of the French line infantry wore a greyish-white woollen *justaucorps* of military pattern. This long single-breasted garment fell to just above the knee. The back was split by a centre vent, which enabled the front and back corners of each skirt to be fastened up, thereby providing greater freedom of movement. The small collar could be worn either up or down, depending on the weather and the whim of the commanding officer. The sleeves ended in deep turn-back cuffs. Pocket flaps were set on the point of the hip.

Individual regiments were identified by the colour of the collar, cuffs, and waistcoat, the shape of the pocket flaps, the colour of buttons and hat braid, and the arrangement of buttons on the pocket flaps and coat cuffs.

Greyish-white woollen breeches, buckled below the knee, were worn with grey or white stockings and black leather shoes with metal buckles. White linen gaiters, worn on parade or with campaign dress, ended an inch or two above the knee, and were fastened below the knee by a black strap.

A mid-thigh-length, collarless waistcoat or *veste* with long sleeves was worn under the frock-coat or as an outer garment for drills, fatigues, undress order, and when on campaign in warm weather. Its colour varied according to the unit. The black felt tricorn was cocked high in front, and worn well down on the brow. It was ornamented with a black or white ribbon cockade, and edged with gold or silver lace. A black neckcloth and white collarless shirt completed the soldier's dress.

The dress distinctions of the régiment de Languedoc on European service were blue collar, cuffs, and waistcoat, brass buttons, and false-gold hat lace. The *justaucorps* had deep shield-shaped pocket flaps with a row of three buttons set along the front and back vertical edges of the flap. Four buttons were set along the edge of the coat cuffs.[2]

When the first six battalions of French regular infantry were posted to Canada in 1755, a special issue of clothing conforming to Ministry of the Navy specifications was made up in France, shipped to Canada, and issued to the troops when they arrived.[3]

The clothing differed slightly from the standard pattern. The Canadian-issue *justaucorps* was collarless, and the distinctive colour of cuffs, waistcoat, buttons, and hat lace for some regiments differed from that prescribed by army regulations. In the case of the Languedoc battalion, however, the only difference from their European issue was the lack of a collar on the *justaucorps*.

There is no evidence of further special Canadian issues of clothing subsequent to that of 1755. It is assumed, therefore, that future clothing issues for regiments posted to Canada were of standard European pattern, and that by 1757 most soldiers were issued European uniforms complete with prescribed regimental distinctions.

The soldier's equipment consisted of a tan leather waist-belt to which was attached a double frog for the brown leather, brass-tipped bayonet and sword scabbards. A tan leather cross-belt supported a brown ammunition pouch on the right hip. All belt buckles and fittings were of brass.

Private soldiers and corporals were armed with a musket and bayonet, and a short straight sword with brass fittings.[4]

The illustration depicts a 1758 officer of the régiment de Languedoc in full dress. His uniform is the same colour and pattern as that of the soldiers, but made of better material. The hat brim and blue waistcoat are trimmed with fine gold lace.

He wears the gilt gorget of officers on duty. His hair is powdered and neatly tied back with a black bow; a white neckcloth and shirt frill are visible above the top of the waistcoat. On formal parade, the officer carried an espontoon or half-pike, and a gilt-mounted straight sword hung from a tan leather sword-belt.[5]

1755-1760
History

The régiment de Béarn was formed in 1684. On the eve of the Seven Years' War, the 1st Battalion was placed on coastal defence duties, while the 2nd sailed for Canada with Dieskau's small force of regulars in 1755.

The battalion arrived at Quebec on 19 June and, after a brief rest, was dispatched with the Guyenne battalion to garrison Fort Frontenac. At the end of autumn it withdrew to winter quarters.[1]

Montcalm succeeded Dieskau as commander of the French forces in May 1756. He quickly moved to Ticonderoga with several regular battalions to block a possible British move against the position. The battalions of the Guyenne and La Sarre were sent to Fort Frontenac. The Béarn battalion was ordered to Niagara, but was recalled at the end of July and sent by boat to reinforce the garrison at Fort Frontenac.[2]

As the British threat failed to materialize, Vaudreuil and Montcalm planned a strike against Oswego, a British post established in the 1720s at the eastern end of the south shore of Lake Ontario. Oswego was intended to attract the fur trade of the western Indians, but it also provided a British base from which to strike at forts Frontenac and Niagara. Montcalm's aim was to eliminate the enemy foothold on Lake Ontario, and to secure the western frontier of New France.

The Oswego position was composed of three fortified posts. Fort Ontario, a recently built star-shaped log fort, was located on high ground on the east side of the Oswego River. On the west bank stood the original Fort Oswego, surrounded by a stone wall and protected to the south and west by earthworks, but exposed to the east. The third post was a fortified cattle pen 1.5 km (1 mi.) upstream from the main defences.[3] The series of fortifications was garrisoned by about a thousand men under the command of Colonel Mercer.

Montcalm swiftly assembled his strike force at Niaouré Bay on 8 August. The battalions of the Béarn, La Sarre, and Guyenne regiments, together with several companies of colonial regulars, militia, and Indians, brought the force to 3,000 men.

Moving at night, the force approached Oswego without being detected by the British, and by 10 August it was in position to attack the fortifications. Led by Captain Pouchot of the régiment de Béarn, the initial advance pressed forward while parallels and batteries were constructed to face the forts. The wooden ramparts of Fort Ontario were useless against the French guns, and the garrison retreated across the river to Fort Oswego. The French occupied the Ontario site dominating Old Fort Oswego, and swept the exposed British position with a fierce bombardment. Mercer was killed, and the garrison surrendered on 14 August.

Montcalm burned the forts, sent his prisoners and captured supplies to Montreal, and hastened his troops back to Ticonderoga before the British learned of the events.[4]

Although Oswego was not a major fortress, its capture and destruction had an immediate effect, for the British were thereafter reduced to using only one inland approach, the Lake Champlain waterway.

The speed and power of the French attack greatly impressed the Indians as well as the British, and French prestige soared as that of the British sank. Furthermore, the Oswego operation demonstrated the value of properly employed regular soldiers even in the Canadian wilderness. As even stout wooden palisades were easy prey for soldiers trained in siege craft, the arrival of French and British regulars changed the character of the war. Battles, not raids and war-parties, would decide the fate of Canada.

The régiment de Béarn accompanied Montcalm to Fort William Henry in 1757.[5] The following year it took part in the defence of Ticonderoga, where, with the Guyenne and La Sarre regiments, the Béarn formed the right flank of the French perimeter.[6] It was against this sector of the French position that the Black Watch launched its impetuous attack.

At the beginning of the 1759 campaign, the Béarn battalion was assigned to the main force defending Quebec. When Montcalm marshalled his small army on the Plains of Abraham, the battalion of the régiment de Béarn was in the centre of the line of battle.

After wintering in Montreal, engaged in the everyday duties of outposts and patrols, the régiment de Béarn took part in Lévis' siege of Quebec and in the final battle at Sainte-Foy on 28 April 1760. On 16 September 1760, eight days after the surrender of Montreal, the Béarn began to embark for the voyage back to France.[7]

1755-1760

Uniform

Illustrations of French regulars in Canada usually depict the *justaucorps* with regimental distinctions as prescribed for European service. However, a special uniform was made in France to Ministry of the Navy specifications, and issued to the first troops to arrive in Canada. As these coats were collarless, the battalions that came to Canada with Dieskau in 1755 could not be identified by the usual system of distinctive collar colour.

The uniforms issued to some regiments differed from their standard dress in other details as well. The European uniform of the régiment de Béarn was distinguished by its red collar, red cuffs with three buttons along the edge, red waistcoat, brass buttons, and gold lace. The special Canadian issue for the regiment, however, had blue cuffs and waistcoat, pewter buttons, and silver lace.[1]

By 1758, the original battalions were no longer supplied with the special Canadian pattern of clothing; all the French regulars were clothed in European dress, complete with prescribed regimental distinctions.

In 1755, the dress of the régiment de Béarn consisted of the traditional greyish-white *justaucorps* with deep cuffs of blue, but without the usual small collar. The skirt, which reached the top of the knee, could be hooked up for greater freedom of movement, or allowed to fall straight for ceremonial occasions or to give additional protection to the legs in inclement weather. The Béarn had a distinctive coat pocket, consisting of a three-pointed double verticle slash with a large button at each point. While this pocket design is clearly shown in the illustration, the artist's retention of regimental pocket distinctions in the Canadian-pattern uniform is purely speculative as documentary evidence is not available.

The greyish-white breeches were buttoned on the side and buckled below the knee. Black shoes with metal buckles were worn over white wool stockings. On campaign and parade, the soldiers wore white canvas gaiters that reached just to the bottom of the coat. These were fastened below the knee by a black leather strap.

All ranks wore the black felt tricorn with black or white cockade. The brim was edged with false-silver tape for privates and corporals, and fine silver lace for sergeants and officers. Other items of dress included a black cravat and white linen shirt.[2]

The officers' uniform was of the same colour and pattern as that of the men, but of better material, and the waistcoat was often trimmed with gold or silver lace. A buff leather sword-belt went around the waist either over or under the waistcoat, but usually under the *justaucorps*. A white cravat, showing a lace frill at the throat, was worn with a white shirt. The gilt gorget denoting commissioned rank was always worn on duty.

In addition to a sword, captains and higher-ranking officers carried an espontoon; junior officers carried a fusil or musket with cartridge-box, as did the men.[3]

The soldier shown in the plate is a corporal of the grenadier company, dressed in the Canadian-issue uniform of 1755. Though grenades were no longer used, grenadiers were still selected from among the biggest soldiers in the battalion. A French grenadier sported a distinctive moustache, although other soldiers were clean shaven. He wore a large grenade pouch with the King's Arms stamped on the flap, and carried a brass-hilted sabre instead of the usual straight-bladed short sword.

Three strips of braid on the cuff formed the usual rank badge for corporals, although the particular pattern and arrangement of the strips differed from regiment to regiment.

The corporal is armed with a 1746 French military musket, and wears the standard infantry waist-belt with double frog for sabre and bayonet. His grenadier cartridge pouch is suspended on the right hip from a buff leather cross-belt.

In the background one can see a fusilier wearing his sleeved blue waistcoat and blue and white forage cap. This serviceable dress was worn on fatigue duties, and also as a warm-weather campaign kit.

History

A battalion of the régiment de La Reine formed part of the six battalions of French regular infantry that set out for Canada in 1755. During the voyage from France, four companies of the La Reine and four of the Languedoc were captured when their transport, le *Lys*, was intercepted by the Royal Navy off Newfoundland.[1]

Shortly after their arrival at Quebec, the remaining men of the La Reine battalion were on their way to Lake Champlain to block the British advance. Two companies of the La Reine and two of the Languedoc were engaged in Dieskau's Battle of Lake George. These two regiments shared the distinction of being the first French regulars to be engaged in battle in North America. Although they failed to drive the English provincials from their hastily fortified camp, Dieskau's troops stalled Johnson's advance on Crown Point.[2]

Dieskau's successor, Montcalm, received reports of the British massing troops to attack Fort Ticonderoga, where the battalions of the La Reine and Languedoc regiments had been posted in May 1756.[3] When Montcalm arrived later that summer, he found the construction of a strong fort well advanced and the British in no great haste to move against the position.

Satisfied with the situation at Ticonderoga, Montcalm turned his attention to the Lake Ontario region. He swiftly launched a successful attack on Fort Oswego, thereby securing the western frontier of New France.

The spring of 1758 brought disturbing news to the French: a strong naval force was being assembled in British ports for a strike at Louisbourg or Quebec. The French regulars were alerted to defend Quebec. In early summer the British fleet anchored at Halifax and was joined by the bulk of the British regulars. Louisbourg was the target. The transfer of local British regulars to Halifax opened the way for a thrust down Lake George, and Montcalm struck quickly.

At Ticonderoga, Montcalm assembled a formidable force of about 7,800 men, including 369 men of the La Reine battalion.[4] By the end of July he was ready to strike. Lévis marched overland with a force of 2,500 while Montcalm moved down Lake George by boat with the remaining 5,300 men. On 3 August the opening shots were fired as parties of militia and Indians harried the British outposts.

Johnson's temporary campsite on Lake George had been transformed into the stoutly constructed Fort William Henry. This post blocked the path to Albany, and provided the British with a firm base for an attack up Lake Champlain into the heart of New France. Fort William Henry was constructed of embankments of gravel with a superstructure of logs and earth, and was protected by swamps and ditches.[5] It was defended by a garrison of 2,200 men, more than half of them provincials, under the command of Lieutenant-Colonel Monro of the 35th of Foot.

Mindful of Dieskau's experience at this very spot, Montcalm decided to undertake a formal siege rather than launch an immediate frontal assault. On the evening of 4 August, the regulars began digging parallels and constructing batteries. Two days later the bombardment began, to the delight of the Indians, who were not needed for their usual scouting and skirmishing assignments and lounged about watching the show.

The soldiers of the La Reine toiled with pick and spade as the trenches grew closer to the fort. They stood their ground, beating off the sorties of the garrison, and firing at the ramparts to check the fire of the defenders. The siege called for all the craft of regular soldiers, and Montcalm's regulars were trained professionals.

As the intensity of the bombardment increased, so did the toll of garrison casualties, yet they refused all demands for capitulation. Finally, with the walls of the fort breached and their last guns disabled, the British asked for and were granted terms on 9 August. After the fort surrendered, the Indians slipped out of control and killed some 200 unarmed soldiers of the garrison and civilians before Montcalm restored order.[6]

The following year, all the regular battalions, including the La Reine, were posted to the Ticonderoga position to block the British thrust up Lake Champlain. During the British attack on Fort Carillon, the La Reine battalion was assigned to the right side of the defence perimeter.[7]

The campaign of 1759 saw the French threatened by Wolfe's drive up the St. Lawrence on Quebec, and Amherst's methodical approach to Montreal by way of Lake Champlain. The La Reine battalion formed part of Bourlamaque's force assigned to block the Lake Champlain approaches,[8] and was therefore not present when Montcalm met Wolfe on the Plains of Abraham.

With the fall of Quebec, the La Reine withdrew to the Montreal area, where the French forces regrouped. The battalion accompanied Lévis on his march back to Quebec in the spring of 1760, and formed part of the French reserve at the spirited Battle of Sainte-Foy. But the arrival of British reinforcements sealed the fate of New France. On 16 September, eight days after the capitulation of Canada, the La Reine returned to France, after campaigning continuously from 1755 to 1760.[9]

Uniform

The second battalion of the La Reine arrived in Canada in 1755 with the first contingent of French regulars, and was issued uniforms made to Ministry of the Navy specifications. The *justaucorps* differed from its regulation coat in that it had no collar. No mention is made of pocket details, which normally constituted a regimental distinction. The Canadian-issue waistcoat for the La Reine was red, although their regulation European *veste* was blue.[1]

The figure in the illustration is a sergeant in Canada after the La Reine returned to full regimentals. The skirts of the greyish-white coat are not hooked up, and the length of this outer garment can be seen clearly. The pocket flaps, set just below the waist, are shield shaped and trimmed with two rows of four buttons set vertically down each side of the flap.

The regiment can be distinguished by the red collar and cuffs, the shape of the pockets, and the pewter buttons. The deep cuffs are trimmed with a row of three large pewter buttons along the edge.[2]

Under the coat, the soldiers of the La Reine wore a long-sleeved blue waistcoat. During the summer, the heavy *justaucorps* sometimes was set aside, and the neat waistcoat was worn as an outer garment. At other times the waistcoat was removed, and only a shirt was worn under the coat.

Greyish-white knee-length breeches were worn with white or grey stockings and black shoes with metal buckles. White duck gaiters, worn over the stockings and breeches, were buttoned down the outside edge and fastened below the knee with a black leather strap.

The black felt tricorn, decorated with a black cockade and pewter button, was bordered with false-silver tape for the men, and fine silver lace for sergeants and officers.

Officers wore a coat of the same colour and pattern as that of the men, but of superior material and tailoring. Their buttons and metal trimmings were silver instead of pewter. The officer's gorget was gilt, and the waistcoat was trimmed with silver lace according to the taste and pocketbook of the wearer. On active service, dismounted officers exchanged the espontoon for a fusil.

Drummers of the régiment de La Reine normally wore the Queen's livery: red coat with blue cuffs and lining; heavy braid along the front opening edge of the coat, pockets, and cuffs, around the buttonholes, and down the seam lines of the sleeves; and Queen's livery lace – a white chain on a blue background – down the back of the coat. The long-sleeved blue waistcoat also was trimmed with Queen's livery lace. The body of the drum was red, the counter hoops blue and white.[3]

When the La Reine battalion arrived in Canada in 1755, the drummers were issued blue coats trimmed with the King's livery lace, red waistcoats, and red breeches. The drummers' black felt tricorns were trimmed with false-gold braid, and their forage caps were white with red flaps.[4]

The plate illustrates a sergeant of the La Reine. His rank is indicated by the silver lace stripe around the top of his coat cuffs. He carries a halberd, with which he can dress the ranks of the company; however, on active service in Canada, the halberd was soon replaced by a musket.

The sergeant's pattern of buff leather sword-belt supporting a brass-hilted sword is clearly shown in the illustration.

1755-1760

History

In the spring of 1755, the 2nd Battalion of the régiment de Guyenne sailed from Brest as part of the small force of regular army troops assigned to Canada. The battalion landed on 23 June and proceeded with the régiment de Béarn to Fort Frontenac, where it remained until ordered to Fort Niagara on 5 October. Leaving a detachment of 200 men to winter at Niagara with the colonial regulars, the remainder of the battalion began its return march to winter quarters in November, and arrived in Montreal on 4 December. This demanding journey gave the Guyenne the distinction of being the unit of French line infantry to penetrate most deeply into the North American wilderness.[1]

In June 1756, Montcalm sent the Guyenne and La Sarre battalions to garrison Fort Frontenac, which guarded the western frontier of New France. Here Montcalm assembled his assault force, which included the Guyenne battalion, for the attack on Oswego.

The following year, the Guyenne formed part of the expedition against Fort William Henry, where the battalion again found itself engaged in siege operations in the midst of the lakes and forests of North America.

Vaudreuil, Dieskau, and Montcalm recognized that the Ticonderoga feature effectively controlled the Lake Champlain gateway to Canada; therefore, the substantial Fort Carillon was constructed on this site.

In the spring of 1758, the British concentrated a force of some 15,000 men, of which 6,500 were regulars, at the south end of Lake George, with the obvious intention to thrust up Lake Champlain into the heart of Canada. Montcalm concentrated the eight regular battalions and a handful of colonial regulars and militia – 3,600 men in all – at Ticonderoga to counter the British threat. The men of the Guyenne, together with the other regulars, fortified the perimeter of the French position with a high loopholed breastwork of logs. Fields of fire were cleared, and an entanglement of felled trees with sharpened branches was placed to cover the entire position.

At noon on 8 July, the French pickets made contact with the skirmishers covering the British main body as it advanced directly against Montcalm's prepared position. The Guyenne moved to its assigned position on the right flank of the roughly semi-circular perimeter, and formed three ranks behind the timber breastwork. As the British lines of attacking infantry reached the tangle of fallen trees, they fell before the disciplined French volleys. The attack broke at the base of the protecting abatis.

The British soldiers, both provincials and regulars, withdrew, regrouped, and advanced again and again. On the fifth attempt, solid columns of British troops, led by the 42nd (Highland) Regiment (Black Watch), crashed into the position held by the Guyenne. The attackers reached the breastwork, and some Highlanders scrambled over. For a few moments the men of the Guyenne and Béarn regiments wavered. Then, at the critical moment, Lévis appeared at the head of the reserve of French grenadiers. The British withdrew, leaving some 500 Black Watch dead or wounded among the tangled branches of the abatis.[2]

Once more the British rallied and advanced; once more the controlled volleys of the French regulars stopped them. Then it was over, and the British withdrew to their boats and the camp on Lake George from which they had embarked with such high expectations.

The victory of Ticonderoga belonged to Montcalm and his regulars. This was no *petite guerre*, but a contest between disciplined professionals. Deserted by their Indian allies, the French soldiers of the line stood against superior numbers, and prevailed. Well might the régiment de Guyenne be proud of its part in the fierce battle fought beside the lakes of this wild country.

Ticonderoga was the zenith of French ascendancy in North America. The following spring, Wolfe was on the move up the St. Lawrence with Quebec as his objective. A week before Wolfe's landing, the Guyenne concentrated on the Plains of Abraham, only to be moved back to the Beauport position the following day. The subsequent movement – or lack of movement – of the Guyenne battalion during that week, while Montcalm attempted to counter Wolfe's moves, has been the subject of some controversy.[3] But regardless of the preliminary disposition of the regiment, it marched out to occupy the left centre of Montcalm's line of battle on the Plains of Abraham.

The Guyenne battalion returned with the Chevalier de Lévis in the spring of 1760 for the final battle of Sainte-Foy. The arrival of British reinforcements forced the battalion to retreat to Montreal; and, after the surrender of New France, it returned to France.

1755-1760

Uniform

When the 2nd Battalion of the régiment de Guyenne arrived in Canada in 1755, the troops were issued colonial-pattern uniforms composed of a collarless grey-white *justaucorps* with red cuffs and brass buttons, a red waistcoat, grey-white breeches, and a hat edged with false-gold lace.[1]

The prescribed European uniform of the régiment de Guyenne included a knee-length greyish-white coat with red collar and cuffs, and brass buttons. The skirt pockets were horizontal with a standard three-button flap, and the cuffs were trimmed with three brass buttons set along the edge. The sleeved red waistcoat, worn under the *justaucorps*, reached well down the thigh.

White linen gaiters to the top of the knee were worn over greyish-white knee-length breeches. Black shoes were fastened with steel buckles.

The black felt hat, with a black cloth cockade and small brass button, was cocked in the traditional three-cornered fashion, and worn low over the eyes. The brim was edged with false-gold tape.

The soldier's equipment consisted of a buff leather waistbelt supporting brown leather, brass-tipped bayonet and sword scabbards. A short strap joined the two ends of the buff leather cross-belt just above the cartridge pouch and held it snugly in position on the hip.

Fusiliers wore a brown leather pouch that held thirty cartridges and closed by means of a flap stamped with the Royal Arms. The grenadiers' pouch had a larger flap, the last vestige of the original grenade pouch that identified the soldiers of the grenadier company.[2]

The regulation uniform was satisfactory for garrison duty in Montreal and Quebec, but was quite unsuitable for service in the forests of the frontier regions. It was hot and cumbersome in the summer, and provided little protection against the biting winter cold. It was not long before the French regulars adapted their dress, as well as their tactics, to meet the demands of warfare in Canada.

The plate illustrates an officer in modified campaign dress. He wears his regimental red waistcoat as an outer garment, the gold-lace trim and gilt gorget indicating commissioned rank. The pattern of the waistcoat is clearly illustrated. Sleeved and collarless, it covers the upper thigh; the cuffs, slit along the back seam, are closed with two small brass buttons.

The black felt tricorn, trimmed with fine gold lace, is light and comfortable, and provides a reasonable degree of protection from both sun and rain. The unpowdered hair is tied at the back with black ribbon. The officer has adopted the black neckcloth of the private soldier, and has dispensed with all frills and ruffles.

His gilt-hilted sword has been replaced by a small hatchet. The espontoon has been discarded in favour of a 1728 military musket, in accordance with the order issued in late 1758 that infantry officers were to carry a light musket and small cartridge-box.[3] A standard fusilier cartridge pouch is suspended on the right hip from a buff leather cross-belt, and a powder-horn hangs above the pouch from a cord. The buff strap over the right shoulder supports the sack-like pack of rations and spare clothing.

This practical officer wears greyish-white breeches of prescribed pattern; but plain buckskin Indian leggings, fastened below the knee with strips of deerskin, have replaced regulation gaiters. He has given up his shoes in favour of moccasins, the most sensible type of footwear for moving through the dense forest underbrush.

All in all, the officer has modified his dress, arms, and equipment to provide a neat and serviceable combat kit adapted to North American campaign conditions.

1756-1760

History

The 2nd Battalion of the régiment Royal-Roussillon sailed from Brest for Canada in April 1756 to reinforce the small contingent of regular French infantry that had arrived the previous summer. The Marquis de Montcalm sailed in the same convoy to take up his new duties as commander of the regular French troops in Canada.

The men of the Royal-Roussillon had no sooner landed on 3 June than reports of an impending British assault on Ticonderoga were brought in by Indian scouting parties. Montcalm went at once to the threatened position, and ordered the Royal-Roussillon to follow as quickly as possible. The regiment arrived at Ticonderoga late in June to join the battalions of La Reine and Languedoc in the construction of Fort Carillon. When he discovered that the reports of British intentions had been grossly exaggerated, Montcalm returned to complete his arrangements for the attack on Oswego, leaving the Royal-Roussillon to strengthen the Ticonderoga position.

The Royal-Roussillon remained at Fort Carillon until well into winter, when all but a few companies of French regulars had withdrawn to winter quarters. In March 1757, a detachment of the regiment, together with one of the Béarn, accompanied Rigaud de Vaudreuil and his force of 1,600 militia, colonial regulars, and Indians on an unsuccessful expedition against Fort William Henry.

When, in August, Montcalm launched his rapid thrust down Lake George to overwhelm Fort William Henry, he employed all six of his regular battalions, including the Royal-Roussillon. The following year the regiment took part in the epic battle of Ticonderoga. Posted at the very centre of the French perimeter, the men fought under the personal command of Montcalm.[1]

After a bitter winter, Quebec received news of a strong British force under Wolfe sailing for the St. Lawrence. Faced with the problem of defending Quebec, Montcalm decided to concentrate the bulk of his troops to the east of the fortress, between the St. Charles and Montmorency rivers. The two battalions of the régiment de Berry and the La Reine battalion were sent to block the British advance up Lake Champlain. The remaining five regular battalions were assigned to the defence of Quebec. The régiment Royal-Roussillon was stationed just outside the city until June, when it was moved to the Beauport position. Along this section of the river-bank the French assembled a force of approximately fourteen thousand men, mainly militia backed by colonial regulars. The French

regulars at the centre of the Beauport position formed the core of the defence.

Quebec remained under siege throughout the entire summer. The city and the fortress were bombarded by the British fleet and by batteries established at Point Lévis. At the end of July, Wolfe attempted to gain a foothold on the eastern sector of the Beauport position with an assault-landing force of grenadiers; but the attack was driven off with considerable British losses.[2]

For the balance of the summer, Wolfe probed the French positions above and below the city, trying to crack the defences of Quebec. With only a few weeks of the campaign season left, the British made one last attempt. Ascending the cliffs above the city by a little-known path, the British appeared in strength on the Plains of Abraham on the morning of 13 September.

Reacting to the unexpected appearance of Wolfe before Quebec, Montcalm hurried his regulars, militia, and Indians over the St. Charles River. Arriving at Quebec, he was shocked to see, not the raiding force he assumed the intruders to be, but a small army drawn up in order of battle.

As they reached the field, the French regular troops took up position facing the red ranks of British regulars. The Royal-Roussillon was on the left of the French line, with its flank covered by a force of militia. By ten o'clock, the French had completed their assembly; at Montcalm's order the whole force advanced to sweep the British into the St. Lawrence.

The British waited until the French had begun their advance. Then the red-coated ranks shouldered muskets, advanced several paces, halted, and waited again. When the line of Montcalm's white-coated regulars came within 50 m (54 yds.), the British muskets came up and fired a volley; platoon firing followed. The French ranks wavered and the British line moved to the attack. The outcome of the battle was settled.[3]

On 19 September, the Royal-Roussillon battalion made its way to Montreal, where the French rallied under Lévis to carry on the struggle. The regiment accompanied Lévis when he moved against Quebec early in 1760, and beat off the British attack at Sainte-Foy. However, with the arrival of a relieving British fleet, the fate of Quebec was decided, and the British tightened their grip around the French colony. In September, the uneven struggle ended, and the Royal-Roussillon returned to France.[4]

1756-1760

Uniform

The 2nd Battalion of the régiment Royal-Roussillon arrived in Canada a year later than did the four battalions that came with General Dieskau, and there is no evidence that the Royal-Roussillon ever wore the Canadian-pattern uniforms issued by the Ministry of the Navy.

Regimental dress of the Royal-Roussillon included the traditional greyish-white single-breasted woollen coat of the French infantry with small collar, deep cuffs, and a single shoulder-strap on the left shoulder to keep the cartridge-box belt in place.

The Royal-Roussillon *justaucorps* was distinguished by blue collar and cuffs, brass buttons, and a simple three-pointed transverse pocket flap with a large brass button at each point. Along the edge of the cuff was a row of six small brass buttons.

The blue, sleeved waistcoat was collarless, reached well down the thigh, and had brass buttons. The black felt tricorn was edged with false-gold lace.

Breeches were greyish white, and buckled below the knees over long white stockings. Steel-buckled black shoes were worn with the breeches. On parade and campaign, white gaiters were worn strapped under the instep of the shoe, buttoned up the outside, and held in place by a black leather strap below the knee. French gaiters were shorter than those of the British, reaching only a few centimetres above the knee.

A black cravat was wound about the throat. The white shirt was visible above the waistcoat and at the wrists.

Officers' coats and breeches were of the same colour and pattern as those of the men, though of finer material. Their blue waistcoats were trimmed with gold lace and gilt buttons, and the tricorn brim was edged with fine gold lace.

Private soldiers were equipped with a buff leather waist-belt supporting a bayonet and a straight brass-hilted sword. A plain brown leather cartridge pouch rested on the right hip, suspended from a buff leather cross-belt buckled on the chest. Grenadiers carried the large grenade pouch with the Royal Arms stamped on the flap, but by this time it was used solely for musket cartridges.[1]

The plate depicts a drummer of the régiment Royal-Roussillon in 1758. He wears the King's small livery – a blue frockcoat with red collar, cuffs, and lining that showed when the skirts were hooked back. The coat is trimmed along the front edge, around the buttonholes, seam lines, and cuffs with King's livery lace, a white chain pattern on a crimson background. The drummer's sleeved red waistcoat is trimmed with royal livery lace. Otherwise, his uniform is like that of a private soldier.[2]

The deep wooden drum shells of the Royal-Roussillon are painted blue with red hoops to indicate that it is a Royal regiment. The front of the shell is emblazoned with the Arms of France, flanked by the colours of the regiment and those of the colonel. The sides of the drum are decorated with large gold *fleurs-de-lis*.[3] The buff leather drum sling is decorated with royal livery lace, and the sword is suspended from a buff leather waist-belt. The drummer in the illustration is dressed for field service. His pack is attached to the large buff leather cross-belt. The braided cords hanging below the shell are used to carry the drum on the march.

The drummers of line infantry regiments in Canada wore the King's small livery, except those of the régiment de La Reine, who wore the Queen's livery of red faced with blue. (See page 24.)

1756-1760
History

In April 1756, the 2nd Battalion of the régiment de La Sarre sailed from France with the Royal-Roussillon battalion in the convoy that carried General Montcalm to Canada. In May, the two battalions disembarked and moved without delay into defensive positions. The La Sarre battalion went to Fort Frontenac.

When the British threat to Ticonderoga failed to materialize, Montcalm assembled a force, including the La Sarre battalion, and overwhelmed the Oswego position. The siege of Oswego was the beginning of four years of steady campaigning in the wilds of New France by the La Sarre.

The following year, the battalion formed part of Montcalm's expedition that swept down Lake George and destroyed Fort William Henry. The La Sarre and Languedoc battalions manned the left side of the Ticonderoga position when the French regulars made their stand against the British thrust up Lake Champlain in 1758. In three successive campaign seasons, the regiment participated in successful major actions.

In 1759, Wolfe sailed into the heart of New France, and the régiment de La Sarre was assigned to the defence of Quebec. The battalion was stationed on the Beauport Heights, where the British seaborne attack on the Montmorency position was beaten off on 31 July.[1] In September, when Wolfe's army appeared on the Plains of Abraham, the La Sarre marched out with four other French regular battalions to meet the British. It was posted on the right of Montcalm's line of regulars, with its flank covered by a force of militia. During the course of the battle, Lieutenant-Colonel de Senezergues, the commanding officer of the la Sarre, was killed while commanding a brigade.

The French battalions were shattered by the rolling volleys of the British line, and streamed back across the St. Charles River to regroup. Bypassing the British, the French withdrew to Montreal where Lévis took over as senior military commander.

As winter approached, the British ships and some troops left Canada, and the new garrison of Quebec settled down to a defensive routine. The French regulars were billeted in Montreal, and the militiamen were sent home to await recall in the spring. Patrols and raiding activities continued throughout the winter, while persistent rumours circulated about French plans to recover Quebec. Lévis worked ceaselessly to gather equipment and supplies for a summer campaign. By April he was on the move toward Quebec with all eight battalions of French regulars, two battalions of colonial regulars, and some 3,000 militia, a total force of more than 7,000 men.

By 26 April, Lévis' troops had landed and advanced to a position in front of the village of Sainte-Foy. Murray, the British commander, decided to attack the French despite being outnumbered, and drew up his small army of 3,800 men in line of battle.

A stubborn battle developed along the Sainte-Foy position, and its outcome was greatly influenced by the attack of the La Sarre battalion on Dumont's house on the right flank of the British position. The strong point changed hands several times; but when it finally fell to the La Sarre attack, the British line began to fold. Murray withdrew his troops to Quebec after suffering 1,000 casualties, and prepared to withstand the siege he knew would follow.

After defeating the British at Sainte-Foy, Lévis pressed his advantage and laid siege to Quebec. However, the arrival of British ships in the St. Lawrence ended Lévis' hopes of recapturing Quebec, and his troops fell back to positions around Montreal.

The British garrison of Quebec, provisioned by the navy, took the offensive, and moved up river toward Montreal. At the same time, Amherst approached Montreal from the Lake Ontario region, and a third British force moved in from Lake Champlain. Assailed simultaneously from three directions, the French were unable to contain the British advance. On 8 September 1760, the articles of capitulation were signed in Montreal, and the hard years of campaigning in Canada came to an end for the régiment de La Sarre.[2]

1756-1760
Uniform

The dress of the régiment de La Sarre followed the same general pattern as that of other regiments of French line infantry. The basic outer garment was the greyish-white wool coat, ending just above the knee. The full skirt could be worn hooked back to give greater freedom of movement or unhooked to give greater protection from the weather. When the skirt was hooked back, the greyish-white lining was clearly visible.

Regimental distinctions on the coat included brass buttons, blue collar, and blue cuffs trimmed with a row of three large brass buttons set along the edge. The skirt pockets had a simple transverse flap with a scalloped edge and three large brass buttons, the centre button set below the edge of the flap.

The cuffs of the sleeved red waistcoat were slit along the back seam and closed with two small brass buttons. Regimental pocket flaps were repeated on the waistcoat and were trimmed with three small brass buttons. The greyish-white knee breeches and thigh-length white linen gaiters, fastened below the knee with a black strap, were of the standard line-infantry pattern.

All companies of the regiment wore the black felt tricorn with black cockade and small brass button. The brim was trimmed with false-gold braid.

The soldier of the La Sarre in the illustration is a corporal of the grenadier company in summer campaign dress. He wears his red waistcoat as an outer garment, with the cuffs turned back for comfort. The greyish-white *justaucorps* can be seen hanging over his pack. The corporal's insignia, three pointed stripes of yellow woollen braid on the cuffs, is clearly visible.

The corporal wears a fatigue cap instead of the usual felt hat. This cap was usually of regimental colours, with the *fleur-de-lis*, headband lace, and tassel the colour of the regimental buttons. Drummers' fatigue caps may have had a blue bag and a red flap trimmed with royal livery lace.[1]

Records of clothing sent to Canada for issue to the four regular infantry battalions in 1755 list similar forage caps of white material. Equal numbers have flaps of white, blue, and red; however, there is no indication of what combination was issued to the particular regiments. Six sets of regimentals were shipped to Canada, of which two had white waistcoats, two red, and two blue. Normal military custom would lead one to expect that the colour of the flap on the cap would match that of the waistcoat. This would allot the La Reine and Guyenne battalions caps with red flaps, the Languedoc and Béarn regiments blue, and the Artois and Bourgogne white. While this assignment is purely speculative, the shipping information does specifically prescribe white caps with red flaps for drummers.[2]

The corporal's equipment consists of a buff leather waist-belt supporting the double frog for the bayonet and, in the case of grenadiers, the sabre, which the corporal has replaced by a hatchet. The buff leather cross-belt over the left shoulder supports the grenade pouch with embellished flap.

The field pack can be seen hanging diagonally across the back. Called *de la Porterie* after its innovator, the pack was simply an open-ended bag, either fur covered or of stout fabric, tied to a buff leather cross-belt.[3] The shipping instructions mentioned above include an issue of water-bottles and mess tins, but the particular design of these items is not indicated. The clay pipe, carried in a leather pouch about the neck, was the soldier's constant companion.

1757-1760
History

By the end of the 1756 campaign season, it was apparent that the British had increased the number of their regular battalions in North America. It was equally obvious that only a larger force of French regular infantry could contain the British strength. The Governor appealed to France for more regular soldiers and, in 1757, two more understrength battalions of French regulars and some colonial regulars were ordered to sail for Canada.

The regular French infantry sent to Canada that year was the 2nd and 3rd battalions of the régiment de Berry. Originally, they were to be sent to Louisbourg; however, plans were altered and both battalions landed at Quebec at the end of July.[1] Each battalion was composed of only nine companies of three officers and sixty other ranks.[2]

The arrival of the régiment de Berry brought to eight the number of Montcalm's regular battalions. Around these regular soldiers Montcalm built his formidable strike forces, in which the French regulars were supported by Canadien militia, colonial regulars, and Indians. The militia, citizens called out for service for the duration of a campaign, made excellent light troops for scouting, skirmishing, and harassing the enemy. The colonial regulars of the *Compagnies franches de la marine* combined experience in fast-moving forest warfare with some of the discipline of regulars.

The Indian allies of the French were demanding, troublesome, and totally unpredictable; but their service in providing information about the enemy was vital to Montcalm. Their skill in scouting the Canadian forest country was equalled only by the French *coureurs des bois*. They were also a means of spreading terror, for the fear of falling into their clutches caused the enemy to withdraw from strong positions on more than one occasion.

Montcalm was able to combine the regulars, militia, and Indians to utilize their respective strengths; but it was the regulars who had the capability of eradicating the forts of the enemy almost at will. The speed with which Oswego and Fort William Henry were reduced by the French was possible only because of the regulars' skill in siege warfare.

The first major test of battle in America for the Berry battalions was the defence of Ticonderoga in 1758. While the British were preparing to embark on Lake George, Montcalm manoeuvred his force around the Ticonderoga area, uncertain of where to face the British advance. The régiment de Berry, positioned on the Ticonderoga feature, was ordered on 5 July to begin construction of a breastwork and abatis on the ridge of high ground in front of Fort Carillon.

Two days later, Montcalm's entire force withdrew to Ticonderoga and completed the work that the Berry battalions had begun. When the French took up their battle positions, the 2nd Berry was posted with the Royal-Roussillon in the centre, under the direct command of Montcalm. The 3rd Berry, under Lieutenant-Colonel de Travis, formed the garrison of Fort Carillon.[3]

In the spring of 1759, the French were faced with a British advance from the south by way of Lake Champlain as well as Wolfe's direct approach on Quebec. Bourlamaque and a force of three battalions, which included both battalions of the régiment de Berry, were ordered to Fort Carillon with instructions to defend the position as long as possible. If forced out, they were to withdraw to Isle-aux-Noix, at the outlet of Lake Champlain.

On 23 July Amherst moved in on the Ticonderoga position and discovered that Bourlamaque had withdrawn, leaving a garrison of only 400 men in Fort Carillon. After a brisk exchange of artillery fire, the French withdrew during the night of 26 July, after setting the fort on fire.

Bourlamaque blew up Fort St-Frederic and withdrew directly to a strong defensive position on Isle-aux-Noix, where the two battalions of the régiment de Berry were stationed when Montcalm faced Wolfe's army on the Plains of Abraham.[4]

Lévis gathered all the regular battalions, including those of Berry, to form the nucleus of a strike force for a return to Quebec early in the spring of 1760. Both Berry battalions fought in the ensuing successful action at Sainte-Foy.

With the arrival of the British fleet, the siege of Quebec was abandoned, and the French withdrew gradually to the Montreal area. The British closed in from the east, south, and west; and by 7 September the combined British force of 17,000 men stood before Montreal.

All that remained of Montcalm's proud and efficient little army was about 2,000 French and colonial regulars: the militia had deserted and returned to their homes; the Indians had melted into the forests.

The French regulars stood alone. They had fought until the last hope of victory was extinguished. France had lost Canada, but the French regular regiments had done all that might have been expected of them and more. Their only course was capitulation.

But Amherst's terms were harsh: there would be no honours of war for the valiant regulars. Lévis protested vehemently, but Amherst was inflexible. Atrocities committed by Indian allies of the French had strengthened his resolve.

A soldier to the end, Lévis ordered his regiments to burn their colours to spare them "the hard conditions of handing them over to the enemy." Then the troops of these fine regiments assembled in the Place d'Armes and laid down their weapons after five years of continuous fighting.[5]

1757-1760
Uniform

The two battalions of the régiment de Berry that arrived in Canada in 1757 were issued standard regular infantry regimental dress. Private soldiers wore the heavy greyish-white single-breasted wool coat so characteristic of the French infantry of the period. The deep cuffs and the small collar, which could be worn turned up or down, were red. The cuffs were trimmed with a row of five large brass buttons along the edge. The skirt pockets had double vertical three-pointed flaps with a large brass button at each point. The design of these pockets can be seen in the illustration.

The sleeved, collarless waistcoat worn under the *justaucorps* was red with a double row of brass buttons. Reaching well down the thigh, it made a serviceable jacket for outer wear in undress or on campaign in warm weather. The black felt cocked hat was edged with false-gold braid.

Breeches were of greyish-white wool and worn with white or grey stockings and buckled shoes. Thigh-length white gaiters were worn on campaign and on formal parades.[1] As clothing wore out during the campaigns, Indian leggings (*mitasses*) were adopted by the soldiers; these proved most practical in the Canadian woods.[2]

White shirts and black cravats were issued to the soldiers of Berry to complete their dress.

Sergeants wore a uniform similar to that of the men. Fine gold lace on the hat, gilt coat buttons, and a band of fine gold lace around the top of the coat cuffs designated the sergeants' rank. A brass-hilted sword was suspended from a buff leather sword-belt.

The men were equipped with buff leather waist-belts holding sword and bayonet scabbards; but the sword was soon found to be useless for Canadian forest warfare, and it was replaced by an axe or hatchet. The cartridge pouch was slung on the right hip from a buff leather cross-belt.

The plate illustrates an officer of the régiment de Berry. His *justaucorps* is of the same pattern and colour as that of his men, but is of finer material and better cut. His buttons are gilt and his hat brim is edged with fine gold lace. The gold lace on his sleeved waistcoat can be seen on the corner of the skirt.

The officer wears regulation greyish-white breeches, although on actual service these were sometimes replaced by hard-wearing yet comfortable velvet breeches. The usual white gaiters have ben discarded in favour of a pair of officers' black-leather campaign leggings, fastened up the outside with straps and brass buckles.

The buff leather sword-belt is worn over the coat to support the straight brass-hilted sword. A pistol is also attached to the sword-belt. Many officers carried light muskets and regulation cartridge pouches on campaign, but the officer in the illustration would have his hands full with the colours. Although his powdered hair seems somewhat out of place for a campaign, some authoritative illustrations of the period show officers on campaign wearing similar hair styles.

The officer carries the regimental colour, which was the same for each battalion within a regiment. The colours of all French line regiments in Canada were of the same basic pattern: a square field with a white cross dividing the colour into quarters. The four quarters of the Berry colour were identical, each containing one violet, one buff, and a second violet horizontal stripe. In the case of the régiment de Languedoc, the first and third quarters were violet, and the second and fourth brown. The Royal-Roussillon colour used another variation of the basic pattern with a white cross covered with golden *fleurs-de-lis*, and quarterings of royal blue, scarlet, green, and brown. The colour staff has a gilded brass head, and is decorated with a white silk scarf and cords of either the colour of the quarters or gold.[3]

History

The 60th (Royal American) Regiment of Foot, better known under its later name, The King's Royal Rifle Corps, has long been associated with Canada. After Braddock's defeat by the French and Indians in 1755, authority was granted to raise a regiment of four battalions to be recruited in Germany and from German colonists in North America. The regiment was named the 62nd, or Royal American, Regiment of Foot; but it was redesignated the 60th (Royal American) Regiment of Foot in February 1757.[1] Recruiting for the Royal Americans in North America was disappointing, and more than half its strength was drafted from men rejected by British regiments in Ireland.[2] From this unlikely collection of foreigners and cast-offs was fashioned one of the most renowned corps of the British Army.

Among the officers recruited in Europe were two able Swiss soldiers, Henri Bouquet and Frederick Haldimand, who commanded respectively the 1st and 2nd battalions of the new regiment. Bouquet trained his battalion as light infantry, emphasizing the skills required for forest warfare. Haldimand also adapted his European experience to war in the American wilderness.[3]

The 1st and 4th battalions of the 60th accompanied General Abercromby's advance up Lake Champlain in 1758, and participated in the disastrous assault on the Ticonderoga position the following July. In November, Bouquet's 1st Battalion played a major role in the successful advance to Fort Duquesne, which secured the western border of New England against the incursions of France's savage Indian allies.

In 1758, the 2nd and 3rd battalions were assigned to the forces of General Amherst for operations in eastern Canada. Both battalions were present at the capture of Louisbourg, and moved on to Quebec with Wolfe the following year. The performance of the 60th at Montmorency Falls on 31 July 1758 won the regimental motto *Celer et Audax* (Swift and Bold) from General Wolfe.[4]

The 2nd and 3rd battalions fought at the Battle of the Plains of Abraham on 13 September 1759. The following year, elements of all four battalions participated in the final advance to Montreal.

From the date of its raising in 1755, at least one battalion of the 60th (Royal American) Regiment of Foot served in North America until 1824, when the name was discontinued and the unit was redesignated The 60th (The Duke of York's Own Rifle Corps and Light Infantry) Regiment. This title was changed to The 60th (Duke of York's Own Rifle Corps) and, in 1830, the regiment was renamed The 60th (The King's Royal Rifle Corps).[5]

In 1844, the 60th returned to Canada, and garrisoned the Quebec and Montreal area until 1847. The 1st and 4th battalions were sent to Canada during the threatened Fenian invasions; the 4th arrived in 1866, and the 1st in 1867. The 1st Battalion accompanied Sir Garnet Wolseley's expedition to Fort Garry to crush the First Riel Rebellion in 1870.[6]

In November 1871, the 1st Battalion marched from the Quebec Citadel to a waiting transport; with its departure, the only British troops remaining in Canada were those manning the naval bases at Halifax and Esquimalt, which remained British garrison stations until early in the twentieth century.

Although the 60th Rifles withdrew from the land of its origin, the memory of this distinguished regiment's North American service was perpetuated in a unique fashion. A large number of the original infantry units comprising the Canadian Volunteer Active Militia – many of which still exist – were designated as Rifles, and wore the green jackets and red facings of The 60th (The King's Royal Rifle Corps).

1755-1760

Uniform

When the corps was raised in December 1755, the 62nd, or Royal American, Regiment of Foot was ordered to dress exactly like a regiment of the British Army, except that the uniform was to have no regimental lace, in recognition of the regiment's proposed role in the forest warfare of North America.[1]

By 1755, British infantry dress had been standardized to a degree. The outer garment was a long red collarless coat falling to just above the knee. The front had wide lapels to the waist, which could be buttoned across in double-breasted fashion when campaigning or in cold weather. The corners of the skirt were hooked up to give the soldier greater freedom of movement. The large turned-back cuff had a deep cleft, above which was set a slashed panel with three buttons. A plain red shoulder-strap on the left shoulder held in place the cross-belt; a transverse pointed pocket flap was set on each hip.

Lapels and cuffs of the 60th were blue, the traditional facing colour of Royal regiments. As the red coats were usually, but not always, lined with the regimental facing colour, the turn-backs on the coats of the 60th were probably blue. A thigh-length sleeved red waistcoat was worn under the red coat. The breeches for Royal regiments were blue, although the Royal Americans also wore leather breeches on some occasions.

Long white gaiters reaching to mid-thigh were strapped under the instep, and fastened below the knee by a black strap. On campaign, the white gaiters were replaced by brown marching gaiters of similar pattern.[2]

Men of the grenadier company wore the tall grenadier cap seen in the illustration of the Louisbourg Grenadiers. Other companies wore a black felt tricorn with black cockade; its brim was edged with white tape for men and silver lace for officers.

A white stock and white shirt completed the soldier's dress.

A wide buff leather belt crossed over the left shoulder to support a black ammunition pouch on the right hip. A narrower buff leather waist-belt, worn over the waistcoat, supported a double frog on the left side, from which hung a bayonet and short brass-hilted hanger. The waist-belt was worn over the closed coat, but under the coat when it was open. A smaller black ammunition pouch was sometimes worn on the middle of the waist-belt.

British troops in North America during this period normally carried the .75-calibre Long Land Musket, popularly known as the Brown Bess.[3]

The private soldier of the 60th depicted in the illustration wears an improvised campaign service dress. The sleeved red waistcoat without lace is worn as an outer garment. Over his blue regimental breeches are green cloth Indian leggings (mitasses) fastened at the ankles and below the knee.[4] Moccasins have replaced regulation shoes. His black felt tricorn has been cut down, leaving only the crown and a narrow brim, which offers some protection without being cumbersome.

The useless brass-hilted infantry hanger has been replaced by a hatchet. He wears the pack high on his back, Indian fashion, as recommended by General Wolfe for his ad hoc battalion of light infantry.[5]

In an effort to reduce the conspicuousness of the contemporary uniform, some soldiers of the light troops wore jackets of blue or green; but these early attempts at camouflage were quite unofficial, and the red coat of the British Army remained the prescribed dress of the 60th for almost half a century.

In December 1797, the 5th Battalion of the 60th, raised in England, was armed with rifles and dressed in green jackets with red facings. This was the introduction of the green jacket that was to become the outstanding feature of regimental dress of the 60th (Royal American) Regiment of Foot.[6]

1757-1763

History

Canada's association with the colourful and distinguished Highland regiments of the British Army dates back almost to the time of their beginnings. Two of the first four regular Highland regiments were raised specifically for service in North America; and, although disbanded on the conclusion of the struggle with France, their influence on Canadian military dress and custom still remains.

The final phase of the 150-year struggle between Britain and France in North America began in 1754. It became evident that large-scale military intervention in the colonial conflict was required if Britain was to prevail. This would necessitate sending British regulars to North America. Therefore, authority was granted for raising two Highland regiments of foot, the 77th Regiment (Montgomerie's Highlanders) and the 78th (Fraser's Highlanders), for service in the New World.

Simon Fraser, Master of Lovat, son of the 11th Lord Lovat who was executed for his part in the Jacobite Rebellion of 1745-46, was commissioned Lieutenant-Colonel Commandant and authorized on 5 January 1757 to raise a regiment of foot. The regiment, designated the 78th Regiment of Foot, 2nd Highland Battalion, was to have a strength of forty-four officers, forty sergeants and corporals, twenty drummers, and ten companies of 100 men each.

The 78th assembled at Inverness, and soon recruited to full strength. In fact, when the regiment embarked at Glasgow in April 1757, it was accompanied by so many volunteers that three additional companies were authorized. When another company was added in 1758, the unit had the formidable strength of 1,542 all ranks.

The Fraser's spent their first North American winter, that of 1757-58, in Connecticut. Some practical soul proposed that the Highlanders should be clad in trews during the cold weather; but the officers and men raised such an uproar that the 78th was permitted to retain its original Highland dress, winter or not!

In the spring of 1758, the regiment joined the force being assembled for the assault on Louisbourg. The 78th took part in the original assault-landing as well as the subsequent siege operations that led to the capitulation of the fortress in July 1758. Fraser's Highlanders then moved to New York, where they were to pass the winter, but they were transferred first to Boston and then, as a result of the disaster at Ticonderoga, to Albany.[1]

Fraser's Highlanders joined General Wolfe's Quebec expedition in the spring of 1759, and served with distinction throughout the campaign. They were the only Highland troops present at the Battle of the Plains of Abraham. The regiment remained in Quebec during the trying winter of 1759-60, and took part in the battle at Sainte-Foy on 28 April 1760. Subsequently, the 78th accompanied General Murray's force in the advance on Montreal, where it met with the 42nd (Royal Highland) Regiment of Foot and the 77th (Montgomerie's Highlanders) Regiment of Foot, both of Amherst's force. Here, for the first time, the three Highland regiments serving in North America during the Seven Years' War came together.

Between 1760 and 1763, the 78th Regiment served in garrison locations in Montreal, Quebec, and Nova Scotia. A detachment formed part of Colonel William Amherst's force that recaptured St. John's in September 1762.[2]

In December 1763, Fraser's Highlanders were ordered to disband in Quebec. Land grants were offered to those who chose to stay in Canada, and many officers and men remained to help build the country they had come to conquer.

1757-1763

Uniform

The colourful dress of the Highland regiments of the British Army borrows nothing from European military fashion. It is based solely on the traditional dress of the Highlands of Scotland. The 78th adopted Highland dress very early, and was one of the first two regiments serving in Canada to do so.

Reliable contemporary evidence on the dress of the Fraser's is sparse. The brief notation, "Seventy-Eighth Regiment – Uniform, Red Faced White, Belted Plaid and Hose," provides little detail.[1]

A veteran of the 78th wrote that "thanks to our generous Chief, we were allowed the garb of our fathers, and in the course of six winters, showed the doctors that they did not understand our constitution for, in the coldest winters, our men were more healthy than those regiments who wore breeches and warm clothing".[2]

"The uniform was full Highland dress with musquett and broad sword, to which many of the soldiers added the dirk, at their own expense, and a purse of badgers or otter skin. The Bonnet was raised or cocked on one side with a slight bend inclining down to the right ear, over which was suspended two or more black feathers".[3] From this information and what is known of Highland military dress of the period, the uniform of the 78th can be reconstructed with some certainty.

The outstanding feature of Highland dress was, of course, the kilt. The 78th wore the belted plaid, which consisted of twelve yards of double-width tartan. The fabric was spread on the ground and neatly pleated over the waist-belt; the soldier lay down on the plaid, fastened his belt, and stood up. The lower part of the plaid formed the kilt proper. The upper portion, which fell over the belt, was gathered behind and fastened at the left shoulder. In inclement weather, the plaid was unfastened and drawn about the shoulders like a cloak.

The filibeg or little kilt was worn by some regiments on occasions when the belted plaid was too cumbersome. But there is no evidence that the 78th possessed both garments.

The tartan of the period was a hard fabric of combed wool, and was harsh on bare flesh. It was not until the 1870s that it was replaced by the present-day softer tartan made from carded wool.[4]

There is much speculation as to the sett or pattern of tartan issued to the 78th, but no hard evidence. Several authorities on Highland dress are of the opinion that the Fraser's wore the government pattern (Black Watch), perhaps with a coloured overstripe.[5]

The regulation red coat of the British infantry was much too long to accommodate the belted plaid, so Highland regiments adopted a short red jacket cut square across the back a few inches below the waist. A 1751 painting depicts a Highland jacket as a short single-breasted garment with a turn-down collar. The small turned-back cuffs have a straight slash edged with white tape, and the buttons and buttonholes have short tape loops. The jacket has a single right shoulder-strap to hold in place the wide sword-belt. The red waistcoat, edged with white tape, is almost as long as the jacket.[6]

The red and white pattern hose, cut from cloth and sewn up the back, were supported a few inches below the knee by a red tape garter. The black leather shoes fastened with metal buckles.

The flat blue-black bonnet of the Highland regiments is shown in contemporary illustrations with a plain or sometimes a red band; the diced band commonly associated with Highland head-gear was not yet in evidence. A small red touri and black ribbon cockade were common adornments of the bonnet.

The white collarless shirt was worn with a white neckcloth or, on active service, a black stock.

Grenadier companies of some early Highland regiments wore a mitre-shaped fur grenadier cap. It seems probable that such a unique Highland distinction would be adopted by the 78th, but there is no evidence to support this speculation.

The sporran or purse was provided at the soldier's own expense. There seems to have been no standard sporran pattern for the regiment, although it is known that some were of otter and others of badger skin.

Officers wore a scarlet jacket and waistcoat similar to those of the soldiers. Although some officers' jackets had plain lapels of facing colour set with buttons but without lace loops, most contemporary illustrations show the officer's jacket without lapels. Cuffs, collars, jacket fronts, and waistcoats were probably trimmed with narrow gold lace, but such embellishments were kept to a minimum on active service.

The Highland soldier's equipment consisted of a black waist-belt with steel buckle to which was attached a small cartridge pouch, a bayonet, and, frequently, a dirk supplied by the soldier. A wide black leather cross-belt with steel buckle, slide, and tip was worn over the right shoulder to hold the basket-hilted Highland broadsword.

The plate illustrates a 1758 private soldier of the 78th in his regimentals. Wearing feathers in the bonnet was a common practice for Highland regiments. The number of feathers gradually increased until the bonnet took the form of the present-day Highland feather bonnet.

It seems that some, if not all, of the 78th carried a lighter musket than the standard forty-six-inch barrel Brown Bess. A military musket with a forty-two-inch barrel, often referred to as the Light Infantry Musket, was issued to some units of the British Army about this time and may have been used by the Fraser's.[7]

The 78th (Highland) Regiment of Foot (Fraser's Highlanders) introduced the colour and distinction of Highland dress to Canada, and it continues to be a part of Canada's military heritage.

1759
History

Some of the most impressive soldiers to serve in Canada were the grenadiers of the British regiments during the Seven Years' War. They were big men, whose tall, colourfully embroidered caps distinguished them from the soldiers of the centre or "hat" companies. Grenadiers were introduced into the British Army in 1677, when the Foot Guards selected two men from each company to be trained to throw grenades.[1] The following year, a grenadier company was added to each infantry regiment.[2]

The grenade of the period was a spherical metal bomb about 7 cm (2 3/4 in.) in diameter, weighing about 1 kg (2 1/2 lb.). The unique percussion-ignition system utilized a hand-lit fuse, which penetrated the casing on impact and ignited the explosive contents of the grenade.[3] Traditionally the biggest men in the regiment were posted to the grenadier company, as throwing grenades required considerable strength. The grenadiers led the assault on fortified positions, cutting through the palisades with hatchets, and clearing the enemy entrenchments with their grenades.

The grenade was discarded by the mid-eighteenth century, probably because of the improved performance of flintlock muskets. However, the grenadier company was retained as the battalion's elite company. It was common practice for commanders to withdraw the grenadier companies from their battalions and form them into special assault units. This was unpopular with both soldiers and unit commanders, as it removed the best soldiers from the parent units and weakened the battalions in quality and numbers.

Nonetheless, this practice was adopted by Wolfe on several occasions. In 1759, he withdrew the grenadier companies from the 22nd, 40th, and 45th regiments of Foot, which had been assigned to garrison the fortress of Louisbourg, and grouped them into a temporary unit called the Louisbourg Grenadiers. This improvised corps accompanied him up the St. Lawrence River to attack Quebec in the late spring.[4]

Sailing up the St. Lawrence was one thing, but the capture of Quebec was quite another. Wolfe initially concluded that his best chance of success lay in landing on the north shore and attacking the fortress from the landward side. Because of the difficulty in moving ships and transports past the batteries of Quebec, the Beauport shore position to the east seemed to offer some advantage. Montcalm evidently agreed, for when the British finally landed on the Ile d'Orléans late in June, they found the French firmly in position on the Beauport shore.

On 31 July, Wolfe attempted to storm the far eastern end of the Beauport position. His thirteen grenadier companies, including those of the Louisbourg Grenadiers, were massed into an assault force. Supported by 200 men of the 60th, the grenadiers stormed ashore; without waiting to form into columns or for the arrival of support, they dashed at the French positions. The impetuous, disorderly assault was beaten off by the French with considerable loss to the attackers. A violent thunderstorm followed, turning the ground into mud; the attack bogged down, and Wolfe ordered his troops to withdraw.[5]

The Louisbourg Grenadiers were on the scene early on 13 September, when the British came ashore above Quebec, and climbed the heights to the Plains of Abraham. By six o'clock, the British line consisted of only three battalions and the Louisbourg Grenadiers, which had been augmented by the grenadier companies of the 2nd and 3rd battalions of the 60th.[6] As more troops arrived on the Plains, Wolfe extended his line, and repositioned the regiments. The right flank of the British force was covered by the 35th, and the unit next in line was the Louisbourg Grenadiers. Wolfe was standing with the Grenadiers when he was mortally wounded during the battle.

The Louisbourg Grenadiers were given the honour of mounting guard at the gates of Quebec when the British took possession of the fortress on 18 September 1759.[7] The companies then returned to their respective regiments.[8]

1759

Uniform

The Louisbourg Grenadiers must have had a very striking appearance on parade, as each of its three companies had facings of a different colour and a unique design of regimental lace and decorative detail on their tall caps.

Apart from their size, grenadiers could be differentiated from the soldiers of the centre companies by unique features of their uniform and equipment. The most prominent distinction of the British grenadier's dress was his tall pointed and embroidered cap. As both hands were needed to light and throw grenades, the grenadier would sling his musket across his back while in action. To facilitate this movement, he wore a tuque-like soft cloth cap with a small turned-up peak and long pointed bag rather than the standard wide-brimmed felt hat. By the early eighteenth century, the bag had been pointed and stiffened, and the resulting mitre-shaped front richly embroidered with cyphers and devices.

The grenadiers of the 22nd, 40th, and 45th regiments of Foot wore this typical cloth "mitre" cap. The twelve-inch stiffened cloth front was of facing colour, edged in white tape, and topped with a worsted tuft. A small turned-up red flap, trimmed in white, bore around the edge the motto *Nec Aspera Terrent* in white letters above the white running horse of Hanover on a red ground. In the centre of the cap front was an embroidered GR (*Georgius Rex*) surmounted by a crown in heraldic colours and flanked with embroidered leaves. The headband around the base of the cap was of facing colour, and embroidered with a grenade at the rear centre flanked by the number of the regiment and assorted scrolls.

The grenadier caps for the 22nd had pale buff fronts and headbands, GR and scrolls in yellow, and white tufts. Caps of the 40th had buff fronts and headbands, GR in black with scrolls in white, and worsted tufts of black and white. The 45th had deep-green cap fronts and headbands, white GR and scrolls, and green and white tufts. The white piping on the red back of the caps can be seen on the right-hand figure in the plate.[1]

The red coats of the grenadiers, of similar pattern to those of the centre companies, had lapels of regimental facing colour to the waist. When buttoned back, the lapels showed their edging and button loops of regimental lace. The lapels could also be buttoned across for added warmth and convenience on campaign.

The deep turned-back cuffs were of regimental facing colour with a deep cleft. A slashed three-button panel in regimental lace set above the edges of the cuffs and pocket flaps was trimmed with a double row of regimental lace.

The skirt of the coat was buttoned back to reveal the lining, usually of regimental facing colour. A plain red shoulder-strap was set on the left shoulder to keep the heavy cross-belt in place. Some grenadier coats had cloth shoulder wings trimmed with regimental lace.

The collarless sleeved waistcoat was trimmed down the front and along the skirt edges with regimental lace. A white shirt and neckcloth were worn beneath the waistcoat.

White gaiters, reaching well up on the thigh, were worn over red cloth breeches. They were buttoned down the outside, and fastened under the knee by a black strap.

The grenadier's equipment consisted of a buff leather waist-belt with a double frog to hold a bayonet and hanger. A narrow buff strap held a small black cartridge pouch in the centre of the waist-belt.

A wide belt with brass buckle and furnishings crossed the left shoulder to support a large black cartridge-box on the right hip. Above the buckle was a brass match case, the last vestige of the grenadier's original equipment.

The British grenadiers of this period carried the Long Land Musket, a forty-six-inch barrel flintlock with socket bayonet, and a hanger, a single-edged curved sword with a twenty-four-inch blade and brass hilt.[2]

The plate illustrates, from left to right, a grenadier of the 22nd, 45th, and 40th regiments of Foot. The various regiments can be distinguished by the detail of their caps, facing colours, and regimental lace. The facings on caps, cuffs, and lapels were pale buff for the 22nd, buff for the 40th, and deep green for the 45th. The different patterns of regimental lace can be seen clearly in the illustration. That of the 22nd is white with two stripes of red and blue dashes, with square-ended loops. That of the 40th is made up of lines of black, buff, and black, with square-ended loops. The lace of the 45th is white with one green line along the outside edge and a row of green stars; the loops of the 45th were pointed.

The plate also illustrates some of the variations in equipment of the period. The grenadier of the 45th, in the centre, wears his equipment in the conventional manner; the grenadier of the 22nd, on the left, wears his waist-belt slung from the right shoulder, an arrangement that soon became regulation practice. The grenadier of the 40th, on the right, is encumbered with full marching order. In addition to his cross-belt and waist-belt, he wears a hide pack fastened to a cross-belt over his right shoulder. A metal water-bottle is suspended on the left from a narrow strap over the right shoulder, and the greyish-white canvas haversack for rations hangs on the right side. The grenadier also wears the brown marching gaiters that replaced white linen ones on active service.

Information on the dress of Wolfe's army is scarce, but there are indications that the officers and men attempted to adapt their dress and equipment to the gruelling conditions of North American campaigns. Clothing was shortened for comfort and ease of movement, and conspicuous ornaments were removed for forest action. Equipment was reduced to the absolute minimum and carried in the easiest possible fashion. Hangers and halberds were replaced by hatchets and muskets.

Nonetheless, even with their dress and equipment faded and worn from campaigning, the companies of the Louisbourg Grenadiers must have presented an impressive appearance as they stood in silent ranks on the Plains of Abraham on the fateful morning of 13 September 1759.

1775-1783

History

Several Loyalist provincial corps were raised in Canada for service with the British Army during the American Revolution. One of the strongest and most colourful of these was the Royal Highland Emigrants, raised chiefly from former soldiers of various Highland corps who had settled in North America.

On 3 April 1775, Lieutenant-Colonel Allan Maclean of Torloisk was granted permission by King George III to raise a regiment from among "our subjects who have at different times emigrated from the northwest parts of North Britain and have transported themselves, with their families, to New York."[1] Armed with the King's permission, Maclean brought his proposal before the British military authorities in Boston.

On 12 June 1775, General Gage authorized Maclean to raise a Highland regiment of two battalions of ten companies each, from any of the provinces in North America, "the whole Corps to be cloathed, armed, and accoutered in like manner with His Majesty's Royal Highland Regiment, and are to be called the Royal Highland Emigrants."[2]

As commanding officer of the 1st Battalion, Royal Highland Emigrants, Maclean set out from Boston to recruit his unit. Hoping to build his battalion around a cadre of veterans of the 42nd and Fraser's 78th who had remained in America after the Seven Years' War, Maclean travelled through the Mohawk Valley, where many of the Highlanders had taken up land. He proceeded to Oswego and then to Canada, where he reported to Governor Guy Carleton with a respectable nucleus of about 150 men.

The Royal Highland Emigrants and their experienced commander were a welcome sight to Governor Carleton, who hoped to block Montgomery's invasion force as it moved up the Lake Champlain-Richelieu River waterway to Canada. Twenty Emigrants were sent to join Major Charles Preston at Fort St-Jean, while Carleton and Maclean planned its relief. One force, under the command of Maclean and made up largely of Emigrants and militia, was to strike out from Quebec to Sorel, and then on to Chambly. The second detachment under the direct command of the Governor included 130 Emigrants and 7th Fusiliers, who provided stiffening for a force consisting chiefly of militia and Indians. This second unit was to cross the St. Lawrence River at Montreal and join Maclean on the Richelieu.

On 30 October, Carleton's column bumped an American outpost at Longueuil. The engagement was badly handled, and Carleton's force stalled the entire operation by turning back. With the collapse of the relief expedition, Preston surrendered after a siege of fifty-five days.

After the fall of Fort St-Jean, Montgomery occupied Montreal on 13 November 1775, and pressed on down the St. Lawrence towards Quebec, where he joined another American force under Benedict Arnold. Maclean and his companies of Emigrants, moving just ahead of the Americans, arrived at Quebec on 12 November to bolster the garrison, both in numbers and in spirit. The Highlanders were further strengthened by the arrival of a draft of ninety recruits, mostly Irish, brought in from St. John's by Captain Malcolm Fraser. This timely addition raised the Royal Highland Emigrants to 230 men, making it the strongest unit of the garrison.[3]

Governor Carleton arrived at Quebec on 19 November, and the city prepared to withstand yet another siege. The strength of the Royal Highland Emigrants and the energy of its commander provided some fibre for the defence.

Detachments of the Emigrants took part in the confused fighting among the houses and barricades of the Lower Town during the American attack of 31 December. During the brief winter battle, Montgomery was killed and a number of Americans were captured. British-born prisoners were given an opportunity to change sides by joining the Royal Highland Emigrants, and some ninety-four men, mostly Irish, enlisted. However, some had a change of heart and escaped over the wall to the American camp. After several episodes of this kind, Carleton "disarmed and disuniformed" the remainder of the reluctant recruits, and locked them up.[4]

The spring of 1776 brought the British navy to Quebec with reinforcements and supplies, and the siege was lifted. The garrison, led by Maclean and his Emigrants, sallied out of the city to force the Americans from the Plains of Abraham.

Until the end of the Revolution, the 1st Battalion served on the Canadian frontier. The 2nd Battalion, under the command of Major John Small, was raised in Nova Scotia. In 1779, the regiment was placed on the regular establishment and given the designation 84th Regiment of Foot (Royal Highland Emigrants).[5]

The 2nd Battalion garrisoned various posts in Nova Scotia until 1781, when five companies were sent to join Cornwallis in South Carolina. Before the end of the year these companies were incorporated into an improvised flank battalion.[6]

When the American Revolution ended in 1783, the 84th Regiment of Foot, the first Highland corps of the British Army to be raised outside of Scotland, was disbanded in Canada. This fine regiment may well be considered the first of Canada's many "Highland" units.

1775-1783

Uniform

Contemporary records of the clothing and equipment of the Royal Highland Emigrants are scarce, and many details of dress are uncertain. However, as we do know that authority was granted for "the whole Corps to be cloathed, armed, and accoutred in like manner with His Majesty's Royal Highland Regiment,"[1] the general features of the uniform may be determined with reasonable certainty.

During this period, a diced band of red, white, and green squares appeared in the Highland bonnet, which began to assume the high-sided Kilmarnock shape, with touri, cockade, regimental button or device, and bunches of feathers.[2]

The coat of the Highland corps was of similar pattern to that of the line infantry, but slightly shorter to accommodate the plaid. Coats were lined in white, with only the front edge of the skirt turned back. By this time, the red coat had a flat collar, small round cuffs, and long lapels, with lapel and cuff buttons set with loops of regimental lace. Being a Royal regiment, the Emigrants' facings were blue.

While the detailed pattern of the regimental lace of the 84th is unknown, there is some suggestion that the lapel loops of the men's jackets were set in pairs.[3] Officers' lace was gold.[4]

Following the dress of the 42nd, the tartan of the 84th was the Government sett. The belted plaid was still in general use by Highland corps, though the filibeg or small kilt was becoming increasingly popular. Some regiments, including the Emigrants, had both the belted plaid and filibeg.[5]

In addition to the Highland bonnet, red jacket with blue facings, and belted plaid of Government tartan, the men wore a sleeved white waistcoat, red and white diced hose, and red garters.

A black cartridge-box was carried on a black cross-belt; a broadsword with a half-basket hilt and a black scabbard were supported from a black sword-belt.[6] The bayonet was attached to the black waist-belt. Regimental sporrans of unknown pattern were said to have been of raccoon rather than badger fur. The sporran was worn only on special parades, and was left behind when the regiment was on campaign.

The plate depicts an officer of the Royal Highland Emigrants in full Highland dress in 1778. His commissioned rank is indicated by the two gold pear-shaped epaulettes, gilt gorget, and crimson sash worn in characteristic Highland fashion over the left shoulder rather than around the waist. Officers also were issued a purse and belt, and a cartouche-box and waist-belt.

Weapons included a fusil with bayonet, a Scottish pistol and strap, a broadsword with black leather sword-belt, and a dirk.[7]

Although Lieutenant-Colonel Maclean ordered Highland clothing from England and Scotland shortly after the Royal Highland Emigrants was authorized, it is unlikely that Highland dress was immediately available when the regiment was recruited in 1775.[8] Evidence shows that the first uniform included green coats with red facings, buff breeches and waistcoat, and the traditional cocked hat.[9] During the siege of Quebec, the Highlanders were issued moccasins, leggings, caps, and *capots* for winter wear.[10]

Clothing wore out rapidly under the severe conditions of service in North America; and the annual issue of uniforms, ordered on contract from England, was frequently delayed by adverse weather, or lost through storms or enemy action. It was often necessary to improvise replacement items of dress from local resources. Entries in the Regimental Order Book indicate that on occasion tartan trousers, white trousers, and even breeches were made up and issued to the 84th.[11]

In 1781, the regiment was requested to accept the clothing of the 21st Regiment as their annual issue. Brigadier-General Maclean, as he was by this time, requested that General Haldimand himself order the regiment to wear the "stockings, bretches, and hats" of the 21st, to deter the soldiers from objecting too violently to the change from Highland dress.[12]

During this period, changes were made in the soldiers' weapons. The Highland broadswords and pistols were cumbersome and of little use in North America. The sword was replaced by the more versatile hatchet, and the pistols were returned to stores, never again to be issued to Highland regiments.[13]

In spite of weather, campaign conditions, and supply problems, the Highland soldier clung to as much of his national dress as was possible. Pride in their unique dress helped to give the Highland regiments a spirit that set them apart from other soldiers.

1803-1816

History

War with the new French Republic strained Britain's military resources to the utmost. It was decided, therefore, to raise a body of regular soldiers in Newfoundland to provide for the defence of England's oldest colony. On 25 April 1795, Major Thomas Skinner, R.E. was authorized to raise the Newfoundland Regiment of Fencible Infantry, sometimes called the Royal Newfoundland Regiment (Skinner's Fencibles).

The Royal Newfoundland Regiment was posted to Halifax in July 1800, and was disbanded there on 31 July 1802, when the British Army was reduced according to the terms of the Treaty of Amiens.[1]

With the resumption of hostilities between England and France in 1803, the recently disbanded colonial regiments of fencibles were reactivated. On 7 June 1803, Brigadier-General John Skerrett was authorized to raise a regiment of fencibles for service in America. It was to consist of one grenadier company, one light company, and eight battalion companies, each composed of five sergeants, five corporals, two drummers, and ninety-five privates. In pay, clothing, arms, and accoutrements the regiment was to be on the same footing as His Majesty's regiments of the line, and was designated the Royal Newfoundland Fencible Infantry.[2]

Through vigorous recruiting, the regiment was 385 strong by Christmas 1803, and by June 1805 it had reached the very respectable figure of 683 men.

On 19 June 1805, the regiment exchanged stations with the Nova Scotia Fencibles, and sailed for Halifax to begin ten years of service in Canada.[3] After spending a year in garrison at Fort Anne, Nova Scotia, the Royal Newfoundland Regiment moved to Halifax in August 1806, and then to Quebec in September 1807 to strengthen the forces in Lower Canada.

As war approached, it became apparent to Major-General Brock and Sir George Prevost that control of the St. Lawrence River and Great Lakes was vital to the security of Upper Canada. However, naval resources were meagre. On 9 May, to help overcome the shortage of manpower, the Royal Newfoundland Fencibles was ordered to form five companies for service as seamen and marines with the naval squadrons on the Great Lakes. Late in May, 360 men left for Kingston, where they were posted in detachments to the ships of the Provincial Marine.[4]

When war against the Americans was formally declared on 18 June 1812, the flank companies were withdrawn from the regiment and, in August, were sent to Kingston under the command of Major Heathcote.

Elements of the Royal Newfoundlanders soon became involved in action around Detroit, as the Americans attempted to mount an attack on Upper Canada. The detachment under Captain Mockler, serving as seamen aboard the *General Hunter* and the *Queen Charlotte*, were brought ashore in August to form a core of regulars for the militia force attacking Detroit. The Newfoundlanders won a special commendation from General Brock on the fall of Detroit.

By the end of 1812, the regiment was scattered in detachments to Quebec, Prescott, Kingston, Fort George, and York. The largest group of the regiment was a detachment of 111 all ranks, which formed part of the garrison of Fort George at the mouth of the Niagara River. The Americans attacked the fort on the night of 26-27 May 1813.

The grenadier company of the Royal Newfoundlanders formed part of the small force of 200 defenders at the point of the original assault-landings. Attacked in overwhelming strength, the British force gradually fell back to Fort George; the grenadier company lost twenty-one men killed and twelve wounded, including both its officers.

A further 100 men of the regiment served as marines with the Lake Erie Squadron under the command of Captain Robert Barclay, R.N. These Newfoundlanders suffered fourteen killed and twenty-five wounded – twenty-eight per cent of the total British casualties – in the naval Battle of Lake Erie fought on 10 September 1813.[5]

In 1814, a detachment of Newfoundlanders carried out a remarkable operation that demonstrated their capability and determination both ashore and on the water. Two companies were ordered to reinforce the isolated British post of Michilimackinac. This involved building a fleet of small open boats and sailing them from Georgian Bay to the northwestern end of Lake Huron. The Royal Newfoundlanders reached their destination in a month.

Early in August, the post was attacked by troops landed from an American naval squadron. The garrison not only beat off the attack, but the Newfoundlanders and a naval detachment took to the water in four small boats and captured the American ships *Tigress* and *Scorpion* in a daring night operation.

In June 1814, the regiment began to return to St. John's by detachments, to be replaced by the Nova Scotia Fencibles. The Royal Newfoundland Fencible Infantry garrisoned St. John's until orders were received for the reduction of all fencible corps in North America. The regiment was formally disbanded on 24 June 1816.[6]

1803-1816
Uniform

Specific details of dress and equipment of the Royal Newfoundland Fencibles no longer exist. The official letter authorizing the raising of the regiment in 1803 specified only that "in pay, clothing, arms, and accoutrements the new corps was to be on the same footing as His Majesty's Regiments of the Line."[1]

Between 1790 and 1800 the uniform of the British infantry underwent drastic change. In 1800, the cocked felt hat was replaced by a shako or cap of black lacquered leather 7 in. high with a black leather peak. The front carried a rectangular stamped brass plate, 6 in. x 4 in. which bore the Royal Cypher enclosed in the Garter and surmounted by a Crown. In the centre of the top was a black rosette with a regimental button in front of a white-over-red worsted plume.[2] In 1806, the leather cap was replaced by a felt shako of similar shape and dimensions, with a black lacquered leather peak. This was commonly referred to as the "stove-pipe" shako.

The "Belgic" or "Waterloo" shako was approved for British infantry in November 1811. This was a felt cylindrical cap 6 in. high with a false front 8½ in. high. It had a black leather peak, a plume and rosette on the left side, cap lines hanging across the front, and a brass cap plate bearing the regimental number. Supplying a regiment that was spread across the entire theatre of operations presented great problems, and it is unlikely that the Royal Newfoundlanders were issued the "Belgic" shako until they returned to St. John's in 1814.

By 1800, the soldier's red coat had developed from a long-skirted garment with wide curved lapels to a single-breasted jacket or coatee, cut square at the waist with the short skirt turned back to show white linings. Its stiff stand-up collar was open at the throat to show the black stock. The jacket front was trimmed with loops of regimental lace, either evenly spaced or in pairs. The small round cuffs in facing colour were trimmed with four buttons set with loops of regimental lace.

Shoulder-straps of facing colour were trimmed with regimental lace. Battalion companies' shoulder-straps ended in white worsted tufts, while those of flank companies had laced wings. The slashed pockets set vertically on the hip were trimmed with four buttons and loops of regimental lace.

The facings of the Royal Newfoundland Fencibles were blue, like those of all Royal regiments; regimental lace was white with a blue line between two red ones. The loops across the breast of the coatee were square ended and evenly spaced.[3]

White woollen knee breeches were worn with black knee-length gaiters. Trousers were worn for fatigues, and gradually replaced breeches for wear on service. Some trousers were white, and buttoned up the outside to the knee like a pair of gaiters. In some cases they were made up locally of brown or grey homespun, or of striped cotton ticking. As trousers became accepted for campaign dress, grey calf-length gaiters were adopted for wear with ankle boots.

The plate illustrates a grenadier of the Royal Newfoundland Fencibles in full marching order for the 1813 campaign.

The soldier's equipment consists of a black leather cartridge pouch suspended on the right hip from a white cross-belt. A second cross-belt over the right shoulder supports the black brass-tipped bayonet scabbard. An off-white canvas haversack and blue wooden water-bottle hang on the left side.

The painted canvas knapsack has some form of regimental identification on the outer flap and is held in place with a white breast harness and shoulder-straps.

Throughout the campaign seasons in the harsh Canadian climate, far from a ready source of supplies, the Royal Newfoundlanders would have had anything but a precise uniform appearance. Dress aboard ship must have been casual, but practical. In winter, regular uniform clothing was supplemented with fur caps, mitts, moccasins, and warm leggings. Although the Royal Newfoundland Fencibles' dress is uncertain, there is no doubt about the magnificent contribution of the regiment to Canada's military heritage.

1803-1817

History

The French Revolution burst upon Europe in 1789. By 1793, Britain was at war with France, and had to defend her North American colonies against raids from bases in the United States.

Three of the four regiments of British regulars stationed in Nova Scotia and New Brunswick were posted to the West Indies; to fill the gap created by their departure, authority was granted to raise four provincial regiments of infantry, one in Nova Scotia, one in Newfoundland, one in Canada, and one in New Brunswick. These regiments were to serve only in their respective provinces, and were not part of the regular British establishment.

In 1799, the status of the provincial regiments was changed to that of fencibles, so they could be committed to serve anywhere in North America. However, they were not called upon to do so, and with the Peace of Amiens in 1802 the regiments were disbanded.[1]

Peace was short-lived, and hostilities recommenced early in 1803. Once again, the shortage of regular British regiments left British North America in a difficult situation, and authority was granted to raise four fencible units, one each in Newfoundland, Nova Scotia, New Brunswick, and Canada.

On 6 July 1803, Brigadier-General Martin Hunter was granted a letter of service authorizing him to raise a corps to be known as His Majesty's New Brunswick Regiment of Fencible Infantry.[2] Unlike the previous unit, the new regiment of fencibles was to be part of the regular establishment of the British Army, although its service was restricted to North America.[3]

In 1808, the regiment volunteered for general service. The offer was rejected; but when it was renewed in 1810, the British authorities accepted, and the fencibles were elevated to an infantry regiment of the line. As the 104th (New Brunswick) Regiment of Foot, the unit could be moved to any British garrison or theatre of operations.[4]

When war with the United States broke out in June 1812, detachments of the 104th were posted throughout New Brunswick. The buildup of American troops in the Sackets Harbor area during the winter of 1812-13 implied that an invasion of Upper Canada would take place in the spring. To strengthen the defences of Upper Canada, Sir George Prevost instructed Sir John Sherbrooke, commanding in Nova Scotia, to send six companies of the 104th overland to Quebec, and then on to Kingston.

The headquarters and grenadier companies set out on snowshoes from Fredericton on 16 February 1813; one battalion company followed each succeeding day, with the light company bringing up the rear. In spite of temperatures of –31°C (–25°F) the detachments arrived in Quebec in mid-March, travelling 550 km (350 mi.) in twenty-four days. After two weeks in garrison at Quebec, the 104th set out for Kingston; they arrived on 12 April having covered a total distance of 1125 km (700 mi.).[5]

In the spring of 1813, the remaining companies sailed to Upper Canada, where the regiment remained for the duration of the war, participating in the battles of Sackets Harbor, Beaver Dam, and Lundy's Lane, the blockade of Fort George, and the assault on Fort Erie.[6]

When the war ended, in December 1814, the 104th (New Brunswick) Regiment was named part of the force of regulars and fencibles assigned to garrison duty in Canada. The regiment was stationed first in Quebec, and later in Montreal. With Napoleon imprisoned on St. Helena and peace established in Europe, Britain wished to reduce the strength of her army, and the 104th (New Brunswick) Regiment of Foot was ordered to disband on 24 May 1817.

1803-1817

Uniform

The letter of service authorizing the raising of the New Brunswick Regiment of Fencible Infantry specified that its pay, clothing, arms, and accoutrements were to be the same as those of the regular British infantry regiments of the line.[1]

By 1803, the dramatic change in the British soldier's dress had almost been completed. At the beginning of the regiment's service, the men would have worn the stove-pipe shako introduced by the General Order of 24 February 1800. Made of black lacquered leather, the shako was 7 in. high with a black leather peak. In a Horse Guards Circular of 1806, the leather cap was replaced by one of a similar design in felt.[2]

It is said that the "Wellington" or "Belgic" shako was introduced on 24 December 1811, at the request of the Duke of Wellington. This new black felt shako was 6 in. high with a false front of $8^{1}/_{2}$ in. and a peak of black leather. The plume, white over red for battalion companies, was set on the left side behind a black rosette. Cap lines fit under the rosette, fell across the front, and fastened high on the right side. Those of the private soldiers were white and ended in white tassels. The cap plate was surmounted by the Crown, and bore the Royal Cypher and the number or badge of the regiment. On service, the cap was provided with an oilskin cover to protect it from the elements.[3]

It is doubtful if the new caps reached regiments serving in Canada, often in company-sized detachments, before the last year of the war. However, the 104th certainly would have received the "Belgic" shako when assigned to peace-time garrison duties in 1814.

The standard infantry outer garment was the single-breasted red coatee with short tails and white turn-backs. The collar and round cuffs were of regimental facing colour. The shoulder-straps were also of facing colour; those of battalion companies ended in white woollen tufts, while those of grenadier and light companies ended in wings. The wings, collar, coatee front, and cuffs were trimmed with regimental lace. The pewter buttons were inscribed with the number and title of the regiment.[4]

The facings of the 104th (New Brunswick) Regiment were light buff; regimental lace was white with red, buff, and blue lines. The loops across the front of the coatee were square ended and set in pairs. Officers' lace was silver.[5]

The plate illustrates a pioneer of the 104th in 1814. Each infantry battalion had a pioneer section of about ten men who were skilled in the use of tools. Their duties included road making, bridge building, and the repair and construction of simple fortifications. Apparently, all the pioneers of the 104th New Brunswick Regiment were black.[6]

The pioneer wears a tan leather apron to protect his clothing during the performance of heavy tasks.[7] His equipment consists of a set of cross-belts supporting a cartridge-box on the right hip and a bayonet on the left. The belts are joined by an oval brass belt-plate inscribed with the number and title of the unit.[8] The canvas haversack and blue water-bottle hang on the left side.

A bill hook, a short heavy-bladed cutting implement, hangs in its black scabbard from a black leather waist-belt. Assorted tools such as saws, hammers, mattocks, and spades were carried by various pioneers. The head of the pioneer's axe was carried in a holster attached to the waist-belt, and the helve was carried across the back.

History

By early 1812, war with the United States was almost inevitable. Lieutenant-General Sir George Prevost, Captain-General and Governor-in-Chief of the Provinces of Upper and Lower Canada, New Brunswick, Nova Scotia, and the Islands of Prince Edward and Cape Breton, planned to increase the military manpower of British North America. On 15 April 1812 he raised a Provincial Corps of Light Infantry, known as the Canadian Voltigeurs, under the authority of the Militia Act of Lower Canada. This corps was a regular unit of full-time soldiers raised and paid by the Province of Lower Canada, and was not part of the regular British Army establishment.

Command of this new and uniquely Canadian regiment was given to a member of a distinguished Quebec family, Major Charles de Salaberry of the 60th (Royal American) Regiment of Foot. Except for the adjutant and quarter-master, who were appointed from regular or fencible regiments, de Salaberry was to select his officers from prominent families of Lower Canada. The six captains and eighteen lieutenants were to receive their commissions on raising the required number of recruits – thirty-six for captains and sixteen for lieutenants. Recruits were to be between the ages of seventeen and thirty-five, and at least 5 ft. 3 in. tall. As light infantry, the regiment was to have one bugle major and ten buglers, but no drummers.[1]

Two volunteer companies of Frontier Light Infantry, recruited in 1813 from the six battalions of the Sedentary Militia of the Eastern Townships, were attached to the Canadian Voltigeurs. They adopted the same dress as the Voltigeurs, and frequently were considered to be the 9th and 10th companies of the regiment.[2]

In the early months of the war, the Canadian Voltigeurs were assigned to the forward defences of the Eastern Townships. In November 1812, General Dearborn moved up from Plattsburg with 6,000 men to invade Lower Canada. Major de Salaberry countered this advance by rushing his Voltigeurs and some Indians to Lacolle on the frontier. Dearborn's advance guard crossed the border; but after several days of skirmishing with the outposts of the Voltigeurs, they withdrew.

In the spring of 1813, four companies of the Voltigeurs were posted to Kingston to assist in the defence of Upper Canada. Two companies were involved in the bungled attack on Sackets Harbor on 29 May. "The timing of the attack on Sackets Harbor," wrote one Canadian historian, "has been one of the more confused moments in a war not noted for its clarity."[3]

The following autumn, the Americans planned to cut the St. Lawrence, thereby isolating British forces in Upper Canada, and then to seize Montreal. As part of this operation, Major-General Hampton led a force of some 4,000 men from the Lake Champlain region up the Châteauguay River. His plan was to cut the St. Lawrence and join forces with General Wilkinson sweeping down the river from Sackets Harbor.

On 25 October, Lieutenant-Colonel de Salaberry, 200 regulars, including two companies of Voltigeurs,[4] and 250 militia, supported by Lieutenant-Colonel George Macdonell with 300 Voltigeurs and 700 militia, checked Hampton's hesitant advance down the Châteauguay River. The so-called Battle of Châteauguay was little more than a skirmish, but it was significant in that all the defenders were Canadians – both English and French – fighting a decisive action without the direct participation of British regular troops.[5]

On 9 November, three companies of the Canadian Voltigeurs formed part of the 900-man force under Lieutenant-Colonel Morrison that checked General Wilkinson's move down river from Sackets Harbor in the second phase of the two-pronged American attack on Montreal. In what was essentially an American rearguard action, the two forces faced each other about halfway between Prescott and Cornwall at Crysler's Farm. The Voltigeurs, extended across the front of the British position in a skirmish line, were struck and brushed aside by the American column on the afternoon of 11 November. However, the enemy was checked by the main body of Morrison's force, and driven from the field by a determined infantry attack. The next day, Wilkinson abandoned his advance on Montreal.

The spring of 1814 found the Voltigeurs and Frontier Light Infantry back on frontier defence in the Eastern Townships. They were brigaded with the Canadian Chasseurs, a new unit formed by a reorganization of the 5th Battalion of Select Embodied Militia. The entire force came under the control of Lieutenant-Colonel de Salaberry, now Inspecting Field Officer of Militia Light Infantry.[6]

In August, three infantry brigades were formed into a division commanded by Major-General Francis de Rottenburg, and were assigned to the force led by George Prevost against Plattsburg. The Voltigeurs formed part of the 2nd Brigade. After a half-hearted attack on the enemy positions at Plattsburg, Prevost withdrew when the naval component of the British force was defeated on Lake Champlain.

On 24 March 1815 the Canadian Voltigeurs was disbanded and the officers placed on half pay.[7] So ended the service of a regiment raised in and paid for by the Province of Lower Canada. It is only fitting that the name of this creditable corps is perpetuated in a regiment of the Canadian Militia.

Uniform

The Canadian Voltigeurs was uniquely Canadian in its origin as a provincial corps, in its officers and men, and in its dress. The document authorizing the raising of the unit specifies "the arms to be rifles or light infantry muskets with black accoutrements: the clothing to be grey with black collars and cuffs and black buttons with Canadian short boots. Light Bear Skin caps."[1]

Subsequent documents record that the men were issued jacket and trousers of mixed grey cloth with black cuffs and collar. As of 1813, the jacket had shoulder wings trimmed with black tape and a black cotton fringe. Sufficient small black buttons were issued to each man to provide one row on the breast of the jacket. For trimming the jacket, staff sergeants were issued nine yards of silver lace, sergeants nine yards of black cotton lace, and the men seven yards of black tape. No evidence of the pattern of this trim exists. Sergeants wore sashes of local manufacture.[2]

There is no available description of the pattern of the "Light Bear Skin caps" mentioned in the original dress instructions. It is known that fur caps were approved for wear both in 1812 and 1813, but subsequent issues of head-gear were of the felt stove-pipe shako.[3] A black and white portrait of Captain Viger of the Canadian Voltigeurs shows him wearing a fur cap with a black leather visor, shaped somewhat like a fusilier's fur cap except that the crown is more sharply pointed. This cap is illustrated in the plate.[4]

The "Canadian short boots" remain a mystery. However, it is known that the regiment was issued with shoes, which probably were worn with short grey gaiters. But from time to time shoes were in short supply, much to the distress of Lieutenant-Colonel de Salaberry.

Light Infantry accoutrements of black leather were sent from England for issue to the regiment.

While there is some question about the exact dress for the men of the regiment, there are several surviving portraits of officers. The surprising feature of the officers' uniform is that it is green, rather than grey.[5]

The green jacket was patterned after that of the Rifles. It had black collar and cuffs, and three rows of black buttons with black braid on the chest. The sash with cords and tassels was scarlet, and the sword-belt was of black leather with gilt clasps.

A portrait of the adjutant, painted about 1814, shows him wearing a tall cylindrical cap with a small peak folded up after the fashion of a cavalry officer's watering cap. This head-gear was commonly affected by officers of Rifles and Light Infantry serving in the Peninsula.[6]

In the illustration, an officer of the Canadian Voltigeurs wears a light fur cap. His green trousers are fitted with leather cuffs, and he wears white metal spurs. It was common practice for officers to ride when feasible, and, as a result, officers of light corps affected such dress details of light cavalry as the fur-trimmed pelisse and leather-bound trousers.

In addition to the bearskin cap, watering cap, and Light Infantry shako, officers still needed a fore-and-aft cocked hat for wear with more informal orders of dress.

The distinctly Canadian pattern and detail of their dress reflected the Voltigeurs' function as a corps of light troops suited to the rigorous Canadian campaign conditions.

History

When Sir George Prevost assumed his duties on 13 September 1811, the rumblings of impending war with the United States were clearly audible. Naturally, one of his first acts was to examine the forces available to him for the defence of British North America. In the Canadas he had 5,600 regular soldiers, of whom only 1,200 were in Upper Canada. With Britain heavily engaged in the war with France, there was no possibility of augmenting his meagre forces in Upper Canada with regulars from England.

In February 1812, without official approval, Sir George directed Colonel Edward Baynes to recruit a small battalion of fencible infantry from Glengarry County in Upper Canada.[1] Glengarry was chosen because it had been settled by men of the Glengarry Fencibles, a unit raised in the Highlands for service in the British Army by the militant priest, Father Alexander Macdonell, later Bishop of Kingston. The regiment had been disbanded after the treaty of Amiens, and many of its members had emigrated to Upper Canada in 1804.[2]

Early in the War of 1812, trained regular soldiers were scarce, and companies were assigned the work of battalions. Detachments of regular regiments like the Glengarry Light Infantry were sent to the various garrisons of Upper Canada as a disciplined nucleus around which the local militia could form.

The regiment was scattered from Quebec to Fort George.[3] Two companies of the Glengarrys at Prescott were involved in an abortive attack on Ogdensburg on 3 October 1812. Together with 600 militiamen, the Glengarrys set out from Prescott to cross the St. Lawrence River. The American artillery quickly ranged on the boats and turned back the force before it was halfway across the river.

On 22 February 1813, Lieutenant-Colonel "Red George" Macdonell of the Glengarrys repeated the attempt on Ogdensburg. With 500 men, including a company of the Glengarry Light Infantry and a number of Glengarry and Stormont militia, Macdonell marched out on the frozen river. British soldiers performing drill on the ice were a common sight, so the American sentries gave little heed to the moving column until it had reached halfway across the river with no sign of wheeling about.

The alarm was given and the Americans opened fire; but Macdonell's troops completed the river crossing, urged on by the church militant in the person of Father Alexander Macdonell. After a brief resistance the Americans fled, leaving Ogdensburg in British hands. Macdonell's men withdrew to Prescott; but the people of Ogdensburg, anxious to avoid further attacks and to continue a clandestine trade with the British, asked Washington not to station another garrison in the town. The authorities complied, and Ogdensburg saw no more American troops until the end of the war.[4]

Throughout the summer campaign of 1813 the Glengarrys fought in Upper Canada with some distinction, but little success. A company was at York when it was attacked and captured by the Americans in April. Another company formed part of the garrison of Fort George on 27 May, when the position was attacked in strength by the Americans. Attempts to meet the enemy assault columns at the landing points were frustrated by effective covering fire from American naval forces. The British evacuated the fort and withdrew to Burlington at the head of Lake Ontario.[5]

Later in May, a company of the Glengarry Light Infantry was involved in the confused British attack on Sackets Harbor,[6] and, in June, it was engaged at Stoney Creek.[7] Although it was a dismal year for the war, the regiment earned a fine reputation for its fighting ability. The Indian allies admiringly called it the "Black Stump Brigade" for both its dark uniforms and its skill in forest warfare.[8]

The 1814 campaign saw an improvement in the fortunes of the Glengarrys. In May, the Light Company accompanied a battalion of Royal Marines in an assault-landing operation to capture Fort Oswego.[9] The entire battalion fought together for the first time in July, when it was sent to York to reinforce Major-General Riall's Right Division of the British Army.[10] As part of Riall's force, the Glengarry Light Infantry fought at the Battle of Lundy's Lane on 25 July 1814.[11] The regiment also saw action at Fort Erie on 17 September, and on 17 October at Cook's Mills; it was commended for its performance on both occasions.[12]

The unit was granted permission to emblazon the battle honour *Niagara* on its colours.[13] The fact that the regiment had colours indicates that, though dressed like a rifle regiment, it was light infantry both in name and custom.

In view of its outstanding service record, it was hoped that the Glengarry Light Infantry would be retained on the regular establishment of the British Army. But the authorities decreed otherwise, and the regiment was disbanded in Kingston on 18 May 1816.[14] Nevertheless, the name of Glengarry and the traditions of the Glengarry Light Infantry are perpetuated by the Stormont, Dundas, and Glengarry Highlanders of the Canadian Militia.

Uniform

The Glengarry Fencible Light Infantry was intended to be uniformed as a Highland corps.[1] In 1811, Lieutenant-General Sir James Craig issued a letter of service on his own authority for the raising of the Glengarrys; and, as the new corps was to be based on the Glengarry Fencibles of the British Army, it would seem reasonable for the new regiment also to adopt Highland dress. But Craig was premature, and had to withdraw his authority because his "zeal had exceeded their ability" to raise men for the Glengarrys as quickly as had been expected.[2]

In February 1812, Sir George Prevost reviewed the proposal to raise a fencible unit in Glengarry County to be uniformed like the 95th Rifles.[3] The first documentation of Glengarry dress lists "white cloth jackets with green cuff and cape, and green foraging caps,"[4] a description that fits the undress uniform of the 95th.[5]

A green uniform like that of the 95th Rifles was issued to the Glengarry Light Infantry. The jacket for the men was dark green with black collar, pointed cuffs, and turn-backs piped with white tape. Cloth pantaloons were green; shoulder-straps were black, piped with white, and ending in a black tuft. The most striking feature of the jacket was the three rows of twelve white metal buttons down the front of the breast.[6]

The cap for both officers and men of the Glengarrys was the black felt "stove-pipe" shako, which remained the head-gear of rifle and light infantry corps even after the introduction of the "Wellington" shako. The officer's cap badge, a silver bugle with cords and the letters GLI, can be seen in the illustration. It is speculated that other ranks wore a cap badge of similar pattern in pewter.[7] The cylindrical felt shako was trimmed with green cap cords and a black cockade; a white metal button in front held a green plume.

The Glengarrys carried the thirty-nine-inch barrel Light Infantry Musket, rather than the Baker rifle of the 95th.[8] Accoutrements consisted of the standard cross-belt equipment of black leather, with regimental belt-plate.

The illustration depicts an officer of the Glengarry Light Infantry in campaign dress. The black collar of his dark-green jacket is laced with black braid, and has a silver button on each side. The rows of silver buttons on the jacket front are laced with black braid across the chest. The black leather cross-belt worn by officers, sergeants, and warrant officers incorporated a silver lion's head, chain, and whistle.[9]

The officer in the illustration wears his crimson sash across the right shoulder.[10] This was probably a regimental affectation to symbolize the Highland origin of the Glengarrys. His sword-belt is black leather with brass fittings; the sword is of the curved light-infantry pattern. Evidence suggests that the sword-knots of the regiment were of green and yellow silk.[11]

Officers of Rifles and Light Infantry frequently adopted clothing styles of Light Cavalry; thus, leather-trimmed overalls, such as those shown in the illustration, were common in these regiments. Some officers wore the cavalry-style dark-green pelisse trimmed with black fur and embellished with silver buttons and black cord across the chest.

It seems only fitting that the green uniform of the Rifles, which was later to figure so prominently in the dress of the Canadian Militia, was worn by one of Canada's first regular regiments.

1859-1873

History

When the settlers of New France first banded together to protect themselves from the Indians and British invaders, military service became compulsory for all male Canadians. Requirements for such service have been included in the provisions of various provincial and federal militia acts; and, although it was ignored in later years, universal military service remained on the books until the introduction of the National Defence Act of 1950.

The militia played a useful role in Canada's defence during the American Revolutionary War, the War of 1812-14, and the rebellions of 1837, although the core of the fighting forces in these conflicts were the British and provincial regulars. By the mid-1840s, there was so little concern for Canadian defence that the Sedentary Militia, as the force was so aptly titled, was little more than a list of names. Training consisted of the annual muster, an excuse for a day-long drinking party for the men of the county. Eventually, even this parody of military duty was allowed to lapse.

For the few who were genuinely interested in part-time military training, the Sedentary Militia was not a satisfactory answer. Therefore, these military enthusiasts banded together in small units, provided their own arms, equipment, and uniforms, and gathered regularly to practise drill and musketry. By 1850, a number of these unofficial companies of volunteers existed in the Canadas and Maritime provinces.

In the spring of 1855, the Legislature of Nova Scotia passed amendments to the Militia Act that authorized the formation of artillery, light infantry, grenadier, and rifle companies of volunteers, independent of the Sedentary Militia. Uniforms and equipment were to be provided by the unpaid volunteer. In effect, the amendment legalized a situation that had existed for fifteen years.[1]

In 1859, the Volunteer Movement swept through Great Britain. The unsatisfactory state of the nation's defence preparations, as revealed by the Crimean War and the Indian Mutiny, disturbed the British public. After a series of public meetings, offers to form volunteer corps poured in from all regions of the country.

Somewhat dazed by this enthusiastic outburst of military zeal, the government sanctioned the establishment of a volunteer force by the War Office Circular of 12 May 1859, based on existing legislation dating back to 5 June 1804.[2] The response was immediate and overwhelming. In June 1860, when Queen Victoria reviewed the South of England corps in Hyde Park, 21,000 volunteers were on parade.

The popularity of amateur soldiering quickly spread to the colonies. By midsummer 1860, thirty volunteer companies numbering some 2,300 men had been granted official approval by the Governor of Nova Scotia. Several volunteer corps were organized in Halifax. The second of these, the Chebucto Greys, was gazetted on 15 December 1859.[3]

The original volunteer companies were administered rather like private clubs, which, in fact, some were. Regular meetings were held with a chairman and secretary; all members had a voice in the financial management, pattern of dress, and appointment of officers. Commissioned officers were elected by a majority vote of the members, which was all that was required by the Adjutant-General to grant a commission.

On 14 May 1860, a meeting of representatives of the various volunteer companies of Halifax passed a resolution "that the Halifax Volunteer Companies be formed into a battalion." So began a regiment that was to have a long and distinguished record of service with the Canadian Army. The newly created battalion consisted of the Scottish Rifles, Chebucto Greys, Mayflower Rifles, Halifax Rifles, Irish Rifles, and Dartmouth Rifles. The right of the line went to the Scottish Rifles, and the left was assigned to the Chebucto Greys.[4]

In 1865, the battalion was reorganized, and a common rifle-green uniform was adopted for all companies. On Confederation, the Volunteers were transferred from colonial to federal authority, and the name of the corps was changed to the Halifax Volunteer Battalion of Rifles. In 1869, it was renamed the 63rd Halifax Battalion of Rifles, much to the disgust of the members, who felt that, in terms of unbroken service, the corps was entitled to third place in the roll of regiments of the Active Militia of Canada.

The Chebucto Greys, now in green, elected to continue their service in the battalion. By 1873, most of the original members had retired, and the name Chebucto Greys was dropped; but the battalion that the Greys helped to create continued its distinguished record for more than a century.

Uniform

In approving the volunteer companies in the United Kingdom, the War Office was careful to limit the role of amateur soldiers. They were not to be trained to stand in line of battle, but rather to perform as auxiliaries to the regulars. Volunteers were to "hang with the most telling effect upon the flanks and communications of a hostile army."[1] In brief, they were to act as irregular light troops.

With this role in mind, some of the more astute commanders of the original volunteer corps, including Lord Elcho of the London Scottish, saw little merit in attracting the attention of the enemy by wearing red jackets and white belts. Instead, they selected neutral colours such as greys, browns, and greens, and designed uniforms for comfort and serviceability.[2]

Like their British counterparts, Canadian volunteer companies had the liberty of selecting such pattern and colours as their imagination might dictate, as they were also allowed the privilege of paying for their own uniforms. Needless to say, there resulted a great variety of patterns and colours of dress from one company to another. Unhampered by preconceived standards of current military fashion, the volunteers produced some uniforms of considerable originality.

The Chebucto Greys adopted a uniform of medium grey with red facings. The clothing was made in England, and the complete uniform was said to be the most costly among those of the Halifax companies.[3]

A grey shako, similar to that of the British 1861-69 pattern, had a red band, and black leather peak and chin-strap; the corps shako plate was a white metal Maltese cross surmounted by a Crown. A surviving example of this shako is fitted with a light-grey horsehair plume,[4] and a similar plume appears in a period illustration of the company uniform. However, an 1862 photograph of a private of the Greys shows the shako embellished with a red ball rather than the hair plume.[5] One concludes that the plume was the original shako fitting, but was soon replaced by the red ball tuft.

The loose-fitting long-skirted grey coat was single-breasted and cut more like a frock-coat than a tunic; its stand-up collar, shoulder-straps, and pointed cuffs were red. The coat front was fastened with five black olivets, and laced with five loops of black cord, the ends of which terminated in a trefoil. The cuffs

were trimmed with black braid formed into an Austrian knot.

The uncreased grey trousers were trimmed down the outside seam with a red welt.[6]

The black leather waist-belt was fastened with a round regimental buckle of white metal. A black leather ball bag was worn on the right front of the belt, and a black bayonet frog and scabbard were suspended from the left. A black leather cross-belt supported a black cartridge pouch resting behind the right hip.

The plate illustrates a private of the Chebucto Greys in the original full-dress uniform of the company. For undress, the Greys wore a grey shell-jacket, which fastened down the front with hooks and eyes, and had plain collar, cuffs, and shoulder-straps. Undress head-gear was a grey pillbox forage cap with red band and black leather chin-strap.[7]

The Volunteer Companies were armed with the 1853-model Long Enfield muzzle-loading rifle with a black sling and triangular bayonet. In 1866, these weapons were replaced by the Short Enfield rifle and sword bayonet.[8]

In the early days of the Halifax Volunteer Battalion, the various companies still wore their individual uniforms and accoutrements, and a battalion parade was a colourful occasion. One observer remarked that, while the battalion lacked something in conformity, its obvious dissimilarities of dress produced variety and a healthy rivalry among the companies.[9]

When the battalion was reorganized in 1865, a green uniform was adopted by all companies except the Scottish Rifles, who refused to give up their national dress. The new uniform consisted of a rifle-green tunic with red collar, cuffs, and piping. A rifle-green shako of the 1861-69 pattern had a black leather peak and chin-strap, bronze shako plate, and green ball. The Chebucto Greys, however, wore a red ball on their shakos as a mark of company distinction.

Officers' tunics were fastened with five black olivets and laced with five rows of black braid across the front. Their red cuffs were trimmed with black braid, ending in an Austrian knot. Black waist-belt, sword slings, pouch belt, gloves, and shoes were worn by officers.[10]

The tradition of rifle regiment dress was retained by the Halifax Rifles when the regiment was incorporated into the Active Militia at the time of Confederation.

1862 to the present
History

By the 1850s, Canada was well on the way to self-government; nonetheless, she still looked to Britain for her defence, and British regulars garrisoned her frontiers and fortresses. Events in the Crimea forced Britain to recall her regiments in 1854, leaving fewer than 1,900 regulars in Canada, and only 1,400 in the Maritime colonies. In order to increase Canadian military resources, a commission was appointed to investigate the state of the militia and to recommend ways to improve its effectiveness.

Based on the commission's report, a new Militia Act was passed in 1855. It retained the Sedentary Militia and the concept of universal military service; but it also created a small, volunteer "Active Militia," to be armed, clothed, and paid at public expense. The Active Militia was to receive regular training, so that it could assemble immediately in a crisis and provide a core for the Sedentary Militia in case of a general mobilization.

The Canadian public's response to the formation of a volunteer force of part-time soldiers was immediate and enthusiastic. On 21 December 1861, a meeting was held in Toronto to discuss the raising of a regiment of volunteers from among the artisans of the city. A motion was passed that "a battalion of Volunteer Rifles, capable of executing field works, be immediately raised. . . ." Steps were taken at once to raise funds by subscription for the purchase of clothing and equipment, to enrol recruits, and to appoint a committee to nominate officers for the battalion.[1]

On 14 March 1862, the new unit was gazetted as the 10th Battalion Volunteer Rifles, Canada. However, a request was granted that the regiment be dressed in scarlet, and be infantry rather than rifles, as were the other companies being raised throughout Canada at the time.[2] On 21 November 1862 the corps was renamed The 10th Battalion Volunteer Militia (Infantry), Canada. On 10 April 1863, the regiment was granted permission to adopt the title Royal, and was redesignated the 10th, or Royal Regiment of Toronto, Volunteers.

The Fenian raids of 1866 provided the 10th Royals with its first taste of active service. The regiment was rushed to the Niagara Peninsula of 1 June; and, while it did not arrive in time to take part in the confused skirmish of Lime Ridge, it was engaged in mopping-up operations. Later that summer, the regiment was called up for a period of continuous service on the frontier with the Corps of Observation under Colonel Garnet Wolseley.

As the threat from the Fenian Brotherhood subsided, so did interest in the militia. The strength and effectiveness of the 10th Royals declined sufficiently that the continued existence of the regiment was seriously questioned. However the fortunes of the unit were revived by a vigorous reorganization. In August 1881, the title Grenadiers was added to its name, and the unit became the 10th Battalion Royal Grenadiers. This distinction was carried by only one other corps in the British service, the Grenadier Guards.[3]

On the outbreak of the Northwest Rebellion in 1885, the Royal Grenadiers mobilized a small battalion, which was sent to join the North West Field Force. The battalion was early on the scene and, as part of General Middleton's own column, took part in the engagements of Fish Creek and Batoche. Throughout the campaign, the regiment served with distinction and earned its first battle honours.

A draft of volunteers from the regiment in 1899 formed part of the 2nd (Special Service) Battalion, Royal Canadian Regiment, which served in South Africa.

In the mobilization muddle of 1914, volunteers from the 10th Royal Grenadiers were incorporated into the 3rd Battalion, Canadian Expeditionary Force. Throughout the war, the regiment maintained a depot, which raised the 123rd Battalion and sent substantial drafts to the 19th, 35th, 58th, and 75th battalions, in addition to maintaining a continual supply of officers and men for the 3rd Battalion. By the end of the First World War, some 4,000 men had passed through the ranks of the 10th Royal Grenadiers to the Canadian Expeditionary Force.[4]

When the militia was reorganized in 1920, numbers were dropped from unit titles, and the regiment became The Royal Grenadiers. In 1936, it was amalgamated with The Toronto Regiment, and titled The Royal Regiment of Toronto Grenadiers. At the request of its members, however, the unit was renamed The Royal Regiment of Canada on 11 February 1939.[5]

The regiment was mobilized on 1 September 1939 and recruited to full war establishment by 19 September. In June 1940, The Royal Regiment was sent to Iceland, and subsequently to England to become part of the 4th Infantry Brigade of the 2nd Canadian Division. With this formation, the Royals took part in the Dieppe Raid and the campaign in North-West Europe.

More than a century after its formation, this distinguished regiment remains on the order of battle of the Canadian Militia.

1862 to the present
Uniform

The Militia Act of 1855 specified that the infantry element of the newly created Active Militia was to be companies of rifles. The rudimentary dress regulations prescribed a uniform of dark green with red facings.[1] The request of the 10th Battalion to be designated infantry rather than rifles implied that its men would be clothed in the traditional red tunic of the British line regiments. The uniforms ordered from England were slow to arrive, and it was not until 6 July 1863, when colours were presented, that the unit appeared on parade in full dress.[2]

Full-dress head-gear was a dark blue shako of the 1861-69 pattern with black leather peak and chin-strap. The front bore a plate of regimental design, and the top was surmounted by a white-over-red ball tuft. The undress was the dark blue pork-pie-shaped Kilmarnock, with blue touri and brass numerals.[3]

The full-skirted single-breasted red tunic had eight buttons and white piping down the front. The dark-blue collar, rounded at the front, was piped with white along the edge; the dark-blue pointed cuffs were edged with white braid ending in an Austrian knot. The tunic skirt was closed behind with a plait on each side; the plaits and centre vent were edged with white cloth. There were two large buttons on each plait, and two at the waist.[4]

The original issue of trousers was dark blue with a red welt down the outside seam.

Rank badges for NCOs were worn on the upper right sleeve. Warrant officers and senior NCOs of the rank of sergeant and above wore a plain red sash over the right shoulder.

Officers' tunics were similar in pattern to those of the men, but of better-quality cloth. The edge of the collar was trimmed with silver lace, and a single left shoulder cord kept in place the crimson sash. Officers' rank badges were worn on the collar. They wore a shako with gilt plate for full dress.

The waist-belt and sword slings were of white leather; the sword was of infantry pattern with gold knot. Junior officers had black scabbards with brass fittings; the adjutant, a steel scabbard; and field officers, brass scabbards.[5]

Undress uniform for officers of the 10th Royals included the round flat forage cap. Rather like a peaked pillbox, the cap had a red band, straight black leather peak, black button, and brass numerals. The loose-fitting undress patrol jacket was of dark blue; the blue collar was trimmed with black tape. Rank badges were worn on the collar, and the jacket was without shoulder-straps or cords.[6]

The jacket front closed with hooks, and was braided across the chest with four rows of black cord ending in drop loops, with olivets in the centre. The front of the jacket and the skirt were edged with black tape. Back seams were trimmed with black braid forming a crow's-foot top and bottom, and double eyes at the waist. Cuffs were trimmed with black braid ending in an Austrian knot.

The dark-blue trousers had a red welt up the outside seam. In undress, the sword-belt was worn under the jacket.

The plate illustrates a private of the 10th Royal Regiment of Toronto Volunteers in full marching order. To the white buff-leather waist-belt is attached a small white leather pouch, called a ball bag, and a white bayonet frog. The wide white leather cross-belt supports a black ammunition pouch on the right hip. The white canvas haversack, worn folded over the bayonet scabbard, is suspended from a white canvas strap over the right shoulder. The square black canvas pack or knapsack is supported by two white shoulder-straps. Although the pack and haversack were rarely issued to militia units, they are included in the illustration to depict the full marching order of the period. This cross-belt equipment of Crimean War vintage served the Canadian Militia through two campaigns, until it was replaced in 1898 with the Oliver equipment.

The weapon first issued to the 10th Royals was the Long Enfield rifle with triangular bayonet. In 1867, the Enfield was replaced twice, first by the Spencer rifle, and then by the Long Snider-Enfield breech-loading rifle.[7]

The regiment adopted the blue home-service pattern helmet in 1879; however, when they were redesignated grenadiers, new forage caps of the Grenadier Guards pattern were issued in 1883.[8] Ultimately, the bearskin cap of the Guards was approved for full dress; it was first worn on parade in November 1893.[9] The full dress of the Grenadier Guards is still worn by detachments of the regiment on special ceremonial occasions.

History

The volunteer militia movement of the early 1850s produced a variety of company-sized units of artillery, cavalry, and infantry. As the movement gathered momentum, it was only natural that companies of engineers should also appear. The first of such units were the Halifax and Dartmouth engineer companies, organized early in 1860. These were soon followed by companies in Ottawa, Montreal, Quebec, Sarnia, and Saint John.

The duties of the military engineer included constructing fortifications and field-works, bridging, signalling, campsite layout and servicing, mining, and handling explosives. For years, engineer officers were involved in such survey expeditions as the establishment of the Canadian-American border. Engineers also required training in basic drill and musketry.

The volunteer engineer companies in Canada faced unique problems, which gave them a relatively brief life expectancy. The officers, particularly those commanding companies, were required to be professional engineers. However, by the very nature of their profession, engineers moved frequently from one major construction project to another. When the company commander moved, his enthusiasm and leadership were usually lost, and the company became ineffective.

The volunteer engineers also had to deal with a lack of trained engineer instructors and an almost total absence of engineer training stores and equipment. For all practical purposes, then, most early engineer companies were trained as infantry, and were engineers in name and dress only.

One of the early volunteer engineer companies that left a lasting impression on Canadian military engineering was the Toronto Engineer Company, authorized on 14 January 1876.[1] The following October, it was renamed the 2nd Military District Engineer Company, but continued to be known by its original title. Its first company commander was Lieutenant-Colonel T.C. Scoble, an energetic and imaginative professional engineer. The Toronto Engineer Company had an establishment of thirty-nine other ranks, and an actual strength of five officers and seventy other ranks, including a band.[2]

The problem of finding a capable instructor was solved by hiring a retired NCO of the Royal Engineers. The members purchased their own uniforms and more than $2,000 worth of engineer stores and equipment.[3]

The lack of support for engineer units was partly due to the absence of military engineers at the command and staff levels of Canada's miniature defence force, as engineer training had been the responsibility of the artillery. However, 1879 saw the first formal inspection of an engineer unit by an Engineer Inspector, when Major G.R. Walker, R.E., of the Royal Military College, inspected the Toronto Engineer Company in camp at Niagara.[4]

Lieutenant-Colonel Scoble proposed the establishment of a School of Military Engineering for Canadian militia units. He also suggested engineer units be formed as field and garrison companies in keeping with the Canadian Militia requirement for military engineering support.[5]

In 1881, Lieutenant-Colonel Scoble left Toronto, and in December the Toronto Engineer Company was removed from the list of Active Militia units.

In 1884, an Engineer Branch was established at headquarters in Ottawa; and, as engineer officers began to graduate from the Royal Military College at Kingston, interest grew in the training and role of engineers in the Canadian Militia. This was evidenced by the authorization of an engineer unit of the Permanent Active Militia on 1 July 1903.[6]

Uniform

When the Toronto Engineer Company was formed in 1876, all units of the Canadian Militia, including engineers, were issued only tunic, trousers, forage cap, and greatcoat.[1] The men were responsible for providing their own boots, and full-dress head-gear was provided from unit funds raised from various sources including public subscription.

Other ranks of the Canadian Engineers were issued a single-breasted scarlet tunic with eight brass buttons. Cuffs, collar, and shoulder-straps were dark blue. The collar was piped top and bottom with yellow braid. Yellow piping along the edge of the pointed cuffs formed an Austrian knot. The shoulder-straps also were edged with yellow braid. Blue cloth edged the tunic front, and the back seams were piped with blue braid from the waist to the hem of the skirt.[2]

The government-issue forage cap was a round pillbox with yellow band, yellow button, and black leather chin-strap. Forage caps of warrant officers and senior NCOs of the rank of sergeant and above had a straight black leather peak. It was then customary for lance-corporals and corporals of engineers to wear their rank insignia in the form of small yellow chevrons, one and two respectively, on the front of the forage cap.[3]

Full-dress head-gear for other ranks was a black fur busby with black leather chin-strap. A Garter-blue bag hung on the right side; on the left was a white horsehair plume in a brass grenade-and-flame plume holder.[4] There is no hard evidence that the Toronto Engineer Company wore the busby; however, as it was a fashionable corps of considerable spirit, it is likely that the busby was provided, either at the soldiers' expense or from unit funds.

The home-service-pattern helmet was introduced to the British Army, including the Royal Engineers, for full dress in 1878. The following year, the Toronto Engineer Company purchased the white foreign-service version of the helmet for its men.[5] In 1880, the white helmet became official head-dress of the Canadian Engineers.[6]

Trousers were dark blue with a wide scarlet stripe down the outside seam. Those originally issued to the Toronto Engineer Company were blue serge of Canadian manufacture; however, they were of poor quality and wore out rapidly. Better quality blue cloth trousers were subsequently purchased by members of the unit.[7] Successive issues of trousers were of cloth rather than serge, and of British manufacture; thereafter, the flood of militia complaints about shoddy trousers stopped.[8]

The equipment of the Engineers consisted of a white buff-leather waist-belt with square brass buckle. The bayonet frog was attached on the left side. A white buff-leather cross-belt supported a black leather ammunition pouch on the right hip. The particular pattern of Snider-Enfield carried by the Toronto Engineer Company is unknown, although the long three-banded model was probably the original issue.

The plate depicts an officer of the Toronto Engineer Company in full-dress mounted order, in 1876. The illustration is based on a photograph of Lieutenant-Colonel Scoble wearing an unusual pattern of busby, which was adopted by officers of the Royal Engineers in 1873.[9] Shaped like the rifles' busby, it was made of black sealskin over a cork frame. Heavy gold cord lines encircled the cap, ending in gold acorns on the left side.[10]

The scarlet cloth tunic, with Garter-blue velvet collar and cuffs, is edged down the front, around the skirt, and down the rear plaits with blue velvet. The cuffs are trimmed with gold cord in the form of an Austrian knot and traced with figured gold braiding. The lace braiding was less elaborate for captains, and lieutenants had only the plain gold-cord Austrian knot.[11]

The officer's shoulder-belt of Russia leather is trimmed with gold embroidery with a wavy gold stripe down the centre. The belt is fastened with a gilt buckle and slide, and supports a black leather binocular case, with a gilt regimental badge on the flap. The Russia leather sword-belt has gold-trimmed sword and sabretache slings of the same material.

Dressed for mounted duties, the field officer in the illustration wears pantaloons with a wide red outside stripe. Dress trousers were trimmed down the outer seam with wide gold lace.

When not in full dress, officers wore a braided blue patrol jacket or scarlet shell-jacket, and a round blue forage cap with a band of gold lace, a scarlet welt around the crown, gold-netted button in the centre, and black leather peak and chin-strap.

1860 to the present

History

The Canadian Militia Act of 1855 provided for the formation of an Active Militia to consist of volunteer troops of cavalry, field batteries and foot companies of artillery, and fifty companies of rifles. By 1856, the full number of rifle companies had been raised, including four from Toronto.

It soon became evident that training at battalion level was desirable, and the Militia Act was amended in 1859 to enable the formation of rifle battalions where practicable. Under the new provisions, nine volunteer rifle companies in Montreal were formed into a battalion designated the First Battalion, Volunteer Militia Rifles of Canada.[1] Today this battalion appears on the order of battle of the Canadian Militia as the Canadian Grenadier Guards.

Not to be outdone by Montreal, the Toronto companies requested the formation of a rifle battalion. As the Act required that a battalion consist of a minimum of six companies from the same locality or district, it was proposed that the rifle companies of Barrie and Brampton be regimented with those of Toronto in the new battalion. In April 1860, the Second Battalion, Volunteer Militia Rifles of Canada was authorized to be formed from the Barrie Rifle Company, the 1st Rifle Company of Toronto, the 3rd Rifle Company of Toronto, the Highland Rifle Company of Toronto, the Rifle Company (formerly the Foot Artillery Company of Toronto), and the Highland Rifle Company of Whitby, which inexplicably had replaced the Brampton Company. The order specified that, regardless of seniority, the Highland companies would take the flank positions when the battalion was on parade.[2]

The possibility of war between the United States and Britain as a result of the *Trent* affair in 1861 produced an enthusiastic expansion of the Volunteer Movement and the formation of several new rifle companies in Toronto. The Second Battalion was reorganized in November 1862: six new Toronto companies were added, and the Barrie and Whitby companies reverted to independent status.[3] Thus, the Second Battalion became an all-Toronto unit and, in March 1863, it was renamed the 2nd Battalion, the Queen's Own Rifles of Toronto.[4]

In 1865, Canada was threatened with invasion from the United States by the Fenian Brotherhood, and militia soldiering became a serious matter. Several provisional battalions made up of drafts from various militia battalions, including the 2nd, were placed on full-time duty on the frontier. In March, there was a general stand to of all militia units; but the provisional battalions were released from duty once the threat of invasion appeared to subside. Suddenly, on 31 May, a force of Fenians crossed the border near Fort Erie. The militia was mobilized and the Queen's Own proceeded to the threatened area at 4 AM on 1 June.[5]

The following day, the Queen's Own and several other militia units detrained at Ridgeway and marched off to join the main body of troops at Stevensville. The Queen's Own were leading when the militia bumped into the Fenians on Lime Ridge. The militia attacked with spirit and was making good headway when one of those frequent blunders of battle occurred. Someone sounded the retreat, and the militiamen withdrew in haste, refusing to be rallied by their officers. More

embarrassed than hurt, the Queen's Own suffered its first battle casualties of seven dead and twenty-one wounded.

The Fenian raids demonstrated that spirit and enthusiasm were inadequate substitutes for training and discipline. Though public interest in the militia declined with the lessening of the Fenian threat, the Queen's Own worked hard to overcome the deficiencies revealed at Lime Ridge.

In January 1882, the unit was redesignated 2nd Battalion, Queen's Own Rifles of Canada.[6]

When the Northwest Rebellion broke out in March 1885, the British regiments had long since left, leaving Canada dependent on her own military resources to restore the situation. The Queen's Own mobilized an active-service battalion of 250 men, which moved west in freezing weather to join Lieutenant-Colonel Otter's column at Swift Current for the relief of Battleford. On reaching Battleford, one company accompanied Otter's flying column and found itself hotly engaged with Poundmaker's Indians at Cut Knife Hill. Once again the Queen's Own counted its casualties.

With the collapse of organized resistance at Batoche, the battalion joined in the search for Big Bear. The regiment reported that "we have with us ten days' provisions and are told to wander with systematic aimlessness for that period over a part of the country known as the Squirrel Plains."[7] The blistering hot days and bitter cold nights of the prairie summer and the ever-present mosquitoes proved more troublesome than either the Plains or Wood Cree.

The Queen's Own provided its quota of volunteers for A Company, 2nd (Special Service) Battalion, Royal Canadian Regiment of Infantry for service in South Africa in 1899; and the battle honour *South Africa* was granted to the Queen's Own in recognition of this contribution.

When the Canadian Expeditionary Force was mobilized in August 1914, the thirty officers and 945 other ranks who volunteered from the Queen's Own were assigned to the 3rd Battalion, C.E.F., along with volunteers from the 10th Royal Grenadiers and the Governor General's Body Guard.[8] The 3rd Battalion served with the 1st Canadian Division throughout the war.

On 24 May 1940, an Active Force battalion of the regiment was mobilized. After a period of garrison duty in Newfoundland, the Queen's Own went overseas as part of the 8th Brigade of the 3rd Canadian Infantry Division. The battalion took part in the Normandy landings on D-Day, and fought continuously with the 3rd Canadian Division in North-West Europe until VE Day.

In May 1951, the Queen's Own provided one company for the 1st Canadian Rifle Battalion for service with Canada's NATO force in Europe. The regiment supplied a further company for the 2nd Canadian Rifle Battalion in April 1952. The two rifle battalions were redesignated the 1st and 2nd battalions, The Queen's Own Rifles of Canada, in October 1953, and taken on the strength of Canada's regular army.[9] After postings to Korea and Europe, the regular battalions were disbanded in 1968, when the strength of the Canadian Army was reduced. The militia battalion still exists and continues to have its headquarters in Toronto.

1860 to the present

Uniform

When the Second Battalion Volunteer Militia Rifles of Canada was formed in 1860, each of the six companies from which it was formed had its own uniform. As the Barrie and Whitby companies were based outside Toronto, the battalion never did parade as a complete unit. However, even a parade of the four Toronto companies was a colourful event: the 2nd and 3rd companies were dressed in rifle green with red facings; the 5th, a converted foot artillery company, continued to parade in its blue artillery dress,[1] while the 4th company, formerly the Highland Rifle Company of Toronto, appeared in full Highland dress.

The Highland company wore a double-breasted rifle-green doublet with Inverness flaps, slashed cuffs, and red facings. Kilts were of Government (Black Watch) tartan, and a plaid of the same pattern crossed the chest diagonally and came forward over the left shoulder. Trews were worn for undress and service dress. The sporran was that of the 93rd Highlanders; the officer's sporran had a badger-head design with tassels set in gilt cups. Red and white diced hose were worn with red garters and tabs, and the head-dress was a Glengarry with long feathers.[2]

After Confederation, the militia companies were required to re-enrol under the terms of the Militia Act of 1868. When the authorities insisted that the Highland company adopt the same dress as the rest of the battalion, the Highlanders were adamant: no kilt, no company! Faced with equally adamant opposition, the colourful unit was dissolved.[3]

The first regimental uniform of the Queen's Own Rifles consisted of a shako of 1864-68 pattern with green ball, rifle-green trousers, and green tunic with red facings.[4] The forage cap was the pork-pie-shaped Kilmarnock; belts and leather equipment were black.

Officers wore a rifle-green tunic faced with red and laced with five rows of black cord across the front. The rifle-green trousers were trimmed with two rows of black braid on a scarlet stripe. Officers and NCOs above the rank of corporal wore a black leather pouch belt with silver chain, whistle, and belt badge.

Officers were ordered to provide a patrol jacket and forage cap for wear on normal drill parades. They were also to supply a winter uniform composed of a dark-grey greatcoat trimmed on the collar and down the front with grey fur, a forage cap with a band of grey fur and black leather peak, knickerbockers reaching to the knees, and long boots.[5]

Several changes in dress took place after 1868: the peaks of officers' forage caps, and the scarlet facings of the collars and cuffs of their patrol jackets were removed. The winter uniform was changed to a black cloth patrol jacket trimmed with black fur, a black wedge-shaped fur cap, dress trousers, and short leggings.[6]

The unpopular Kilmarnock cap was replaced by the Glengarry in 1871; it, in turn, gave way to a rifle-green field service cap with red ball. In 1877, the black fur rifle busby was adopted for full dress.[7]

A complete new issue of clothing was made in 1877, and it was in this pattern of uniform that the Queen's Own went West in 1885. The plate illustrates a private of the Queen's Own Rifles on active service in what is now Saskatchewan in 1885. The green tunic is closed with seven bronze buttons and trimmed down the front with red cloth. The red collar is edged with black braid; the green shoulder-straps with red piping bear the letters QOR in red. The pointed green cuffs are trimmed with black braid edged with red, and the trousers have a red welt down the outside seam.[8]

The soldier wears a Glengarry forage cap, issued after supplies of the regimental field service cap were exhausted. Because of supply difficulties and hard wear on uniforms that already had seen four or five years' service, the red infantry tunic was issued in the field to some of the Queen's Own.[9]

Equipment consisted of a black leather waist-belt to which was attached a black ball bag and a bayonet frog and scabbard. The black cross-belt supported a black cartridge-box on the right hip. Also issued for active service were a square canvas knapsack, a water-bottle, and a black haversack. The Queen's Own was armed with the short two-banded Snider-Enfield rifle and long sword bayonet.

With the arrival of hot weather in late June, the Queen's Own adopted an improvised summer-service dress of havelocks, peaked low round caps with white cover and neckcloth, and grey flannel blouses made up for the regiment by the ladies of Toronto. The blouses were loose fitting and had low collars, shoulder-straps, and breast pockets. Though not the height of military fashion, these comfortable blouses were welcomed by the troops, as their rifle-green tunics had become badly worn.[10]

While full dress was unsuitable for active service, it was the only clothing available to Canada's soldiers, and even it was in short supply. White foreign-service-pattern helmets and suits of grey Halifax tweed were ordered for summer wear, but arrived after the campaign was over.[11] However, the Northwest Rebellion was the last campaign in which Canadians were required to fight in full dress.

1873-1904
History

In 1870, the vast area known as Rupert's Land was transferred from the Hudson's Bay Company to the new Dominion of Canada. The sudden shift of authority and resultant uncertainty and unrest among the inhabitants of the region erupted into the Red River Rebellion of 1869-70. Alarming reports of whisky trading and of restlessness and inter-tribal warfare among the Indians of the plains reached the newly formed federal government in Ottawa. It was essential that order be restored and maintained if the Canadian Northwest was to attract settlers.

In 1872, Colonel P. Robertson-Ross, Adjutant-General of the Canadian Militia, was dispatched into the Northwest on a fact-finding journey for the Canadian government. He recommended that a regiment of 550 mounted riflemen be organized to preserve order in the territory and to protect the surveyors and railway builders who were working their way to the Pacific coast.[1]

On 3 May 1873, Sir John A. Macdonald introduced a bill to establish a police force, para-military in nature, in the Northwest Territories. On 23 May the bill was passed; and, after receiving royal assent, the North West Mounted Police came into being.

In October, Lieutenant-Colonel George Arthur French, former commandant of the School of Gunnery at Kingston, was appointed Commissioner of the Force, and recruits were assembled at Toronto and Fort Garry, Manitoba. In June 1874, the two groups assembled at Dufferin, Manitoba, to complete preparations for a march west to intercept the whisky traders from Montana. When clothing and equipment had been issued and the divisions adjusted to equal strength, all ranks were assembled for a full-dress ceremonial parade. This is the only occasion in the history of the Force on which it paraded at full strength.

On 8 July, the Force began its march with a strength of 275 officers and men, 114 Red River carts, 73 wagons, and two 9-pounder field guns. The beef ration, still on the hoof, was herded along at the end of the column.[2] Commissioner French planned to move directly to the forks of the Belly and Bow rivers, where Fort Whoop-up, headquarters of the whisky traders, was rumoured to be. He would leave a garrison to police the area, and would return with the remainder of the Force to establish headquarters at Fort Ellice. Another division of the Force was to leave the column at Roche Percée and proceed to the north of what is now Saskatchewan.

On 18 September, after failing to locate Fort Whoop-up, the column halted at a suitable site for winter quarters in the Sweet Grass Hills. In seventy-two days they had covered more than 1700 km (1000 mi.) under most difficult conditions. The B, C, and F divisions were left under the command of Assistant Commissioner Macleod, while D and E divisions returned with the commissioner to Fort Ellice. The A Division was stationed in Edmonton.

Before winter set in, Macleod learned of the real location of the infamous Fort Whoop-up. He appeared with his men before the palisaded structure only to find that the traders had left for winter quarters south of the boundary. Though he failed to catch up with the whisky traders, Macleod did discover an excellent site for a permanent camp near the present city of Lethbridge. Here he built Fort Macleod and established the permanent presence of the North West Mounted Police in the Canadian West.

From the moment the Force was established, demands for its services multiplied. It was called upon to control and contain the migration to Canada of Sitting Bull's Sioux after Custer's disaster at the Little Bighorn. The Northwest Rebellion of 1885 taxed the Force to its limit, as the West was threatened with a general Indian uprising. The opening of the far North and the discovery of gold in the Yukon also tested the Force's ability to preserve order. The Force supplied many officers and NCOs for the Canadian mounted regiments that went to South Africa in 1899. For excellence of service performed in the course of these many duties, King Edward VII conferred the title Royal upon the North West Mounted Police in 1904.[3]

In 1920, the jurisdiction of the RNWMP was extended throughout the entire nation and, in recognition of this added responsibility, the name of the Force was changed to the Royal Canadian Mounted Police. The wheel had come full circle: the Force that marched from east to west marched back east fifty years later.

1873-1904
Uniform

When a western constabulary was first considered, Sir John A. Macdonald was determined that there be as little gold lace, fuss, and feathers as possible. He believed that the appearance of the unit should reflect its purpose: an efficient police force for the ready enforcement of the law in Western Canada.[1] In keeping with this spirit, the original dress was extremely simple.

A loose-fitting red Norfolk jacket without lace or facings, having a roll collar and large skirt pockets, was worn with steel-grey Bedford cord breeches. Dark-blue trousers with a double white stripe were issued for dismounted duties. The white cork helmet of Indian pattern was worn with the ends of the pug-gree hanging behind.[2] The round blue pillbox forage cap had a band and button, white for the men, and gold for sergeants, warrant officers, and officers. Black Wellington boots with steel spurs were worn in full dress; brown riding boots were provided for service wear. White gauntlets and haversack, and brown leather pistol belt with S buckle completed the men's dress. The only deference to officers' rank was a gold Austrian knot on the jacket cuffs, and badges of rank on the collar.

For winter wear, the officers and men were supplied with a short buffalo coat, fur cap and mittens, moccasins, and long woollen stockings. This sensible and serviceable winter dress remained practically unchanged as long as the Force was mounted.

Although practical, the Norfolk jacket was most unpopular; and a new pattern of uniform was introduced in 1876.[3] Full dress for officers consisted of a scarlet tunic, cut and braided like that of the 13th Hussars, with dark-blue collar and cuffs, and dark-blue overalls with a gold outside stripe.[4] The white helmet was fitted with a gilt chain and spike, and a white horsehair plume. The heavily gold-laced red Russia-leather pouch belt and sword slings had gilt metal fittings. White gloves, Russia-leather sword-knot with gold acorn, black half-Wellingtons, and steel spurs completed the uniform.[5]

For undress uniform officers wore a scarlet jacket fastened with hooks. It was trimmed around the blue collar, down both front edges, and around the hem with gold braid. The skirt pocket openings and back seams were trimmed, hussar fashion, with gold cord ending in a crow's-foot; the cuffs were edged with an Austrian knot of gold cord. Twisted gold cords were fastened on each shoulder by a small gilt regimental button.[6] Dark-blue pantaloons with a red stripe were worn with black riding boots. A black binocular case was carried on the brown leather pouch belt; brown sword slings and a black sabretache with regimental badge were supported by a sword-belt worn under the jacket.[7] A blue forage cap was worn with this undress uniform.

Full dress for the men is illustrated in the plate. It consisted of a scarlet tunic of dragoon pattern without facings. The collar was trimmed all around with yellow cord. The cuffs were edged with an Austrian knot of yellow cord, while the shoulder-straps, tunic front, and skirt edges were piped with yellow. The dark-blue pantaloons initially had a red stripe, but it was later changed to yellow; the pantaloons were worn with black riding boots. The white helmet, of a new pattern, had a brass spike and chain, but no puggree.[8]

The helmet was a most cumbersome and unpopular form of head-gear; carried in the wagons whenever possible, it soon became badly battered. Though preferred to the helmet, the forage cap was a useless adornment, giving protection from neither sun nor rain. The soft felt western hat, though quite unofficial, was commonly worn from the earliest days of the Force. It was light and comfortable, and provided good cover from the elements. Though repeatedly recommended for official approval, it was not until the turn of the century that the Stetson became a formally recognized item of dress.[9]

A plain red serge jacket was worn on routine duties and patrols to prolong the presentable appearance of the tunic. Brown cotton jacket and trousers were issued for stables and other fatigues. This sombre uniform was worn as an improvised service dress during the Northwest Rebellion.[10]

The original weapons of the Force were the .577 Snider-Enfield carbine, Mk. III, and the .450 Adams revolver, first model. The single-shot carbine was satisfactory for the first few years; however, as the Indians soon began to carry repeating rifles, equality of fire-power had to be restored. The police experimented with the Winchester repeating rifle, and finally adopted the .45-.75 Winchester Model 1876 military carbine in 1878.[11]

The Force left Dufferin equipped with the British Army universal saddle. However, the steel buckles and stirrups rusted and became unbearably cold in winter, and the saddle slipped from side to side in rough going. After trying several types of saddle, the California saddle was adopted and proved most satisfactory. The new saddle altered the carriage of the carbine from a bucket to a strap fastened to the pommel.[12]

The dress and equipment of the Royal Canadian Mounted Police has changed over the years to meet changing roles and conditions. However, the scarlet jacket that immediately identified a "Mountie" still remains a symbol of the Force more than a century after its founding.

1862 to the present

History

The Black Watch (Royal Highland Regiment) of Canada is the senior Scottish regiment of the Canadian Militia. Though it has seen more than 100 years of unbroken service, the regiment has not always been a completely Highland unit. On 31 January 1862 the 5th Battalion, Volunteer Militia Rifles of Canada was formed from six existing rifle companies in Montreal.[1] In November, the unit was renamed the 5th Battalion, The Royal Light Infantry of Montreal, re-establishing a unit that originated with the volunteer corps of 1837.[2]

By General Order of 9 October 1863, the Highland Rifle Company of Montreal, one of the first volunteer companies authorized under the Militia Act of 1855, was transferred from the First (Prince of Wales's) Regiment of Volunteer Rifles of Canadian Militia to The Royal Light Infantry.[3] This was to have a profound influence on the regiment. To retain its Highland identity, the company wore a diced band on its forage caps, and from this modest distinction it evolved into a full Highland regiment.

The regiment first saw active service during the Fenian raids of 1866 and 1870. On both occasions, the entire unit was mobilized and rushed to the region of St-Jean, not far from the American frontier.

In 1871, a strange incident almost ended the young regiment's existence. General Orders of 2 June 1871 tersely announced that the 5th Battalion, The Royal Light Infantry, "having become disorganized is removed from the list of Active Militia corps."[4] Somewhat shaken, the officers of the regiment took their case directly to the Minister of Militia, Sir George Etienne Cartier, Member of Parliament for Montreal. Cartier apparently was quite unaware of the offending order or its cause.[5] In August, authority was granted for the re-enrolment of two companies of the regiment; a further order of 12 April 1872 stated that "the 5th Battalion, 'Royal Light Infantry', Montreal, is hereby authorized to be reorganized, and will be reinstated with its former position and precedence in the Active Militia of the Dominion of Canada."[6]

By 1875, the regiment had recruited to a strength of ten companies, including a second Highland company, and in November the name of the unit was changed to the 5th Battalion, Fusileers [sic], Montreal. This was amended the following January to the 5th Battalion, Royal Fusiliers, Montreal.[7] As the strength of the regiment increased, so did its Scottish character; and in 1880, at its own request, the unit was redesignated the 5th Battalion, Royal Scots Fusiliers.[8] In 1884, the regiment again was renamed, this time the 5th Battalion, Royal Scots of Canada.[9]

The services of the regiment were not required for the Northwest Rebellion of 1885; however, it did have an opportunity for active service in 1899, when volunteers were required for the 2nd (Special Service) Battalion, Royal Canadian Regiment of Infantry for service in South Africa. The Royal Scots of Canada soon filled its quota of volunteers, and earned its first battle honour: *South Africa, 1899-1900.*

The regiment's approach to full Highland status was reflected in 1904 by a further change in title to 5th Regiment, Royal Scots of Canada, Highlanders.[10] In 1906, the regiment was designated the 5th Regiment, Royal Highlanders of Canada, and became formally associated with the Black Watch of the British Army.[11]

The regiment raised three active-service battalions during the First World War: the 13th Battalion (RHC), the 42nd Battalion (RHC), and the 73rd Battalion (RHC). It was not by accident that Canadian units of the Black Watch bore the two historic numbers of their parent unit of the British Army.[12] All three battalions were in action at the Battle of Vimy Ridge on 9 April 1917. However, the 73rd RHC was broken up after the battle to reinforce the 13th and 42nd battalions.

When the militia was reorganized after the war, the Royal Highlanders of Canada became a two-battalion regiment. To conform with the redesignation of its British counterpart, the regiment was twice retitled. In 1934, it became The Black Watch (Royal Highlanders) of Canada and, in 1935, it was given its present title, The Black Watch (Royal Highland Regiment) of Canada.[13]

On the outbreak of the Second World War in 1939, the 1st Battalion was mobilized and assigned to the 5th Infantry Brigade of the 2nd Canadian Division. The 1st RHC was heavily committed throughout the campaign in North-West Europe. It lost some 150 officers and more than 2,000 other ranks, giving it tragic distinction of suffering the most casualties of any unit in 21st Army Group.[14]

The 2nd RHC, mobilized in March 1942, was broken up to provide reinforcements for battalions in Italy and England.

After the War, the RHC was reorganized as a one-battalion regiment of the Reserve Army. The regiment supplied one company for each of the 1st and 2nd Canadian Highland battalions, which formed part of Canada's NATO brigade. In 1953, these battalions of regulars were redesignated the 1st and 2nd battalions, The Black Watch (Royal Highland Regiment) of Canada.[15] With the reduction of the Regular Army, the two regular battalions of the regiment were disbanded in 1969, leaving the militia battalion to represent the regiment. The Black Watch of Canada, as a regiment of Canadian Militia, forges a link with those Scottish soldiers who came to Canada to fight, but remained to build this country.[16]

1862 to the present

Uniform

When the regiment was formed in 1862, the dress of the 5th Battalion, The Royal Light Infantry of Montreal was that of the British Army light infantry except that its lace and buttons were silver rather than gold.[1] The head-dress was a black shako of 1861-69 pattern with a green ball. The collar, shoulder-straps, and slashed cuffs of the long-skirted red tunic were dark blue. The forage cap was a high pillbox, similar to that of the British guards, with a red band.[2]

In undress, the officers wore the long double-breasted dark-blue frock-coat and a low round forage cap with straight black peak and red band. A loose single-breasted four-button patrol jacket was worn over the sword-belt on active service.[3]

When transferred to The Royal Light Infantry in 1863, the Highland Rifle Company of Montreal adopted the standard light infantry uniform when on parade with the unit. Only a diced band on the forage cap indicated the Highland origin of the company. Off parade, however, the company was permitted to wear trews of Black Watch tartan and a feather bonnet with red hackle.[4]

Upon being reorganized as the 5th Battalion, Royal Fusiliers, Montreal in 1876, the regiment adopted fusilier dress: a fusilier busby with white plume, and the standard Canadian-pattern red tunic with dark-blue facings and pointed cuffs trimmed with a white crow's-foot.[5] Both flank companies were designated as Highland, and dressed in Scottish doublets with gauntlet cuffs, trews of Black Watch tartan, and fusilier busbies. Glengarrys with diced bands were adopted as the forage cap of the Highland companies.[6] In 1879, the entire regiment adopted this dress, and shortly thereafter changed its title to the 5th Battalion, Royal Scots Fusiliers.[7]

When the kilt was adopted in 1883, the fusilier busby was replaced by the white helmet for full dress until enough bonnets could be purchased to supply the entire regiment. This was achieved with the assistance of several prominent citizens of Montreal and, in 1895, the feather bonnet became part of the official full-dress uniform of the regiment.[8] In the same year, the red hackle was authorized for all ranks.[9]

When the regiment adopted the kilt, the Lorne tartan was selected in honour of the Marquis of Lorne, then Governor-General of Canada. This proved an unfortunate choice because of the inconsistency of pattern and dye of succeeding lots of tartan. Within a few years, the Lorne tartan was replaced by the Black Watch. As it was a sealed pattern of the British Army, it was reproduced with great uniformity.

The plate depicts a field officer of the 5th Battalion Royal Scots of Canada in full dress in 1891. The scarlet Highland doublet is faced with blue; the collar is edged with gold lace, and piped around the seam with gold cord. The blue gauntlet cuffs are decorated with three vertical loops of gold lace, each terminating in a regimental button; the cuffs are trimmed with broad gold lace and edged in white. White piping runs down the front of the doublet and along the edges of the Inverness flaps, which are trimmed with gold lace and decorated with three vertical lace loops with a regimental button at the base of each loop.[10] A Highland broadsword is attached to the traditional white Scottish cross-belt by white sword slings; a dirk is carried on the brown leather waist-belt. The regiment wore a white sporran with two black tails; the official Black Watch five-tailed sporran was not adopted until after the outbreak of the First World War.

The officer in the illustration wears the usual red and white diced hose of the Highland regiments. In 1899, authority was granted for the adoption of the black and red hose tops of the Black Watch.[11]

In 1891, the other ranks of the regiment still wore antiquated equipment of Crimea vintage: white waist-belt, ball bag, and bayonet frog, and a white cross-belt supporting a black cartridge pouch on the right hip. The ancient Snider-Enfield, the original breech-loading rifle of the British Army, was still the standard long arm of Canadian militia infantry regiments.[12]

When, in 1895, feather bonnets were issued, the transition from Light Infantry to full Highland status was completed. This long and costly process was effected only with considerable personal sacrifice by all ranks. But the result was not merely a unit in full Highland dress: the effort required to bring about these changes created a regiment with great pride and spirit, a unit that achieved a remarkable record of service in two world conflicts.

1883 to the present

History

The often inadequate performance of the Canadian militia during the Fenian raids of 1866-1870 clearly demonstrated a need for better training at all levels. The British Army had long been the source of qualified instructors; but the British regiments sailed for home in 1870, leaving Canadians to their own resources. In 1883, to replace the personnel and expertise lost through the British departure, approval was granted for the creation of a small Canadian regular force of cavalry, artillery, and infantry.[1]

On 21 December 1883, Lieutenant-Colonel J.F. Turnbull was authorized to raise and command A Troop, Cavalry School Corps and School of Cavalry. During the following year recruiting brought A Troop to its established strength of three officers, forty men, and a number of horses. However, proper saddlery, valises, and carbines were not provided, and these items had to be borrowed from A Battery of the regular artillery and from the Queen's Own Canadian Hussars, a militia unit in Quebec City.[2]

Active service came quickly for the Cavalry School Corps. On the outbreak of the Northwest Rebellion in April 1885, A Troop was joined by the Winnipeg Troop of Cavalry to form a mounted unit of General Middleton's North West Field Force. When the Rebellion had been crushed, the Cavalry School Corps resumed its normal peace-time task of training the volunteer militia cavalry.

On 15 July 1887, the title Royal was conferred on the School of Cavalry.[3] In 1891, it was recommended that the Permanent Force adopt the regimental system. The Cavalry School Corps was redesignated the Canadian Dragoons on 14 May 1892. On 27 June, the Canadian Mounted Rifle Corps at Winnipeg was amalgamated with the regiment and designated B Troop, Canadian Dragoons.[4] In May 1893, the corps was given its present title, The Royal Canadian Dragoons.[5]

In December 1899, the Canadian government's offer of more troops for South Africa was accepted by the British War Office. A brigade of field artillery and two battalions of mounted rifles, designated the 1st and 2nd battalions Canadian Mounted Rifles (CMR), were mobilized. The Royal Canadian Dragoons provided most of the trained officers and men for the 1st Battalion. At the request of the unit while in South Africa, it was redesignated The Royal Canadian Dragoons on 22 August 1900.[6]

Upon landing in South Africa, the regiment was posted to the 1st Mounted Infantry Brigade. Within days it had seen its first action, and was in continuous contact with the enemy for almost nine months. When the unit was withdrawn from active service in November 1900, it had marched 2740 km (1700 mi.), taken part in twenty-eight engagements, and was reduced from a strength of 400 to three officers and eighty-three other ranks.[7] In the performance of this demanding service, the unit had been awarded thirteen decorations including three Victoria Crosses.[8]

When war broke out in 1914, The Royal Canadian Dragoons, Lord Strathcona's Horse (Royal Canadians), and the RCHA Brigade went overseas with the 1st Canadian Contingent. From this group the Canadian Cavalry Brigade was formed in January 1915. Initially, the 2nd King Edward's Horse was the third regiment; but it was replaced in September by the Fort Garry Horse, making the Brigade an all-Canadian formation.[9]

The Brigade landed in France in May, just in time to take part in the Battle of Festubert – as infantry! For the duration of the war, the Dragoons performed as infantry and cavalry. Its most memorable action took place on 30 March 1918, when the entire Brigade carried out a classic cavalry charge at Moreuil Wood.

In 1919, the regiment resumed the peace-time routine of a regular cavalry unit. Although there was much debate on the future of horsed cavalry, the question really had been settled at Moreuil Wood, where machine guns cost the Brigade some 300 men and 800 horses in only ninety minutes. Nonetheless, when war was again declared in September 1939, The Royal Canadian Dragoons was still a regiment of horsed cavalry.

With precious little demand for horse-soldiers, the regiment remained behind while the infantry divisions proceeded overseas. With the formation of the Canadian Armoured Corps in August 1940, however, The Royal Canadian Dragoons went on active service as an armoured car regiment, first as a unit of the 5th Canadian Armoured Division, and later as corps troops with the 1st Canadian Corps in Italy and North-West Europe.

After the war, the regiment exchanged its armoured cars for tanks, and became Canada's senior armoured regiment; but the graceful South African springbok on its badge remains a constant reminder of the service performed by The Royal Canadian Dragoons as horsed cavalry.

1883 to the present
Uniform

The original recruits of the Cavalry School Corps were issued· the standard Canadian militia cavalry uniform of hussar pattern in 1884.[1] It consisted of a dark-blue hussar jacket heavily braided on the chest, back seams, hems, and cuffs with yellow woollen cord. Described in dress regulations as buff, the collar was, with the characteristic perversity of British military custom, white. Dark-blue overalls with a double white stripe were worn in dismounted dress, and similar pantaloons were worn with black Wellingtons and steel spurs in mounted order.[2]

The dark-blue pillbox forage cap was trimmed with a band of gold lace for officers and senior NCOs, and with white cloth for other ranks. The hussar busby with white plume and bag, and gilt chin chain was prescribed for full dress, although militia cavalry was issued only forage caps. Full-dress head-gear was purchased privately with non-public funds by some units.[3] The officers of the permanent cavalry were required to provide themselves with full dress, including busbies. However, it is not known whether busbies or helmets were issued to the men. Given the character of Lieutenant-Colonel Turnbull, it is likely that his regular cavalrymen were properly turned out, even if this meant borrowing busbies from his former unit, the Queen's Own Canadian Hussars.

Officers' dress was similar in pattern to that of the men, with gold lace and braid replacing the yellow worsted cord. The amount of braiding on collar and cuffs increased with rank. A dark-blue patrol jacket trimmed with black mohair braid was worn for normal parades and duties. A blue frock-coat elaborately braided with black mohair was adopted for dismounted undress order.[4]

The handsome hussar uniform required a great deal of upkeep. Pipeclay was used to clean the white collar; the yellow braiding was treated with a wash of chrome yellow to restore its colour. The General Officer Commanding the Militia thought the choice of the hussar-pattern uniform for militia cavalry a most unhappy one. It was his view that "the quantity of braid on the tunic requires great care and trouble to keep clean, and with, very often, uncleaned sword, boots and spurs (the two latter being very much according to the fancy of the wearer) the cavalryman presents a tawdry appearance which is not pleasing to the eye."[5]

Once a cavalry school was established, the General recommended the adoption of a simplified uniform of dark blue with scarlet facings, a belt of black or brown leather, and a helmet. Although some of these sensible recommendations were adopted, most were ignored, probably because of the cost of obtaining new uniforms for the volunteer cavalry.[6]

The original equipment of the Cavalry School Corps consisted of a white buff-leather pouch belt with black pouch, and white sword slings and sword-knots. The sword issued to the troopers appears to be the 1882-pattern British cavalry sword. Their carbine was the Snider-Enfield,[7] although Turnbull complained bitterly about this weapon as it was useless beyond 400 metres.[8] On dispatch to the Northwest Rebellion, A

Troop was armed with the Winchester Model 1876 carbine. It was vastly superior to the Snider, but Turnbull continued to press for the new Martini-Henry cavalry carbine.

When the corps was redesignated Canadian Dragoons in 1892, and subsequently The Royal Canadian Dragoons, the dress was changed completely to that of dragoon pattern: scarlet cavalry tunic with dark-blue collar, cuffs, and shoulder-straps. The collar was trimmed top and bottom with yellow cord, the yellow cord of the cuffs formed an Austrian knot, and the shoulder-straps were edged with yellow. Blue cloth edged the front of the tunic, which closed with eight brass regimental buttons. Dark-blue overalls and pantaloons were trimmed down the outside seam with a single wide yellow stripe.[9]

The granting of the title Royal also was accompanied by authorization of unit badges of the Royal Cypher surmounted by the Imperial Crown.[10] A white Canadian-pattern helmet with brass spike, chin chain, and helmet plate was worn in full dress. The band on the dark-blue pillbox forage cap was yellow cloth for the men and gold lace for officers and senior NCOs.

In keeping with the recommendations of the General Officer Commanding the Militia, the pouch belt, waist-belt, sword slings and gauntlets were of brown leather, which did not require cleaning with messy pipeclay. Black Wellington boots with steel jack spurs were worn in mounted orders of dress.[11] For drill and service dress the men were issued a red serge five-buttoned frock with blue collar and shoulder-straps, and plain cuffs.[12]

At the same time the corps finally received the Martini-Henry carbine.[13] It also carried the 1882- and 1885-pattern British cavalry sword with steel scabbard. Lances were carried on some occasions, although this was not normally a weapon for dragoons.[14]

The plate depicts a field officer of The Royal Canadian Dragoons in full-dress mounted order in 1897. The heavy gold braiding on the cuffs is indicative of his senior rank. In the background is an officer in the dark-blue patrol jacket trimmed with black mohair tapes and braid.

During one engagement in South Africa, the stealthy approach of a party of Boers was signalled by unusual activity among a herd of nervous springbok. Heeding the warning of the graceful animals, the detachment stood to in time to beat off a determined enemy attack. To perpetuate this event, authority was granted to adopt the springbok as an official badge of the regiment, in addition to the Royal Cypher.[15] The bounding springbok is still worn by the regiment as the cap and collar badges of The Royal Canadian Dragoons.[16]

Shortly before the outbreak of war in 1914, the regiment replaced the white helmet by the brass dragoon helmet with black plume. Once again, white buff-leather belts and slings made their appearance to differentiate between service dress and the full dress reserved for ceremonial parades.[17]

1848 to the present
History

At the close of the American Revolution, the men of several disbanded Loyalist regiments settled in the valleys of the Saint John and Kennebecasis rivers, then part of Nova Scotia. These men brought with them a tradition of military service that was to develop into one of Canada's best known regiments of cavalry, the 8th Canadian Hussars (Princess Louise's).

Although military service came naturally to the new settlers, conditions were not conducive to the formation of cavalry units. The primitive pioneer farms cut out of the surrounding forest had few horses and fewer roads. As the settlements developed into a group of thriving communities connected by road, the number of horses increased, and with the horses came cavalry. In 1825, the Militia Act of the Province of New Brunswick provided for the raising of troops of volunteer cavalry, attached to a county militia battalion of infantry.[1]

The story of the regiment began with Militia General Order No. 1 of April 1848, which authorized the amalgamation of eleven independent troops of cavalry to form a regiment designated the New Brunswick Yeomanry Cavalry. Major Robert James, formerly of the 7th Hussars of the British Army, became the first commanding officer of the new regiment.[2]

In 1865, Captain John Saunders, grandson of the John Saunders who commanded a mounted troop of the Queen's Rangers, replaced Lieutenant-Colonel James as commanding officer. Thus, a link was forged between the Queen's Rangers and the New Brunswick Yeomanry Cavalry. His enthusiastic and effective leadership in these formative years earned Saunders his reputation as the father of the regiment.[3]

On Confederation, the unit became a regiment of the Canadian militia, a change in status formally acknowledged in General Orders of 30 April 1869, which designated it the New Brunswick Regiment of Yeomanry Cavalry.[4] It was retitled the 8th Regiment of Cavalry in May 1872; that particular number was assigned because New Brunswick constituted Military District No. 8. The regiment was recognized as one of the best-trained units of volunteer cavalry in Canada, with summer training carried out at Fox Hill, the home of Lieutenant-Colonel Saunders.[5]

Governor-General the Marquis of Lorne paid an official visit to New Brunswick in 1879, accompanied by his wife, Princess Louise, daughter of Queen Victoria. This charming woman captivated the men of the vice-regal mounted escort provided by the 8th Regiment of Cavalry, and they applied immediately to have the regiment renamed for her.[6] After following the usual convoluted path of such requests, the unit was officially redesignated the 8th Princess Louise's New Brunswick Regiment of Cavalry in July 1884,[7] and proudly bears her name to this day.

The regiment had acquired a distinctive title, and was recognized as a very efficient cavalry unit; but it still lacked battle experience. The commanding officer offered the services of the regiment to Britain during the Sudan campaign of 1884. The proposal was acknowledged but declined.[8] Neither was the unit invited to participate in the Northwest Rebellion of 1885, much to its disgust. However, the regiment was officially recognized as a hussar unit when it became the 8th Princess Louise's New Brunswick Hussars in 1892.

While some of the 8th Hussars saw active service when the regiment volunteered both infantry and mounted units for South Africa in 1900, there was considerable disappointment when the regiment was not mobilized immediately on the outbreak of war in 1914. Not until January 1915 was the 6th Canadian Mounted Rifles raised, with A Squadron coming from the 8th Princess Louise's New Brunswick Hussars.

When the militia was reorganized after the First World War, the regiment resumed its pre-war title and peace-time routine. But the days of horsed cavalry were over, and in 1936 the unit went to camp to train in rented automobiles as a motorized cavalry regiment.[9]

The 8th Hussars was not mobilized on the outbreak of the Second World War in 1939. In July 1940, however, it was placed on active service as a motorcycle regiment, and was converted to an armoured regiment in February 1941. As the 5th Armoured Regiment (8th Princess Louise's (New Brunswick) Hussars), the regiment served with distinction in Italy and North-West Europe as a unit of the 5th Canadian Armoured Division.

After the war, the regiment returned to reserve status, and to the training grounds of Sussex, New Brunswick, where it carried on its tradition of hard work, enthusiasm, and efficiency. Widely regarded as one of Canada's most effective militia armoured units, the regiment was designated the 8th Canadian Hussars (Princess Louise's) in 1957, and contributed a regular component to the Canadian Army. The militia unit continues to serve in New Brunswick, and maintains close relations with the regular regiment.

In June 1973, the regiment celebrated the 125th anniversary of its formation. On that occasion, as a tribute to its origins, the commanding officer of the regulars led the formal march past mounted on a horse.[10] Parades were held at Petawawa, the home base of the regulars, and at Moncton, where the 8th Canadian Hussars (Princess Louise's) (Militia) received the freedom of the city.

1848 to the present

Uniform

Volunteer cavalry troops raised in New Brunswick under the Militia Act of 1825 were required to provide their own horses, uniforms, and equipment. As each troop designed its own uniform, the resulting military splendour was curbed only by imagination and funds. Some wore red jackets, others wore blue, and at least one troop imported hussar uniforms from England.[1]

Early in its existence the regiment adopted the hussar uniform, and the mounted escort for the Prince of Wales during his visit to New Brunswick in 1860 was dressed in blue.[2]

After Confederation, the unit obtained cavalry uniforms through government supply channels: a dark-blue hussar jacket with white collar, braided on the chest, cuffs, back seams, and skirt edges with yellow worsted cord. Blue cloth overalls were trimmed down the outside seam with a double white stripe. The round pillbox forage cap with white band and button, and black leather chin-strap was the only headgear issued by government stores.[3] However, the regiment purchased hussar busbies with white plumes and bags for ceremonial wear.[4]

The men were equipped with a white pouch belt, black leather pouch, and a sword-belt with white leather slings, worn under the jacket. In the early years the unit was issued the Enfield rifle; but its length made it difficult to carry on horseback,[5] and it was replaced by the Spencer carbine in the late 1860s. In turn, the Spencer was succeeded by the Snider carbine in 1872.[6]

The basic dress of the 8th Hussars changed little during the final years of the nineteenth century. The white helmet with brass spike, chin chain, and helmet plate was issued for full dress in 1885. For service dress, the officers adopted a dark-blue patrol jacket trimmed with black mohair braid and tapes, a plain brown leather pouch belt, and black leather sabretache with regimental badge.[7]

The plate illustrates a mounted junior officer of the mid-1890s in full dress. On each side of his dark-blue hussar jacket are six loops of gold chain lace with caps and drops, fastening with six gold-net-covered olivets. The entire jacket is edged with gold chain lace. On each back seam is a double row of the same lace forming a crow's-foot at the top, passing under a netted cap at the waist and terminating in an Austrian knot at the hem of the skirt. The white collar is trimmed top and bottom with gold lace, and the blue cuffs are trimmed with a gold-chain Austrian knot.

The busby has a gold oval cockade in front of the eight-inch white plume. The white busby bag is trimmed with gold braid and a single gold-lace-covered button. The gold cord cap lines fasten about the neck with the free ends looped up on the right shoulder.

Dark-blue pantaloons with double white stripe are worn with black Wellington boots and steel spurs.

The shoulder-belt is of gold lace with a white silk centre stripe, silver buckle and slide, and silver prickers and chain. The pouch is of black leather with silver flap ornamented with Queen Victoria's Cypher. The sword slings are of gold lace with a white centre stripe and gilt fittings. The sabretache is of white cloth edged in gold lace with the Queen's Cypher and regimental device embroidered in gold and red. White leather gloves complete the rider's dress.[8]

A black lambskin covers the saddle, while the dark-blue shabraque edged with gold lace has a regimental device in the rear corner. The throat plume is white, and a regimental badge is worn on the circular breastplate.[9]

In addition to full dress, officers provided themselves with a plain dark-blue patrol jacket with breast pockets, blue collar, plain cuffs, and white shoulder-straps. A dark-blue folding field service cap with chin-strap was worn with this order of dress. Pouch belt, sword slings, and gloves were of brown leather. Blue overalls with black boots were worn in dismounted order, while blue pantaloons with black Wellingtons and steel spurs were worn for mounted duties.[10]

The men were issued a new-pattern serge patrol jacket with breast pockets, white collar, and blue shoulder-straps and cuffs piped with yellow braid.[11] Blue breeches were worn with black Stohwasser-pattern leggings or blue woollen puttees.[12]

By 1907, all ranks had adopted the dark-blue naval pattern cap. Officers' caps were worn with a white cover, while those of the men had a white welt around the edge of the crown and a white band. Shoulder-chains replaced the white shoulder-straps on officers' jackets. The men were issued a plain blue patrol jacket with white shoulder-straps.[13]

Weapons also changed. The ancient Snider carbine was replaced by the magazine-loading Lee-Metford carbine in 1898. In 1911, the regiment was armed with the controversial Canadian Ross Rifle, Mark II.[14]

Though details of regimental dress and equipment changed over the years, the basic uniform retained the hussar pattern. In 1966, when the regular component of the regiment received its guidon, a mounted escort in the colourful full dress of the 8th Canadian Hussars served as a reminder of the origins of this distinguished corps.

1855 to the present

History

The Governor General's Horse Guards is the senior regiment of the Canadian militia, and claims the longest period of unbroken service for a mounted unit of the Canadian Army. The regiment traces its beginning to the reorganization of the militia of Upper Canada after the War of 1812-14, when the provincial Militia Act provided for a troop of cavalry for each regimental district. In 1822, Colonel Chewett of the 1st West York Regiment of Militia persuaded Captain George Taylor Denison of Bellevue, Toronto to raise and command such a troop for his regiment. The Denison family was to maintain a long association with the newly formed unit.[1]

Though not provided with weapons until 1831, Denison's troop, which assumed the title of York Dragoons, continued voluntary training.[2] This was most unusual for a militia unit of the period, but it proved its worth. When the Rebellion of 1837 confronted Toronto, Denison's troop was taken immediately into regular British service, and performed so effectively that it was granted the honorary designation of Queen's Light Dragoons. The corps was relieved from service in May 1839 after two six-month periods of active duty.[3]

The Militia Act of 1846, enacted to standardize militia regulations in the recently united provinces of Lower and Upper Canada, authorized the formation of volunteer units of infantry, artillery, and cavalry. Such units had existed previously, but the new Act provided the first official recognition of volunteer corps by Canadian authorities. Some reorganization of the militia followed, and in 1847 the Queen's Light Dragoons was regazetted the 1st Toronto Independent Troop of Cavalry.[4] In 1853, a regiment of volunteer cavalry designated the 1st Regiment, York Light Dragoons was formed in the county of York, and Denison's Independent Troop of Cavalry was named the 1st Troop of the new regiment.[5]

The Militia Act of 1855 provided for the formation of the Active Militia of selected volunteer units, to be equipped and paid by the government. It also authorized the enrolment of troops of cavalry, rather than regiments. The 1st Troop, York Light Dragoons was selected for the new force and designated 1st Troop, Volunteer Militia Cavalry of the County of York (1st York Cavalry).[6]

As one of the better trained and mounted units in Toronto, the 1st York Cavalry and its predecessor, the 1st Toronto Independent Troop, were called on frequently to furnish an escort for the Governor-General of the day. Because of this long tradition of vice-regal service, a memorial was presented to His Excellency in 1861 requesting that the troop be granted the title of the Governor General's Body Guard. No reply was received.[7] When, in April 1866, the Royal Guides of Montreal was gazetted the Governor General's Body Guard, the 1st York Cavalry protested vigorously. As a result, an order of 27 April 1866 directed that the Royal Guides be designated the Governor General's Body Guard for Lower Canada, and the 1st York Cavalry be titled the Governor General's Body Guard for Upper Canada.[8] The latter designation was changed to the Governor General's Body Guard for Ontario on 1 July 1867.

The Body Guard was placed on active service during the Fenian raids of 1866, serving in the Fort Erie area with the British regulars. The corps made a creditable showing during these operations despite the inadequacy of its weapons and equipment.[9]

In 1874, it was proposed that the strength of the unit be raised to two troops. The second troop was soon recruited, although authority for the increase in establishment was not forthcoming until May 1876.[10] It was with a strength of two troops that the Body Guard went on active service with General Middleton's North West Field Force in 1885; and during the ensuing campaign the unit was assigned a protective role on the right flank of Middleton's advance to Batoche.

In May 1889, the Body Guard was raised to the status of a cavalry regiment of four troops. The new regiment was designated the Governor General's Body Guard in 1895, as the Royal Guides had been disbanded in 1869.[11]

Although it was not mobilized as a mounted unit on the outbreak of the First World War, the regiment contributed volunteers to the 3rd Battalion, CEF, on the assembly of the First Canadian Contingent in 1914. Subsequently, the unit recruited for the 4th Regiment, Canadian Mounted Rifles, which served in France with the 2nd Canadian Mounted Rifle Brigade.[12]

After the 1918 armistice, the Governor General's Body Guard resumed its role as a horsed regiment of cavalry. When the Canadian militia was again reorganized in 1936, the regiment was amalgamated with the Mississauga Horse of Toronto and redesignated the Governor General's Horse Guards.[13]

The Horse Guards, like most Canadian cavalry regiments, took on a modern mechanized role on active service during the Second World War. Mobilized in 1940, the unit was equipped first with motorcycles and later with tanks. As the 3rd Canadian Armoured Reconnaissance Regiment (GGHG), the unit formed part of the 5th Canadian Armoured Division, and served with that formation in Italy and North-West Europe until the end of the war.

The Governor General's Horse Guards remains on the roll of active regiments of the Canadian militia. Although its horses have been replaced by armoured vehicles for normal service, a special mounted troop of the regiment parades in full dress on very special occasions, adding a welcome dash of colour to Canada's mechanized army.

1855 to the present

Uniform

When raised in 1822, Captain Denison's troop of volunteer cavalry provided its own weapons, equipment, and clothing. While searching for a suitable uniform, Denison discovered that a retired master tailor of the 13th Light Dragoons had set up shop in Toronto. The tailor was engaged immediately to outfit the troop in a uniform that, understandably, bore a strong resemblance to that of the 13th Light Dragoons.[1]

This early uniform of the York Dragoons consisted of a dark-blue coatee with buff facings, heavily laced across wide buff lapels and along the back and sleeve seams with silver braid for officers and white for other ranks. The dark overalls were trimmed with a double white stripe down the outside seam. A girdle was worn at the waist. A bearskin crest and a side plume of red and white feathers decorated the helmet-shaped head-dress.[2]

During the Rebellion of 1837, the troop was issued with accoutrements, weapons (including flintlock carbines), and some items of clothing, such as cloaks and fur caps, from British Army supply channels.[3] The coatee was simplified by removing the wide lapels and fastening the braid to the plain blue cloth front.[4] About the same time, the bearskin-crested helmet was replaced by a bell-topped light dragoon shako with white plume.[5]

On becoming a unit of the Active Militia in 1855, the 1st York Cavalry was issued with new pouches and pouch belts, swords, sword-belts, and pistols carried in a leather holster fastened to the sword-belt.[6] The dress of the troop was described as a jacket of fine blue cloth with white facings, and the old bell-topped shako.[7]

A marked change in regimental dress came in 1871, when the light dragoon uniform was discarded in favour of one of heavy cavalry design. A dragoon helmet of German silver with brass binding, chin scales, spike, and white horsehair plume replaced the bell-topped shako. The dark-blue dragoon tunic was edged with braid, silver for officers and white for other ranks. The white collar of the officer's tunic was edged with silver lace, and the pointed cuffs were trimmed with an Austrian knot of silver cord and tracing braid. The back of the skirt had three-pointed flaps of standard cavalry pattern. Edged with silver lace, the flaps had a silver button at each point and two at the waist. Shoulder-straps were of flat braided silver cord with blue lining. The front of the officer's tunic was fastened with six silver olivets, a regimental distinction that was carried over into succeeding patterns of patrol jacket and frock, including the khaki service-dress tunic worn until the introduction of the green Canadian Forces uniform.

The officer's waist-belt was of silver lace, lined with white morocco leather and edged with white velvet, with white metal fittings and snake buckle. The shoulder-belt was of silver lace with white metal buckle, tips, and slide; the silver chain and prickers were of light cavalry origin. The silver flap of the black leather pouch was mounted with the inscription GGBG in gilt metal.

Dark-blue overalls with a double stripe of silver were worn in full dress, while pantaloons with a double white stripe were worn with black butcher boots and steel jack spurs in mounted order. A white sabretache was trimmed with silver lace and mounted with an embroidered regimental badge. Sword slings were of silver lace, the sword-knot was of white leather with silver acorn, and gauntlets were of white leather.[8]

The men's uniform was similar to that of the officers, except that white braid and cord were worn in place of the officers' silver, and white shoulder cords replaced the officers' heavy silver shoulder-straps. Waist-belts and cross-belts were of white leather for troopers and NCOs.[9]

Special permission was granted by the War Office for all ranks of the regiment to wear aiguillettes in full dress. Those of the officers were of heavy silver cord and were worn on the right shoulder. The regimental sergeant-major, quartermaster-sergeant, and bandmaster wore aiguillettes of small silver cord, while those of NCOs and men were of white cord; both were worn on the left shoulder.[10]

The simple and dignified full-dress uniform illustrated in the plate went almost unchanged until 1936, when the regiment was amalgamated with the Mississauga Horse and re-designated the Governor General's Horse Guards; at this time the white plumes and facings were changed to scarlet.[11]

Various patterns of jacket and frock were worn for undress and drill order. During the Northwest Rebellion both officers and men wore stable jackets and round pillbox forage caps. Shortly after the campaign, the men were issued a dark-blue serge frock with breast pockets for undress. A white helmet or round forage cap was worn with this order of dress. In the late 1890s, the unit received a new pattern of blue serge frock with white collar and shoulder-straps, and a crow's-foot in white cord on the cuffs.[12]

Ultimately, the colourful blue uniforms of the Horse Guards were replaced by various forms of khaki service dress and by the black coveralls of armoured crewmen; but the mounted detachment can still be seen in full dress wearing the century-old dragoon helmets of German silver on special ceremonial occasions.

1855 to the present

History

Although there has been an organized militia in Canada for more than 300 years, militia artillery units have a more recent origin. Not until 1725 was it reported that militiamen were being trained in gunnery at Quebec, and that a nominal roll of militia artillerymen was maintained.[1] The Loyal Company of Artillery of Saint John, which still exists, was raised in 1793.[2] A Royal Militia Artillery Company was formed in Montreal in 1812,[3] and at least three militia artillery companies and two troops of drivers were embodied during the War of 1812-14.[4] The Royal Quebec Volunteer Artillery, a militia unit for many years, originated in 1830,[5] and it was the guns of the 1st Toronto Artillery Company that blew Mackenzie's rebels out of Montgomery's Tavern on 7 December 1837.[6] In 1838, a General Order dated 28 February constituted the New Brunswick Regiment of Artillery under Lieutenant-Colonel Richard Hayne.

For the most part, these early artillery corps disappeared with the circumstances that stimulated their creation. For our purposes, the artillery of Canada originated with the Militia Act of 1855, which provided for seven field batteries and five foot companies of artillery in a new volunteer active militia.[7] One of the first of the new artillery units was the Montreal Field Battery, which was gazetted on 27 September 1855.[8] By the spring of 1856 the battery had recruited to its full establishment of seventy-five all ranks, and had been equipped with three 6-pounder brass smooth-bore muzzle-loading guns and one 12-pounder howitzer.[9]

Its commander, Major W.F. Coffin, set an exacting standard for his battery. He paraded it for gun drill each Wednesday afternoon, and for foot drill every morning at 5 AM![10] He demanded and received full attendance at all parades. As a result, the Montreal Field Battery gained an excellent reputation throughout the British Army.[11]

One of the more unusual feats of the battery was climbing Mount Royal with all of its guns on 10 November 1862 to fire a Royal Salute in celebration of the Prince of Wales' twenty-first birthday. Until this time the mountain had been considered inaccessible to horse-drawn vehicles, and the battery's ascent led to the acquisition of Mount Royal as a public park by the City of Montreal.[12]

On 1 June 1866, the Fenians crossed the border and the battery was ordered to the frontier near Huntingdon. While it fired no shots at the enemy, the unit became deeply involved in a battle of administrative mismanagement. On 25 May 1870, armed with 9-pounder smooth bores, the battery was dispatched again to the Huntingdon area to repel the Fenians. Again it returned to Montreal without firing a shot.

One of the more unpleasant duties of the militia was to aid the civil authorities when the local police were unable to maintain public order. The militia units of Montreal were called on to perform more than their fair share of such service. Elections were spirited events in the 1860s, and Montreal mayoralty contests were especially vigorous. On one such occasion the battery was under arms for four days.[13]

In 1872, the Government purchased a number of British 9-pounder muzzle-loading rifled wrought-iron guns. This was ideal equipment for the Canadian artillery, for "during its service the 9-pounder proved a simple, robust gun, admirably suited to the rough handling of a half trained but enthusiastic force in a rugged, little-developed country."[14] During the next six years, all the field batteries were equipped with this serviceable piece of ordnance.

When numbers were assigned to the militia artillery units in 1895, the corps was officially designated the 3rd "Montreal" Field Battery, Canadian Artillery.[15]

There was great excitement in the battery when, in the spring of 1898, it was rearmed with six 12-pounder breech-loading rifled guns, the most up-to-date field equipment in the British Army.[16] However, subsequent experience in South Africa demonstrated that the recently acquired 12-pounder was totally inadequate for modern warfare. It was replaced by the 18-pounder quick-firing gun, which began to arrive in Canada in 1906 and soon became the standard armament of the Canadian Field Artillery.[17]

In August 1914, the 3rd "Montreal" Field Battery finally went to war. At Valcartier, the 3rd "Montreal" and the 22nd "Sherbrooke" batteries were amalgamated under the command of Major A.G.L. McNaughton to form the 4th Battery, Canadian Field Artillery (CFA). It was assigned to the 2nd Brigade, CFA, of the 1st Canadian Divisional Artillery. In November, the unit was redesignated the 7th Battery, CFA, when the field-artillery brigade establishment was changed from three six-gun batteries to four four-gun batteries.[18]

Four years later, the battery returned from the First World War with battle-proven professional competence, and resumed militia duties in Montreal. The militia was mobilized again in 1939, and the 7th "Montreal" Battery served throughout the war as a unit of the 2nd Field Regiment, RCA, of the 1st Canadian Division.

In the 1946 reorganization of the militia, the 7th Field Battery remained on the order of battle to preserve the traditions and continuity of service of one of the most venerable units of the Royal Canadian Artillery, the 3rd "Montreal" Field Battery.[19]

1855 to the present

Uniform

The first uniform of the Montreal Field Battery, selected by the officers in 1855, was highly original. The officers' dress consisted of a dark-blue frock-coat like that of the Royal Artillery, with two rows of eight gilt buttons and a plain high blue collar that carried the rank badges. In period photographs, the pointed cuffs appear to be of a different colour from the coat – probably red – and the shoulder scales end in solid metal crescents.[1]

Dark-blue trousers trimmed with a wide scarlet stripe were worn over black boots with steel spurs. Major Coffin, the battery commander, wore riding boots that came well up on the thigh and were fitted with jack spurs.[2]

A crimson net sash was worn over the left shoulder, and the white leather sword-belt, fastened with a square metal belt-plate, was worn about the waist. Sword-slings were of white leather.

The most unusual feature of the uniform was the shaggy black monkey-fur cap. It was similar to a guardsman's bearskin except that the front of the crown projected slightly, and the front of the cap was ornamented with a large bullion tassel suspended by a gold cord.[3]

The dark-blue round forage cap with gold lace band and black leather dropped peak had a full crown, and was similar to the forage caps of British officers of the Crimean War period. A large embroidered grenade was worn on the front of the forage cap.

The sole period description of the original dress of the men states only that they wore blue uniforms and black monkey-skin busbies.[4]

Officers' winter dress included a round black astrakhan cap and a long double-breasted greatcoat of dark cloth with collar and front opening trim of black astrakhan. The coat was braided across the front with six loops of black cord, each ending in a crow's-foot, and the cuffs were trimmed with an Austrian knot of black braid. The white leather sword-belt was worn over the greatcoat. Knee-length winter boots were worn with jack spurs.[5]

The original uniform of the battery was short-lived, as a standard artillery uniform was adopted in 1863. Thereafter, the general pattern remained much the same until full dress was discarded in 1914.[6]

For full dress, the battery adopted the fur busby of horse-artillery pattern with gilt curb chain, red bag, and a white plume – feathers for officers and hair for other ranks – fixed at the front of the cap. A gold cord cockade was set top centre in the front of the officer's busby, and the gold cap lines were fastened around the neck and looped up on the left breast.[7] Yellow woollen cord appeared on the busbies of other ranks.

The plate illustrates a subaltern officer of the 3rd "Montreal" Field Battery in mounted review order in 1893. The dark-blue cloth tunic had nine buttons in front and two behind at the waist; the front was edged in scarlet cloth. The coat was split behind to the waist with a blue flap on the back of each skirt; the skirt opening was edged with scarlet cloth. Each flap was edged with gold cord and ornamented with three gilt buttons.

The scarlet collar was edged with gold lace, and trimmed around the base with gold cord; embroidered grenades in frosted silver were set at each side of the collar opening. The blue cuffs were trimmed with an Austrian knot of gold cord and laced according to rank. The shoulder-straps were edged with gold cord with rank badges embroidered in silver. In 1893, the shoulder-straps of militia artillery officers were ordered to be of red cloth.[8]

Dark-blue trousers with a wide scarlet stripe down the outside seam were worn over black Wellington boots fitted with steel spurs; pantaloons were worn with black butcher boots and steel jack spurs. As can be seen in the plate, the officers of the battery wore a white leather pouch belt and sword-belt with sword slings of white leather, and a plain black sabretache with gilt badge and white slings.

The dress of the NCOs and gunners was like that of the officers except that the collar and cuffs were edged with yellow cord, and the backs of the skirts were without flaps. In 1883, the gunners discarded the black leather leggings issued to field batteries and replaced them at their own expense with black riding boots and pantaloons.[9]

Other ranks carried swords with steel scabbards, and white leather sword-knots and slings. The white waist-belt was fastened by a gilt belt-plate ornamented with the battery badge; the white pouch belt held a black leather pouch.[10]

In addition to full dress, the men were issued with a blue serge service dress, which was worn with the round blue pill-box forage cap.

1883 to the present
History

The Canadian Militia Act of 1883 provided for the establishment of a small regular force of one troop of cavalry, three batteries of artillery (two of which had been formed in 1870), and not more than three companies of infantry to serve as schools of military instruction for the volunteer militia.[1]

An order of 21 December 1883 authorized the formation of three schools of infantry formed into one corps to be known as the Infantry School Corps. Each school was based on a company of the Corps; A Company was located at Fredericton, B Company at St-Jean, Quebec, and C Company at Toronto.[2] Although the companies, consisting of some one hundred NCOs and men, were not fully raised until early 1884, the first schools of military instruction were opened in April 1883.[3]

Canada's newly organized miniature force of regular infantry had just completed recruitment when it was required to furnish a company for the North West Field Force for service during the Northwest Rebellion of 1885. The five officers and eighty-five NCOs and men of C Company were assigned to this duty.[4] During the final battle of the campaign at Batoche, part of the company served as marines aboard the paddle-wheeler *Northcote*, a unique duty for infantry in the heart of the Canadian prairies.[5]

A fourth infantry company was authorized in August 1887 to be raised and stationed at London, Ontario. However, its formation was not completed until early in 1888.[6] Both the schools of infantry formed by these companies and the School of Cavalry were designated Royal in July 1887.[7]

Major-General Herbert, General Officer Commanding the Militia, recommended that Canada's regular force adopt the regimental system. Accordingly, the four companies of the Infantry School Corps were raised to regimental status in May 1892 and titled the Canadian Regiment of Infantry.[8] In May 1893, the regiment was granted the prefix Royal by Queen Victoria and redesignated the Royal Regiment of Canadian Infantry.[9]

The four companies of the regiment were together as a unit for the first time in 1894, at the Engineers' Camp, Lévis, Quebec. Lieutenant-Colonel William Otter of the Toronto company acted as the commanding officer on this occasion. In 1896, Lieutenant-Colonel G.J. Maunsell was appointed the first full-time commanding officer of the regiment. Prior to this appointment the four companies had been commanded from militia headquarters in Ottawa by Colonel Walker Powell, the Adjutant-General.[10]

In 1897, gold was discovered in the Yukon; and Dawson, the tiny capital of the territory, became the largest city west of Winnipeg, with a population of 18,000. The local resources of the North West Mounted Police were taxed to capacity and the Canadian government dispatched a small force of regular troops to help maintain law and order. The Yukon Field Force was authorized on 21 March 1898 to consist of twelve officers and 191 other ranks to be drawn from the three regular regiments. Lieutenant-Colonel T.B. Evans of The Royal Canadian Dragoons was appointed Commanding Officer, and the Royal Regiment of Canadian Infantry supplied three officers and 130 other ranks for this unusual force.[11]

The Yukon Field Force departed from Ottawa by train on 6 May for Vancouver. From there it proceeded by coastal steamer, river boat, overland, and by home-made scow to its base at Fort Selkirk. A fifty-man detachment was dispatched immediately to Dawson to augment the NWMP detachment under Superintendent Sam B. Steele. The march to the Yukon took 160 days and demonstrated the resourcefulness of the Canadian regular soldier. After guarding banks and gold shipments, fighting fires, and subduing the occasional riot, the force was withdrawn in June 1900.[12]

In April 1899, the name of the unit was changed to The Royal Canadian Regiment of Infantry and, on 1 November 1901, this title was officially shortened to The Royal Canadian Regiment, a designation that remains unchanged to this day.[13]

In the autumn of 1899, Canada's offer to send a battalion of infantry to South Africa was accepted by the British government, and on 14 October orders were issued to raise the force. The regiment provided a nucleus of trained officers and NCOs for the new battalion, and this contribution was acknowledged by designating it the 2nd (Special Service) Battalion, The Royal Canadian Regiment of Infantry.[14] The battalion distinguished itself at the Battle of Paardeberg on 27 February 1900, and returned to Canada the following December.

A 3rd (Special Service) Battalion of the regiment garrisoned Halifax from March 1900 to September 1902, to release the regular British battalion, the 1st Prince of Wales' Leinster Regiment (Royal Canadians), for service in South Africa.[15]

The regiment was placed on active service in September 1914 and posted to Bermuda to relieve the regular British garrison. In August 1915, the unit returned to Canada, but was sent immediately to England and from there to France; there, in December, it joined the 3rd Canadian Division as a unit of the 7th Infantry Brigade. The regiment served with this formation until the end of hostilities.

After the war, the regiment was reduced to its peace-time establishment, and resumed its original role of providing instruction for militia infantry units.

On the outbreak of the Second World War, the unit was recruited to its war establishment and assigned to the 1st Infantry Brigade, 1st Canadian Division. In June 1940, the regiment landed in Brittany after the evacuation of Dunkirk, as part of the "Second British Expeditionary Force." However, its stay was short-lived as the force was withdrawn without seeing action.

The regiment took part in the Sicily landings in July 1943, and in subsequent operations of 1st Canadian Division in Italy and North-West Europe.

In more recent times, battalions of The Royal Canadian Regiment have seen active service in Korea, formed part of Canada's NATO force, and served in UN peace-keeping operations in Cyprus and the Middle East. But it seems fitting that particular attention should be directed to what might be regarded as a relatively small part of this proud regiment's distinguished record, the provision of the first troops to serve in Canada's northland.

1883 to the present

Uniform

A soldier of the Canadian volunteer militia of the early 1880s received a government issue of clothing that included a tunic, trousers, greatcoat, and forage cap. In the official language of the day, "as the means available for the purchase of uniform clothing for the Active Militia is not at present sufficient to permit the issue of both helmets, busbies or shakos and forage caps, there will be no objection to corps . . . wearing helmets, busbies or shakos procured at their own expense."[1] As no boots were issued, there was no objection to the volunteer providing these at his own expense. Indeed, he was expected to do so.

In 1884, the first soldiers of the permanent Infantry School Corps received the standard government clothing, boots, a special issue of personal clothing including shirts, socks, and underwear, a suit of fatigue clothing, and some cleaning equipment.

The infantry uniform consisted of a scarlet cloth tunic with dark-blue collar, cuffs, and shoulder-straps. The front opening, collar base, and shoulder-straps were piped with white tape; the pointed cuffs were trimmed with a crow's-foot of white braid. The tunic skirt was closed behind, and had a plait on each side edged with white braid. There were eight buttons down the front of the tunic, and two at the waist behind. Dark-blue trousers were trimmed with a narrow red welt down the outside seam. The forage cap was a blue Glengarry with scarlet tuft and a black cockade on the left side. The badge was mounted on a scarlet backing, and worn on the cockade.[2]

Officers' full dress was similar to that of the men, with the addition of gold braid trim on the blue collar and cuffs of the scarlet cloth tunic. On state occasions and in formal dress, their trousers were trimmed with a wide gold lace stripe with a fine crimson silk line down the centre. Mounted officers wore blue cloth pantaloons with scarlet welts, black riding boots, and spurs.

A crimson sash was worn over the left shoulder, knotting on the right side. The sword-belt was white enamelled leather with a round gilt clasp of regimental design and white leather slings. The full-dress sword-knot was gold and crimson with gold acorn, while the undress knot was of white buff leather.[3]

For undress, officers wore a blue patrol jacket that closed with hooks. Edged all around and trimmed on the back seams with black mohair braid, the jacket had four double rows of black cord across the front. The round blue forage cap had a drooping black leather peak with gold-laced edge and a scarlet cloth band. Officers wore the Glengarry as a forage cap on some occasions.[4]

Officers were required to supply a scarlet shell-jacket with blue collar and cuffs, and a blue waistcoat for wear as mess dress.

For winter wear, the men were issued a grey greatcoat, black wedge-shaped fur cap, and black leather mitts. Officers' greatcoats were of grey cloth with a collar of otter fur, and four rows of black cord across the front. The mitts and cap were of black otter fur; the cap had a dark-blue bag on the left side.[5]

When first equipped in 1884, the Infantry School Corps complained about the lack of an issue of helmets for the men, and about the poor quality serge trousers.[6]

When C Company of the corps joined General Middleton in 1885, the men wore the uniform described above. The scarlet tunic was the service dress of the day. Equipment included a white buff-leather waist-belt with white ball bag and bayonet frog, white cross-belt over the left shoulder supporting a black ammunition pouch, white haversack on the left side, water-bottle, and square canvas pack. Like the volunteers, the regulars were armed with the three-banded Snider-Enfield rifle and triangular bayonet.[7] Officers wore braided blue patrol jackets with peaked forage caps, and a double Sam Browne belt with sword and pistol. High boots were common on active service.[8]

One of the more original uniforms worn by the regiment was that adopted by the Yukon Field Force in 1898. A private in this dress is depicted in the illustration. The basic uniform was the standard scarlet infantry frock with blue collar, cuffs and shoulder-straps. The base of the collar and the shoulder-straps were piped with white, and the pointed cuffs were trimmed with a crow's-foot of white braid. The frock had two breast pockets, and closed with five brass regimental buttons.

Blue trousers were tucked well down into high beef boots that laced all the way up the front.[9]

The white helmet, with brass spike and helmet plate, was worn on special occasions. In addition, the troops were issued a tan felt hat, creased down the centre, looped up on the left side and fitted with a puggree.[10]

The recently adopted Oliver-pattern equipment and a single ammunition pouch in the centre of the waist-belt was worn on the expedition. A small kit bat was worn high on the back to supplement the small valise. The unit was armed with the long Lee-Enfield magazine rifle.

A special issue of winter clothing included a fur cap of Yukon pattern, a dark-grey pea-jacket with detachable fur collar, knee-length woollen stockings and buckskin-covered woollen mitts.[11] For extreme northern temperatures the men wore practical caribou-skin parkas and mukluks.[12]

Duck fatigue dress was worn on long hot arctic summer days as the force toiled up the northern waterways to the base camp at Fort Selkirk. Yet, even during this vigorous overland trek, the men were not allowed to forget that they were soldiers. On 24 May 1898, the Yukon Field Force paraded in scarlet and blue frocks and white helmets to celebrate Her Majesty's birthday.[13]

1900 to the present

History

In 1899, Canada took the unprecedented step of committing troops to overseas service. One infantry battalion, two battalions of mounted rifles, and a field artillery brigade were sent to South Africa. In addition, the Right Honourable Lord Strathcona and Mount Royal offered to raise, equip, and transport a mounted corps to South Africa to serve with the British Army. His proposal to the British government of 10 January 1900 was formally accepted by the War Office three days later.

At Lord Strathcona's suggestion, the corps was recruited in Western Canada from ranchers and members of the NWMP who already could ride and shoot. Major Sam B. Steele, recently transferred from the NWMP to the 2nd Canadian Mounted Rifles, was appointed Commanding Officer of Strathcona's Horse. The regiment left Ottawa for Halifax on 12 March 1900 with twenty-eight officers and 512 other ranks.

Arriving in South Africa on 10 April after a difficult voyage, the regiment was dispatched on an independent operation deep inside enemy territory, but was recalled because of a breach of security. However, the unit did see action with the 3rd Mounted Brigade of General Buller's Natal Field Force and with the 6th Brigade, to which it was posted in October. In November 1900, the unit was officially redesignated Lord Strathcona's Corps.[1]

In January 1901, the regiment returned to Canada by way of London, where, on 15 February, it was inspected by King Edward VII and presented with a King's Colour. This caused some discussion in military circles. As Strathcona's Corps was classified as mounted infantry, it was not entitled to carry any colours, let alone a King's Colour, which normally would be carried only by infantry units. Although never carried on parade since its presentation, the King's Colour of the Strathcona's remains a treasured possession of the regiment.[2]

In the strictest sense, the original Lord Strathcona's Corps was not a Canadian unit at all, but a regiment of the British Army recruited in Canada and equipped, mounted, transported, and partially paid for by a private Canadian citizen.

On 9 March 1901, the corps was paid off in Halifax and officially passed out of existence. However, a subsequent proposal suggested that the service of Lord Strathcona be acknowledged by raising a unit of the permanent force that would bear his name. As the budget did not permit the creation of a new corps, it was decided to retitle an existing unit in the appropriate manner. The unit selected was The Royal Canadian Mounted Rifles. On 1 October 1909, with His Majesty's permission and the unanimous consent of all ranks, the name was changed to Strathcona's Horse (Royal Canadians).[3] In 1911, it received its present official designation of Lord Strathcona's Horse (Royal Canadians).[4]

The selection of The Royal Canadian Mounted Rifles to perpetuate Lord Strathcona's service was most fitting, as the corps had a long association with Western Canada, the recruiting ground of the original Strathconas, and traced its origin to the School of Mounted Infantry established at Winnipeg in September 1885. The Company of Mounted Infantry was redesignated the Canadian Mounted Rifle Corps in 1891; it, in turn, was amalgamated with the Canadian Dragoons the following year, becoming B Troop of the regiment.[5]

On the basis of South African battle experience, nine militia squadrons of Canadian Mounted Rifles, designated A through I, were authorized in June 1901. B Squadron of The Royal Canadian Dragoons at Winnipeg was renamed A Squadron (Permanent), Canadian Mounted Rifles, to provide a regular nucleus for training the newly created mounted force.[6] On 1 October 1903, the regular squadron was granted the title Royal, and became The Royal Canadian Mounted Rifles.[7] This was the unit selected to honour the remarkable contribution of Lord Strathcona.

When war was declared in August 1914, the unit moved to Valcartier where, in September, it was taken on the strength of the Canadian Expeditionary Force. On its arrival in England, the regiment was posted to the Canadian Cavalry Brigade, and served with this formation in both mounted and dismounted roles until the end of the war.

The Strathcona's was still a regiment of horsed cavalry when war was again declared in 1939. In 1940, however, it was converted to an armoured unit. As the 2nd Armoured Regiment (Lord Strathcona's Horse (Royal Canadians)), the unit formed part of the 5th Canadian Armoured Division and served with that formation in Italy and North-West Europe throughout the war.

In the post-war years, elements of the regiment have fought in Korea, formed part of Canada's NATO force in Europe, and served with the UN peace-keeping forces in Cyprus and the Middle East. The record of this regiment is a worthy tribute to the distinguished Canadian whose name it bears and the traditions of the original Lord Strathcona's Corps.

1900 to the present

Uniform

When the Canadian contingents were mobilized for South Africa, clothing reserves were neither sufficient nor of appropriate pattern for active service. The problem was overcome by contracting for the immediate delivery of uniforms of special design. This clothing was made available to Strathcona's Horse.[1]

The men of the regiment were issued two types of uniform, one of blue serge and one of khaki duck.[2] The seven-button blue serge frock had two pleated breast pockets with pointed flaps and buttons, as well as two inside skirt pockets with buttonless pointed flaps. The base of the white collar and the edges of the blue shoulder-straps were trimmed with dark-crimson tape. The blue cuffs were closed with two brass buttons and trimmed with crimson tape in a crow's-foot. Both trousers and pantaloons of blue serge were trimmed along the outside seam with a narrow red stripe.[3] The pantaloons were worn either with black puttees and laced boots or with high brown boots specially made for the regiment by the Slater Shoe Company of Montreal. These "Strathcona boots" were similar in pattern to those worn today by the Royal Canadian Mounted Police.[4]

Head-gear consisted of a drab field service cap, a tan felt Stetson with brown leather band, worn peaked like that of the RCMP, and a woollen tuque.[5]

The khaki field service dress included a five-button frock of heavy duck with a stand-and-fall collar, pleated breast pockets with buttoned flaps, and skirt pockets with plain flaps.[6] Khaki pantaloons were worn with Strathcona boots on mounted parades and for walking out, and with drab woollen puttees and ankle boots on all other occasions.[7] The regiment wore brass letters SH on the shoulder-straps, and brass regimental badges on the collar and field service cap.[8]

The Canadian-made khaki uniforms soon washed out almost to white under service conditions.[9] The duck service dress was not warm enough for the South African winter, and the men were issued a drab serge frock of British pattern.[10]

Equipment consisted of a brown leather belt with S buckle, haversack, water-bottle, and web "Orndorff" bandolier. A Colt .44 revolver in a brown leather holster and a pistol ammunition pouch were attached to the waist-belt,[11] although the trooper's main weapon was the long Lee-Enfield .303 rifle. The regiment was equipped with the NWMP-pattern saddle with a horn and large wooden stirrups. All ranks carried a western lariat on their saddles.[12]

Depicted in the illustration are the service dress and equipment worn by the officers of the regiment in South Africa. The pattern of the Strathcona boots can be seen quite clearly. A pistol and sword were attached to the Sam Browne belt, which was worn with a double brace.[13]

The Canadian Mounted Rifles, formed in 1901, wore a white helmet with brass spike and chin chain. A white puggree was added in 1906.[14] The tunic was scarlet with green facings; the front was edged in green cloth and closed with eight buttons. The back of the skirt was ornamented with red flaps of cavalry pattern edged with yellow braid and set with three large buttons. The trousers and pantaloons were dark blue with a wide yellow stripe down the outside seam. Black leather butcher boots and steel spurs were worn in mounted order.[15] The pouch belt, sword-belt and slings, sword-knot, and gauntlets were of brown leather.

When granted the prefix Royal in 1903, the unit retained its green facings, rather than adopting the traditional blue of Royal corps.[16]

When redesignated Strathcona's Horse (Royal Canadians) in 1909, dress remained virtually unchanged, except for the badges. In 1912, the white helmet worn in full dress was replaced by the dragoon-pattern helmet of white metal. The plume was red and white, the plate and ornaments of gilt metal. At the same time, the facing colour of the regiment was specified as olive green.[17]

The original SH worn on the shoulder-straps subsequently became LSH. During the Second World War, at the suggestion of King George VI, it was again changed, to Ld SH.[18]

When the regiment returned to full dress after the First World War, the facings were described as myrtle green, and white leather belts, slings, and gauntlets made their appearance. Other than these minor changes, the full-dress uniform of the Strathcona's has remained unaltered to the present day.

1903-1929
History

At the end of the nineteenth century, the Canadian defence forces consisted primarily of cavalry, artillery, infantry, and engineer units of the Non-Permanent Active Militia. The small Permanent Active Militia provided a training and administrative cadre for the volunteers. The South African experience taught Canadian defence authorities the necessity of providing specialized services and departments to support the fighting arms. As part of a programme to create a more effective citizen army for Canada, an Intelligence Department was formed in 1903, and a Corps of Guides was authorized to provide officers and men trained to perform intelligence duties at the various headquarters.[1]

The Corps of Guides was a mounted corps of the Non-Permanent Militia with precedence immediately following the Canadian Engineers.[2] The officers, NCOs, and men were appointed individually to the headquarters staffs of various commands and districts to carry out intelligence duties. From the authorizing order, it was apparent that one of the functions of the Corps was to ensure that, in the event of war on Canadian soil, the defenders would possess detailed and accurate information of the area of operations.[3]

The ranks of the Corps of Guides were filled quickly, and by the end of 1903 the General Officer Commanding the Militia was able to report that "the formation of the Corps has been attended by the best possible results. Canada is now being covered by a network of intelligent and capable men, who will be of great service to the country in collecting information of a military character and in fitting themselves to act as guides in their own districts to forces in the field. I have much satisfaction in stating that there is much competition among the best men in the country for admission into the Corps of Guides. Nobody is admitted into the Corps unless he is a man whose services are likely to be of real use to the country."[4]

The training of the Corps began at once under the supervision of the Director of Intelligence. Special courses stressed the organization of foreign armies, military topography, military reconnaissance, and the staff duties of intelligence officers. Instruction in drill and parade movements was kept to a minimum.[5]

Although primarily made up of individual officers and men, there was also an establishment for a mounted company of the Corps with one company allocated to each division. The strength of the company was forty all ranks.[6]

The Corps of Guides was not mobilized for service with the Canadian Expeditionary Force of 1914-18; however, many of the original members of the Corps served as intelligence officers with overseas formations or were transferred to other mobilized service.[7] The Corps of Guides was disbanded in 1929, but its traditions were carried on when the Canadian Intelligence Corps, formed in 1942, adopted the badges of the original Corps of Guides.

1903-1929

Uniform

The uniform of the Corps of Guides reflected its early twentieth-century origin, combining the khaki colour of the new service dress with the colourful full dress of the late-Victorian army.

Head-gear was the universal-pattern white helmet with brass spike and curb chain.[1] The muslin puggree had six folds, the two centre folds of scarlet and the remainder of khaki.[2] A silver puggree badge was worn on the front of the helmet, and a khaki silk helmet cord was attached in review order.[3]

The double-breasted tunic was of fine khaki serge with a scarlet plastron fastened with two rows of seven gilt buttons. The scarlet collar and cuffs were trimmed with khaki braid, and the three-pointed flap at the rear of each skirt was piped in scarlet and ornamented with three buttons. Back seams, rear sleeve seams, and skirt edges were piped with scarlet cloth. White metal rank badges were worn on the brown twisted-silk shoulder cords. The khaki silk girdle with two scarlet stripes was $2^{1}/_{4}$ in. wide.[4]

Fine khaki serge trousers with a $1^{3}/_{4}$ in. scarlet stripe were worn with black Wellingtons and steel box spurs. In mounted order, khaki serge pantaloons with a scarlet stripe were worn with brown butcher boots and steel jack spurs. Gauntlets were of brown leather.[5]

A brown leather shoulder-belt, $2^{1}/_{2}$-in. wide, supported a pouch bearing the corps badge in silver. The sword-belt, worn under the tunic, had square gilt buckles, and supported a cavalry-pattern sword with brown leather sword-knot and slings.[6]

The khaki mess jacket with scarlet roll collar was edged with scarlet cloth; the scarlet cuffs were edged with khaki braid. Embroidered rank badges were worn on the scarlet shoulder-straps. The scarlet vest closed with four small regimental buttons.[7]

Undress consisted of a dark-blue universal-pattern patrol jacket with gilt corps buttons and metal rank badges, dark-blue trousers with a 2-in. scarlet stripe, black Wellingtons, and steel box spurs. The naval-pattern cap was dark blue with scarlet band.[8]

Officers of the Corps also wore an undress uniform of khaki. Their serge jacket of 1903 service pattern had scarlet shoulder-straps with the corps title, Guides, in gilt metal. Khaki serge trousers with a scarlet stripe were worn with brown laced boots. In mounted order, khaki Bedford cord breeches with a scarlet stripe were worn with brown laced boots, brown puttee-pattern pigskin leggings, and steel jack spurs. The sword and brown leather scabbard were carried on the brown Sam Browne belt. The staff-pattern cap was of fine khaki serge with a silver corps cap badge.[9]

The smart business-like uniform of the Guides, with its dash of scarlet to brighten the sombre khaki, was unique in Canadian military fashion. It was a dress well suited to a corps whose unobtrusive efficiency was the key to its function.

1901-1972

History

For many years, supplies and transport for the British Army were furnished through local contracts arranged by the commissariat officer, a civilian official at army headquarters responsible to the treasury. Gradually a system of military control of supply and transport evolved, and became the special concern of the Army Service Corps created in 1888.[1]

During military operations in Canada, British staff officers were responsible for organizing supply and transport. However, when British troops withdrew from Canada in 1871, this responsibility fell to Canadian authorities.

The deficiencies of the support services of the Canadian militia were dramatically demonstrated during the Northwest Rebellion in 1885. Transport of the North West Field Force from eastern Canada to what is now Saskatchewan was arranged by officials of the partially completed Canadian Pacific Railway. Field transport, rations, and forage were provided by the Hudson's Bay Company.[2] Wagons, teams, and drivers to accompany the advancing columns were hired from among the settlers of the territory. Obviously, such scattered arrangements proved both complicated and costly.

Succeeding General Officers Commanding the Militia recommended the establishment of a military supply department; however, it was not until the turn of the century that any serious attempt was made to form the militia into an organized military force with trained staff and supporting administrative departments. As part of this effort, four militia companies of the Canadian Army Service Corps were authorized in November 1901.[3] In December, Lieutenant-Colonel James Lyon Biggar, a Canadian officer with considerable service with a supply and transport column in South Africa, was appointed Assistant Quartermaster-General and detailed to command the new corps.[4] In order to provide a training cadre of regulars for the militia companies, a small permanent unit of the Corps was authorized in 1903, and designated the Canadian Permanent Army Service Corps in 1906.[5]

The militia companies of the Corps were set to work at the various summer camps, where they made an immediate and favourable impression on all ranks.[6] As a result, four additional militia companies were authorized in December 1903, and three more in August 1905. By 1912, there were eighteen Service Corps companies, each with an establishment of 106 all ranks.[7] In 1912, a Mechanical Transport Branch of the Corps was established as the potential of the automobile as a means of transport became recognized.[8]

On the outbreak of the First World War in August 1914, the Canadian Army Service Corps, both regulars and militia, numbered approximately 2,000 all ranks. By the end of the war, more than 590 officers and 16,500 men had served with the Corps.[9] While horsed transport played an important part in the movement of supplies, motor transport proved a reliable and modern means of supplying an army in the field, and the Corps emerged from the war as a highly mechanized component of the Canadian Army.

The Canadian Permanent Army Service Corps was granted the title Royal in 1919, and, in 1936, the coveted honour was bestowed on the militia units.[10]

Between the wars, military transport became increasingly mechanized. The last parade of the horse transport of The Royal Canadian Army Service Corps was held in 1936,[11] and by 1939, the Corps was completely motorized. While motor vehicles were indispensable to the modern army, they contributed to the supply problem by their heavy demand for petrol. Although it entered the Second World War with an acute shortage of motor vehicles, the Corps developed into a magnificent organization, which moved and supplied Canadian soldiers wherever they fought, whether by driving mule companies in Italy or manning fleets of gigantic tank transporters.

The Corps continued to play an important part in Canada's post-war army. In 1961, the sixtieth anniversary of the Corps, 7,000 of Canada's 49,000 regular soldiers were members of the RCASC.[12] The strength of the Corps remained second only to that of the infantry until 1972, when it was merged with other corps and services to form the Logistics Branch of the Canadian Forces. Although the name of The Royal Canadian Army Service Corps has disappeared, supply and transport functions remain vital to the effectiveness of the Canadian Forces.

Uniform

The fact that The Canadian Army Service Corps was raised in 1901 as a mounted combatant corps determined some details of its original dress.[1] The plate depicts an officer of the Corps in full-dress dismounted order, between 1901 and 1912.

His universal-pattern Canadian white helmet had a gilt ball, helmet plate, and curb chain. His dark-blue tunic had eight buttons in front and two behind at the waist; it was edged down the front and around the skirt with white cloth. The back of the skirt was open half-way to the waist, and edged with white cloth; the three-pointed slash on each skirt was trimmed with gold cord and ornamented with three buttons. The white collar was edged with gold lace and trimmed with gold cord along the base. The pointed white cuffs were trimmed with an Austrian knot of gold cord, traced on each side with Russia braid. Rank badges were worn on twisted-gold shoulder cords, which were lined with blue and fastened with a small regimental button.[2]

In dismounted order, blue cloth overalls with a double white stripe down the outside seam were worn with black Wellington boots and steel box spurs. Blue pantaloons with a double white stripe were worn with black butcher boots and steel jack spurs in mounted order.

The sword-belt and slings were of gold lace with a dark-blue centre stripe; the belt was lined with dark-blue morocco leather. The sword had a slightly curved, 35½-in. blade, and a half-basket steel hilt with two fluted bars on the outside. The sword-knot and acorn were of gold and blue.

A shoulder-belt of gold lace with a dark-blue centre stripe supported a black patent-leather pouch ornamented with the Service Corps badge. White gloves completed the full dress.

In 1912, the white Wolseley helmet with gilt ball and white puggree replaced the Canadian-pattern helmet for full dress. Otherwise, the full dress of the Corps remained unchanged throughout its existence.[3]

The mess dress of the period consisted of a blue cloth mess jacket with white roll collar, pointed white cuffs, and blue shoulder-straps. There were no buttons, gold braid or piping on any part of the jacket. A white waistcoat with four regimental buttons was worn under the jacket.[4]

The undress uniform included a dark-blue forage cap of naval pattern with a white welt around the crown and a dark-blue band edged top and bottom with white cloth welts. The dark-blue fine-serge patrol jacket had five buttons on the front. Two patch breast pockets with three-pointed flaps closed with a small regimental button; the two patch pockets on the skirts had pointed flaps but no buttons. Badges of rank were worn on the white cloth shoulder-straps. The pointed blue cuffs were slit and closed with two small buttons.

Blue serge trousers with two white stripes down the outside were worn with black boots; pantaloons with black butcher boots and spurs were worn on mounted duties.[5]

For undress, the NCOs and men wore a blue forage cap like that of the officers. The blue serge jacket had pleated breast pockets with buttoned flaps, seven buttons down the front, and white cloth shoulder-straps. Blue serge trousers with a double white stripe down the outside were worn with black laced boots.

For mounted duties, blue serge pantaloons with a double white stripe were worn with black Stohwasser-pattern leggings, black boots, and jack spurs.[6]

For service dress, the NCOs and men wore the 1903-pattern drab serge jacket, serge pantaloons, drab woollen puttees, and laced boots. The cavalry-pattern brown leather ammunition bandolier was worn in mounted order.[7]

The character of the Corps changed as petrol fumes replaced the smell of the horse and harness, and the Corps' dress reflected that change. However, the blue dress uniform and scarlet mess kit introduced after the Second World War retained the overalls, spurs, and curved sword blades as a reminder of the days when horsemanship was an essential feature of The Royal Canadian Army Service Corps.

1914-1919

History

On 4 August 1914, the German armies swept into Belgium, and Britain took Canada with her to war. When the Canadian government decided to raise a division for overseas service, Colonel Sam Hughes, the energetic but willful Minister of Militia and Defence, jettisoned existing mobilization plans[1] and called for volunteers to assemble at Valcartier. More than 30,000 men poured into the new camp, where they were organized into sixteen provisional infantry battalions numbered in sequence, and units of the various supporting arms and services.

Sailing from Canada on 3 October 1914, the 1st Canadian Contingent completed its training at Salisbury Plain, where it became the 1st Canadian Division. After a cold wet winter, the division moved to France in February 1915. Hardly had the first contingent cleared Valcartier than the 2nd Division was mobilized. Its battalions moved to England in May and June 1915 and, after further training, crossed the Channel in mid-September. With the arrival of the 2nd Division, the Canadian Corps was formed of the two Canadian divisions.[2]

The 3rd Canadian Division was raised in December 1915, chiefly from units already overseas; the 4th Division was formed in England in April 1916 and moved to France in August. Both these divisions joined the Canadian Corps, which was placed under the command of Lieutenant-General Sir Julian Byng in May 1916. Under the command of this experienced and able British soldier, the Corps matured and developed into an efficient fighting formation. With the transfer of command to Lieutenant-General Arthur Currie in 1917, the Corps became Canadian led as well as Canadian manned.

From the time of their arrival in France, the Canadians were almost continuously in action. In April 1915, the inexperienced 1st Division stood firm at Ypres in the face of the first gas attack. Later the same year, Canadians took part in the attacks on Festubert and Givenchy. Early in 1916, hard fighting at Saint-Eloi and Mount Sorrel added to Canadian experience at considerable cost. In September, the Canadian Corps moved to the Somme front to take part in those costly battles of attrition.

The Canadian Corps came of age in an operation planned and executed by Byng. On 9 April 1917, all four Canadian divisions stormed the strongly fortified position of Vimy Ridge. With meticulously prepared artillery support, the assault swept the enemy from the ridge in a single day's fighting.[3]

Later in the summer, the tactics of Vimy again succeeded as Hill 70 fell to the Corps under Currie's command. Moved to the sodden Flanders sector for the autumn offensive, the Corps struggled under inhuman conditions to take the village of Passchendaele, a name synonymous with the greatest horrors of the Western Front.

After stemming the dangerous German spring offensive of 1918, the British mounted a summer counter-offensive. The Canadian Corps led the attack with a drive on Amiens that completely routed the German defenders. With complete victory in sight, the Canadians were moved quickly to the Arras sector, where the Corps broke through the Drocourt-Quéant Line (an extension of the Hindenburg defences), and then stormed across the Canal du Nord into open country. Cambrai was engulfed as the Corps maintained the vigorous pursuit that brought it to Mons on 9 November. On 11 November, the Armistice was signed, and General Currie entered the city where the war had begun for the British in 1914.

The Canadians had come a long way since the frantic days of 1914, when volunteers in their thousands had thronged into Valcartier. "Under General Currie's leadership, the Canadian Corps became, without any doubt, the most formidable battle formation of its size on the Western Front."[4] The price of victory was high – one in every ten Canadian soldiers died – but Canada had been carried into true nationhood on the backs of her sturdy fighting men.

Uniform

Prior to 1914, several steps were taken to modernize the dress and equipment of the Canadian militia. A drab serge service dress was adopted in 1903, and the ancient cross-belts were replaced with leather Oliver valise equipment in 1898.[1] Forty thousand Lee-Enfield magazine rifles purchased in 1895 were withdrawn in favour of the Canadian-made Ross rifle.[2] Reserves of clothing and military stores were, however, practically non-existent when the first contingent was mobilized in 1914, and orders were placed for the immediate delivery of uniforms, boots, shirts, underwear, and various items of personal kit. Before the greatcoats and serge uniforms could be made up, the wool had to be specially woven into suitable cloth.[3]

Canadian service dress was similar, but not identical, to the British pattern. The Canadian jacket had a stand-up collar, seven buttons down the front, and skirt pockets with plain flaps; the British garment had a stand-and-fall collar, five buttons down the front, and buttons on the skirt flaps.[4] The British jacket, cut to give a loose and comfortable fit, was preferred to the tight-fitting Canadian uniform, which caused much chafing.[5] In France, Canadian service dress gradually disappeared as it became unusable and was replaced by the British uniform.[6]

Experience in South Africa revealed serious deficiencies in the Oliver equipment, and the adoption of the 1908-pattern British web equipment was recommended for use by the mobilized troops.[7] The Oliver equipment was modified by adding a pair of ammunition pouches, and fitting it with a British-style web pack, haversack, and water-bottle.[8] This was certainly an improvement over the original, but even the modified equipment was unsatisfactory.[9] Although most Canadian units were issued British web equipment before proceeding to France, some battalions wore the modified Oliver equipment in action as late as 1916.[10]

The most controversial item of Canadian equipment was the Ross rifle. Though it was a good target weapon, the Ross was not "soldier-proof," and tended to jam when repeatedly fired under wet and muddy conditions. Canadian front-line troops lost confidence in the weapon, and armed themselves with the Lee-Enfields of their fallen British comrades when possible.[11] Because of the personal involvement of the Hon. Sam Hughes, Canadian Minister of Militia, the deficiencies of the Ross rifle caused a violent political controversy that continued until August 1916, when, to the delight of the troops, General Sir Douglas Haig, Commander-in-Chief of the British armies in France, ordered that all troops of the Canadian Corps be armed with the Lee-Enfield rifle.[12]

The plate illustrates a Canadian infantryman during the Somme battles of November 1916. He wears the steel helmet introduced in April 1916, the Canadian service-dress jacket, and British boots; he carries a Short Magazine Lee-Enfield rifle. The goatskin jerkin was preferred to the greatcoat for cold weather in the trenches, as the coat's long skirts became heavily coated with mud.[13]

The soldier's unit and formation can be determined by the distinguishing patches on the upper sleeve, which were adopted by the Canadian Corps late in 1916. Evidence suggests that the distinguishing insignia sometimes was painted on the helmet.[14] The division is identified by the colour of the rectangular patch: red for the 1st Division, blue for the 2nd, black (later changed to French grey) for the 3rd, and green for the 4th. The Brigade and unit are indicated by the cloth device worn above the coloured rectangle. The colour of the device – green, red or blue – denoted in that order the first, second, and third brigade within the division; the shape – a circle, semi-circle, triangle, or square – indicated in order of seniority the four battalions of the brigade.[15] The soldier in the plate displays a green semi-circle above a red rectangle; this identifies his unit as the 2nd Battalion, 1st Brigade of the 1st Canadian Division.[16]

These small bits of coloured cloth, which distinguished the Canadians from other troops of the British Army, became proud symbols of the Canadian Corps.

1914 to the present

History

On 3 August 1914, a wealthy Montreal militia officer and veteran of the South African War, Captain Hamilton Gault, offered to raise and finance a unit for overseas service in the event of war. The following day war was declared. Gault's offer was accepted, and authority to raise a battalion of infantry was granted on 8 August.[1] Lieutenant-Colonel Farquhar, Military Secretary to the Duke of Connaught, then Governor-General of Canada, was appointed commanding officer of the new battalion. Through an appeal to former regular soldiers of the British Army then residing in Canada, Farquhar had, by 18 August, recruited 1,100 men, of whom more than 1,000 had previous service.

It was suggested that the new battalion bear the name of the youngest daughter of the Governor-General. The Princess and the Duke agreed, and the unit officially became Princess Patricia's Canadian Light Infantry. Though it was certainly fitting, the full unit title was somewhat unwieldly, so the battalion was commonly designated by its initials, PPCLI, or simply as the Patricia's.

When the Patricia's arrived in England in October 1914, they were almost fully trained because of the previous service of most of the officers and men. The battalion was posted to the 27th British Division, which proceeded to France on 20 December 1914.[2] This gave the Patricia's the distinction of being the first Canadian unit in the field in the First World War.

While serving with the 27th Division, the PPCLI distinguished itself during the Battle of Frezenberg in May 1915. Commemorated by the battalion to this day, Frezenberg cost the Patricia's dearly; its strength was reduced by casualties to four officers and 150 other ranks.[3]

In December 1915, the Patricia's rejoined the Canadian Corps to become part of the newly formed 3rd Canadian Division. It was joined by The Royal Canadian Regiment, the 42nd Battalion (Black Watch) and the 49th (Edmonton) Battalion to form the 7th Canadian Infantry Brigade.

The battalion returned to Canada in March 1919 with a most distinguished battle record. During the course of the war some 5,000 officers and men served in the Patricia's; more than 4,000 of these became casualties.[4] Because it drew recruits from all parts of Canada and was not associated with any single geographic location, the battalion captured the imagination of the public; and it seemed only natural that the Patricia's be selected as one of the new infantry units of the post-war Regular Army. The peace-time battalion of the PPCLI was formed at Toronto and, after a brief stay in London, moved west in 1920 to establish headquarters and two companies at Winnipeg and one company at Esquimalt. From these bases the unit provided instructors for the militia battalions of Western Canada during the lean years between the wars.

The PPCLI was again mobilized for active service on 1 September 1939. After recruiting to full war establishment, it proceeded to England in December as part of the 2nd Canadian Infantry Brigade of the 1st Canadian Division. After more than three years of training and coastal defence duties, the Patricia's, as part of the 1st Division, took part in the assault-landings on Sicily in July 1943 and in the invasion of Italy in September. The battalion rejoined the First Canadian Army in March 1945, and fought in North-West Europe until the end of the European campaign.

In October 1946, the regiment once more became a unit of Canada's Regular Army, with headquarters in Calgary.[5] As part of their peace-time soldiering, the Patricia's underwent training in arctic warfare and airborne techniques and tactics.

In August 1950, the 2nd Battalion of the regiment was raised as part of the Special Force for service in Korea. As in the First World War, the Patricia's became the first Canadians in the field when the battalion was assigned to the 27th British Commonwealth Brigade. The 2nd Patricia's was awarded the United States Distinguished Unit Citation for its defence of the Kap'yong position on 24 April 1951.[6]

In June, the battalion rejoined the 25th Canadian Infantry Brigade, which became part of the 1st Commonwealth Division to the great satisfaction of the Canadians. Before the end of the Korean conflict, a 3rd Battalion of the regiment was formed.

The regiment remains based in Western Canada, and its three battalions continue to serve abroad with Canada's NATO contingent and the United Nations peace-keeping forces.

1914 to the present

Uniform

Mobilized originally as an active-service battalion, the only uniform Princess Patricia's Canadian Light Infantry had for several years was the drab service dress of First World War pattern. Even in this most uniform of uniforms, however, a regimental dress distinction was introduced by Lieutenant-Colonel Farquhar, DSO, the first commanding officer of the battalion. The unique shoulder badge of PPCLI, white on a red background, appeared on the regiment's service dress from November 1914 until the introduction of the Canadian Forces' green uniform.[1]

When the regiment became a part of Canada's Permanent Force, a full-dress uniform was introduced.[2] French grey was selected as the facing colour to commemorate the regiment's first entry into the line, in January 1914, beside the French army. It also symbolized its service with the 3rd Canadian Division, whose divisional patch was French grey.[3]

A white Wolseley helmet with brass spike and curb chain was worn with a French-grey puggree until 1927, when the regiment was ordered to revert to a white puggree: authority for adopting the French-grey puggree had not been obtained through proper channels! After the Second World War a proper request for the restoration of the French-grey puggree was officially approved.[4]

The officers' full-dress scarlet tunic had eight gilt regimental buttons in front and two behind at the waist. The French-grey collar was edged in gold lace with a single line of gold braid around the base. French-grey cuffs were trimmed with gold lace; a tracing of gold braid formed an Austrian knot above the lace and a small eye below. The rear of the skirts was ornamented with an infantry-pattern two-pointed plait on each side of a centre vent. The tunic front, skirt plaits, and centre vent were edged with white cloth. Badges of rank were carried on twisted round gold shoulder cords lined with French grey.[5]

Dark-blue trousers with a scarlet welt down the outside seam were worn with black shoes. A crimson net sash encircled the waist with the tassels falling over the left hip. The infantry-pattern sword was attached by gold lace sword slings to the web sword-belt, which was worn under the tunic. White gloves were worn in review order.

The forage cap, worn with undress blue patrols, was dark green with a black band and a black patent-leather peak and chin-strap.[6] The officers' mess jacket was scarlet with French-grey roll collar and pointed cuffs. The waistcoat was French grey with four small regimental buttons.[7]

The scarlet cloth tunic of the NCOs and men was similar in pattern to that of the officers, but had less ornate trimming. The rear skirts had two vents running from the rear button at the waist to the bottom of the skirt. The vents were edged with white cloth. The French-grey collar was piped with white along the base, and the pointed French-grey cuffs were edged with white braid in a crow's-foot. Shoulder-straps were French grey edged with white cloth. The men's waist-belts were of white leather with regimental belt-plate.[8]

The illustration depicts a drummer of the Patricia's in 1926. On his helmet are the original French-grey puggree and the first cap badge of the regiment, which was replaced in 1934 by the present badge. The tunic has drummer's shoulder wings. The collar, back and front sleeve seams, and back tunic seam are trimmed with the traditional drummer's lace of red crowns on white braid.[9]

Full dress was retained by the band of the Regiment and the Corps of Drums until the introduction of the Canadian Forces' uniform of dark green. The traditional scarlet and French grey is still worn by the Corps of Drums on very special occasions.

1905-1936
History

At the turn of the century, the government authorized a reorganization of the Canadian militia with the object of providing a peace-time training establishment that could be expanded rapidly to provide a balanced force of 100,000 men in a national emergency. The proposed plan required an increase in the number of cavalry units, as the General Officer Commanding the Militia felt that "with Canada's immense extent of frontier and the great distances involved, it is of the utmost importance that the Cavalry should be increased, not only in some places in the East, but especially in the Northwest. No country in the world is in greater need of large numbers of efficient Cavalry, armed with the rifle, than is Canada."[1]

One of the first steps taken to expand the mounted arm, particularly in the Northwest, was the authorization, in 1900, to raise eight squadrons of the Canadian Mounted Rifles in Military District No. 10, which included Manitoba and the Northwest Territories. The squadrons were designated A through I; A Squadron, located at Winnipeg, was to be a Permanent Active Militia squadron.[2] Within a few years, most of the squadrons had been raised, augmented, and converted into regiments of cavalry. Between 1900 and 1914, twenty-five new cavalry regiments were formed, fifteen of them in Western Canada.[3]

As early as 1885, General Middleton, General Officer Commanding the Canadian Militia, had recognized the usefulness of the mounted rifleman, particularly in the Canadian west, and had established a School of Mounted Infantry at Winnipeg. Lieutenant-Colonel G.T. Denison of the Governor General's Body Guard had won the Czar's prize in 1877 for his book, *History of Cavalry*, in which he emphasized the role of the modern mounted soldier as a rifleman transported on horseback. The views of these officers were upheld by the experience of the South African War, and it was intended that the mounted troops of Western Canada be mounted rifles both in nature and name.

The 16th Mounted Rifles was one of the mounted units raised in the west as a result of the reorganization of the militia. It was authorized in 1905 and recruited from several communities in the area of Regina.[4] In 1908 the unit was redesignated The 16th Light Horse.[5]

In August 1914, details of The 16th Light Horse were placed on active service for local protective duties.[6] Ironically, most of the mounted units raised and trained in Western Canada, including The 16th Light Horse, were not to fight in their traditional role. The unit contributed recruits to the 5th Western Cavalry, which was converted to the 5th Battalion (Infantry) of the Canadian Expeditionary Force.[7]

When the militia was reorganized in 1920, there were nineteen mounted units east of the Great Lakes, and fourteen in the West, including The 16th Canadian Light Horse of Yorkton.[8] In spite of experience in South Africa and the First World War, which cavalrymen viewed as a vulgar brawl among foot soldiers, there was a concerted movement by mounted units to become traditional cavalry, rather than mounted infantry, the role for which they had been trained and armed.[9] As early as 1885 General Middleton had foreseen such a move, and had recommended that all mounted units be designated as mounted infantry. His observation that, as soon as their title was changed, these units would assume the trappings and outlook of cavalry and thus lose sight of their true function was borne out some forty years later.[10]

In the militia reorganization of 1936, the 16th and 22nd regiments of Canadian Light Horse were amalgamated to form the 16th/22nd Saskatchewan Horse. On mobilization in 1940 the regiment was converted to infantry, although it was later reconverted to an armoured regiment, a role more suited to its mounted origins. The regiment did not see active service as such, but was broken up in 1943 to provide trained reinforcements for the 4th and 5th Canadian Armoured Divisions.[11]

1905-1936
Uniform

Although a drab service dress had been authorized for the Canadian militia in 1903, the issue for rural units was kept in stores until they were ordered out on service.[1] Western mounted units, therefore, wore pre-1900 service dress until the First World War. That of The 16th Light Horse consisted of a dark-blue naval-pattern forage cap with yellow band and yellow welt around the crown. The peak and chin-strap were of black patent leather.

The jacket was a scarlet serge frock with scarlet shoulder-straps, cuffs, and square stand-up collar. It closed with seven brass buttons; the pleated breast pockets with pointed flaps also fastened with brass buttons. There were two vents at the rear of the skirt opening along the back seams.

Unit collar badges were worn, and the shoulder-straps bore brass letters and numerals [A/16] to designate the squadron and the regiment.

Dark-blue pantaloons with a wide yellow stripe were worn with black leather Stohwasser-pattern leggings, black boots, and steel jack spurs.

For undress, officers and NCOs wore a blue serge patrol jacket with blue collar, cuffs, and shoulder-straps. Brass titles were worn on the shoulder-straps of the patrol jacket with the brass title, Light Horse, under the numerals and letters [A/16]. All ranks wore dark blue overalls with a wide yellow stripe, black Wellingtons, and steel box spurs.[2]

The facings of the unit were officially listed as yellow; however, only the undress scarlet frock with plain collar and cuffs seems to have been issued.[3]

Light Horse units wore a brown leather waist-belt with S buckle and brown leather bandolier. For camp and fatigue duties the mounted troops were issued khaki duck breeches, drab wool puttees, khaki cotton shirts, and straw hats worn with the left side turned up.[4] The troops were armed first with the long Lee-Enfield .303 and later with the Canadian Ross rifle.

When the regiment was reconstituted after the First World War, the drab serge service dress of cavalry pattern served for both service and ceremonial dress. With the service dress, the troopers and NCOs wore the new-pattern cavalry bandolier without a waist-belt. Fatigues, complete with straw hat, remained practically the same as the pre-war issue. The personal weapon was the No. 3 Short Magazine Lee-Enfield .303 rifle.

Some of the more fashionable cavalry regiments wished to return to the former splendour of full-dress uniforms, but there was little likelihood of being issued anything other than the drab serge service dress as long as large stocks were available from stores.[5] Nevertheless, some units made an effort to introduce some form of unit dress for ceremonial occasions by improvising and refurbishing pre-war issues.

The plate depicts a trooper of The 16th Canadian Light Horse in the improvised dress uniform worn by a mounted escort in 1923. His white Wolseley helmet was adopted by both British and Canadian armies in 1911. The dark-blue pre-war patrol jacket is worn with cotton drill cavalry breeches, washed to near-white. The brown laced high-topped boots are worn with steel jack spurs.[6]

Of particular interest are the trooper's sword and lance. Lances were not issued to Canadian cavalry, and swords were in such short supply that only the permanent cavalry units and the four mounted militia regiments designated as heavy cavalry were issued more than six swords per unit![7] The lance pennants were crimped after the fashion of the 16th Lancers, the British regiment with which the Canadian unit was affiliated. Like The 16th Canadian Light Horse, most militia units, by one means or another, managed to preserve some element of style and colour in a period when funds were scanty, and equipment and clothing were old, dull, and obsolete.

1903-1968

History

The Royal Canadian Corps of Signals is the oldest signal corps in the Commonwealth.[1] General Order 167, October 1903, authorized the organization of a Signalling Corps (Militia) with an establishment of ninety all ranks.

The basic concept of an organized corps of signallers grew out of Canada's experience in the South African War. There is an unsubstantiated legend that Lieutenant Bruce Carruthers of the 2nd Canadian Mounted Rifles overheard Winston Churchill comment at the end of a battle how much more efficient "those fellows with flags" would have been had they been properly trained and organized.[2] Carruthers shared the great man's grasp of the necessity for good communications during mobile warfare. He returned to Canada to carry on his crusade for an independent signalling service.

Fortunately, his campaign came to the attention of an understanding authority. The General Officer Commanding the Militia reported to his minister that, in the event of a war, it would be quite impossible to improvise good signallers; their training must have been completed before mobilization. To insure that signallers would receive adequate training, the GOC recommended the establishment of a Signalling Corps and the formation of a School of Signalling.[3] The recommendations were approved, and the new corps was authorized with Major Bruce Carruthers appointed as Inspector of Signals.

At the time, military signalling consisted essentially of visual communication by means of flags, signal lamps, and heliographs operated by any soldier of the regiment who might be particularly interested in the process. Telephone and telegraph were the responsibility of the engineers, and wireless telegraphy was regarded as only an entertaining toy. Forward signals, as a trained body of specialists, did not exist in any army of the Empire.

The new Signalling Corps was a cadre of officers and NCOs with an interest in signalling, drawn from various units of the Permanent Force. Its function was the training of unit signallers and the establishment of a uniform system of signalling. While most instruction was in visual signalling, the key and sounder was introduced in 1908, and this hesitant step toward telegraphy brought the signals into the hitherto private preserve of the engineers.

Originally, the Signalling Corps was composed of a small permanent staff, District Signalling Officers, and the regimental signallers of the militia, who were carried on the strength of their respective units. In 1913, the Corps was reorganized. Authority was given for the formation of signal units, signal companies for divisions, and signal troops for mounted brigades.[4] At the same time, the Corps was redesignated The Canadian Signal Corps.[5]

The First World War saw the formation of signal companies and the introduction of motorcyclists with blue and white armbands as dispatch riders. Telephone and telegraph communications and the embryonic wireless systems were still the responsibility of engineers, although the development of massive static positions saw the gradual merging of visual signals and telephony, and the unification of all signalling services under central control. However, the resulting organization remained a hybrid – part signals and part engineers.

In the post-war reorganization of the Canadian Army, there was a complete separation of all signal functions from engineers.[6] Signals had come of age through experience and service in massive conflict, and, in 1921, in recognition of this service, Canadian signallers were granted the title Royal and a change in designation to The Royal Canadian Corps of Signals.[7] The badge that was adopted at that time is still worn by the Corps.

With full corps status and a clear and unique role in battle, Signals were given corps precedence over The Royal Canadian Army Service Corps, immediately following The Corps of Royal Canadian Engineers.

No sooner had the Corps been accorded recognition for distinguished war service than it was plunged into a major contribution to the development of Canada's Northland. The Corps had established a ground-to-air system of wireless communication with Royal Canadian Air Force forestry patrols in the northern areas of the western provinces, and it was requested to set up a wireless system to serve the Northwest Territories and the Yukon. The first stations were set up at Dawson and Mayo in 1923. The following year, the control station was established at Simpson, and a terminal station in Edmonton linked the system into the telegraph network of the Canadian National and Canadian Pacific railways. By 1933, the system had been expanded to include twelve year-round stations.[8]

The Northwest Territories and Yukon Radio System became a normal part of life for The Royal Canadian Corps of Signals. Although a tour of duty in the north meant long periods of isolation in bitter arctic weather, northern service brought some moments of excitement: two signalmen were involved in the successful manhunt for Albert Johnson, the "Mad Trapper of Rat River," in the winter of 1932.

The demands on the NWT and Yukon Radio System grew as requests for meteorological information increased. The system continued to be operated and manned by the RCC of S until it was handed over to the Department of Transport in 1957.[9]

The wealth of skill and experience in wireless operations that they had gained through continuous practice admirably prepared the men of The Royal Canadian Corps of Signals to meet the requirements of mobile operations during the Second World War.

Uniform

When the Signalling Corps was established in 1903, officers and men wore the uniform of their former regiment or corps. They continued to do so until 1908, when the Corps was given its own distinctive dress. For facings, Major Carruthers chose French grey, the facing colour of the 21st Lancers in which he had served when commissioned in the British Army.[1]

The new uniform included the universal-pattern white helmet with gilt spike, brown leather chin-strap, and French-grey puggree. The tunic was of fine drab serge with French-grey collar and cuffs edged with drab braid. The base of the collar and the front edge of the tunic were trimmed with French grey; officers' rank badges were worn on French-grey shoulder-straps.

Trousers of fine serge, with a 1-in. stripe of facing colour, were worn with black Wellingtons and box spurs. A crimson net sash was worn over the sword-belt, which supported the infantry-pattern sword fitted with brown leather sword-knot, and slings.[2]

Service dress of khaki serge with shoulder-straps edged in French grey was prescribed for all ranks.[3]

A full-dress uniform for NCOs and men, approved in 1912, consisted of a dark-blue tunic with eight buttons in front and two behind at the waist; collar, cuffs, and shoulder-straps were of French grey. The blue cloth trousers were trimmed down the outside seam with a French-grey welt.[4]

Early in 1914, the officers' khaki full dress was replaced by a more conventional blue uniform, the recently adopted white Wolseley helmet with gilt spike and curb chain, and French-grey puggree. The dark-blue cloth tunic had eight buttons in front and a French-grey collar edged with gold lace and trimmed around the base with gold braid. French-grey cuffs were pointed with 5/8 in. gold lace. A tracing of gold Russia braid formed an Austrian knot above the lace and a small eye beneath it. The skirt was closed behind and trimmed with French grey along the seam. Three-pointed slashes on each side had a button at each point. The twisted round gold shoulder cords were lined in blue and had a small button at the top.

The dark-blue trousers were trimmed with a double French-grey stripe and worn with black Wellingtons and steel box spurs. Pantaloons with a similar stripe were worn with butcher boots and jack spurs in mounted order.

An infantry-pattern sword and scabbard were attached to a gold lace sword-belt with gold lace slings and gilt buckles. The sword-knot was a gold and crimson strap with a gold acorn.[5]

With the reorganization of the army after the First World War, the Corps became affiliated with the Royal Corps of Signals, and adopted the dress of its British counterpart in 1922.[6]

Officers' full dress included a black fur busby with black leather chin-strap, black bag on the right side, and scarlet plume in a gilt socket on the left. The tunic of scarlet cloth had eight buttons in front and two at the waist behind. The black collar was edged with gold lace and trimmed with gold braid around the base. Black cuffs were pointed with gold Russia braid and a tracing of gold cord above forming an Austrian knot. The skirt was open at the back, with the tunic front and back skirts edged with black cloth.

The dark-blue overalls with a 2-in. scarlet stripe down the outside seam were worn with black Wellingtons and steel box spurs. In mounted order, pantaloons with a scarlet stripe were worn with butcher boots and steel jack spurs.

The waist-belt, shoulder-belt and sword slings were of gold lace with black centre stripe; the waist plate was gold. On the black patent-leather pouch was the Royal Cypher and Crown badge in gilt. The infantry-pattern sword with gold cord and acorn sword-knot was carried in a steel scabbard. Gloves were of white buckskin.[7]

For most parades and duties, the men wore drab service dress of First World War pattern. Signals was a mounted corps, ranking immediately after the Engineers, and followed such dress affectations of mounted troops as jack spurs, and breeches worn with puttees rolled cavalry fashion.[8]

The men of the Signals serving the NWT and Yukon Radio System were issued a special muskrat cap of Yukon pattern, a short buffalo-hide coat like that worn by the Royal Canadian Mounted Police, and locally made moccasins and mittens.[9] The pattern of the cap and coat can be seen in the plate, which depicts a signalman in the Northwest Territories. Although the illustration shows the signaller wearing puttees and boots, these would be discarded in cold weather in favour of long woollen stockings and deer-skin moccasins. Locally made parkas were preferred to the heavy coats for normal working conditions.[10]

Few corps of the Canadian Army have gone through as many changes of dress as have the Signals. Today, they wear the green Canadian Forces' uniform, common to all ranks.

1939-1946

History

On 3 September 1939, Britain and France declared war on Germany after her armies invaded Poland. Canada was not automatically committed to the conflict as she had been in 1914. The Canadian Parliament met in emergency session to formally declare war on Germany on 10 September.

The mobilization of a Canadian Active Service Force of two divisions proceeded smoothly, as previously chosen militia units were placed on active service. It was decided that one infantry division should be sent overseas, and the 1st Canadian Division sailed for England in December to complete training and equipping prior to joining the British Army in France. However, in the spring of 1940, before the Canadians had left England, German armour crashed through the brittle Allied front to the Channel, and the British streamed back through Dunkirk. A Canadian brigade landed at Brest, as Britain made a desperate effort to bolster the rapidly disintegrating front; but it was recalled immediately when French resistance completely collapsed.

After the fall of France in 1940, Britain stood alone. The 2nd Canadian Division was sent to England to help meet the urgent need for troops. Two additional divisions, the 3rd and 4th, were formed in Canada to replace those dispatched overseas.

The buildup of Canadian troops in England continued through 1941. With armoured formations in great demand, the 1st Canadian Army Tank Brigade was formed and sent to England early in the year. The 3rd Canadian Division proceeded overseas in late summer, and the 5th Canadian Armoured Division arrived in England in November.

The concentration of Canadian formations overseas was completed when a second army tank brigade was formed from units already in England, and the 4th Division, converted from infantry to armour, sailed from Canada in early autumn 1942. Only weeks earlier, Canadians had experienced their first real test of war on the Continent: 5,000 men of the 2nd Division stormed ashore at Dieppe on 19 August. In less than nine hours' fighting more than 3,300 had become casualties.

In the summer of 1943, Canadians were committed to a major theatre when the 1st Canadian Division and the 1st Canadian Armoured Brigade landed on the beaches of Sicily on 10 July. Within two months the island was cleared of the enemy, and the Canadians were on their way to Italy. Both Canadian infantry and armour saw bitter fighting, particularly on the Adriatic at Ortona, as the Allies slowly clawed their way up the Italian peninsula. Canadian strength in Italy was increased markedly with the arrival of the 5th Canadian Armoured Division in November. As a result, the 1st Canadian Corps became operational in February 1944. The newly formed corps broke through the Hitler Line in the Liri Valley, and then swung to the Adriatic coast to smash through the Gothic Line to the Lombardy Plain.

While the 1st Canadian Corps was fighting its way from one Italian defence line to the next, Canadians in England were preparing for the invasion of France. On 6 June, the 3rd Canadian Division and the 2nd Canadian Armoured Brigade landed on the beaches of Normandy. The 2nd Division joined the fighting shortly afterwards, while 4th Canadian Armoured Division crossed the Channel during the last week of July.

First Canadian Army was launched into the Battle of Falaise, which terminated in the destruction of the German 7th army. The pursuit that followed took the Canadians through France and Belgium before they finally halted that winter on the Maas River in Holland. In February 1945, the British and Canadian divisions overcame stubborn resistance to clear the west bank of the Rhine. As the Allies prepared to cross the river, the 1st Canadian Corps arrived from Italy. Thus, all Canadian overseas formations were brought under the command of First Canadian Army for the final stages of the war.

Long before the momentous events in Italy and France, a small force of Canadian soldiers engaged the enemy in a hopeless defence action on another front. Two battalions of Canadians sent to reinforce the garrison of Hong Kong were lost when the Japanese overwhelmed the defenders of the colony in December 1941.

By the time the war ended, Canadian soldiers had served in locations scattered from the Pacific to Gibralter. For the second time in twenty-five years, Canadian citizens had formed themselves into a formidable fighting force. Some 630,000 volunteers joined the Canadian Army between 1939 and 1946; 368,000 of these proceeded overseas to uphold Canada's creditable record of achievement in battle.[1]

Uniform

In September 1939, the Canadian soldier looked remarkably like his counterpart in November 1918. The 1914-18 khaki service dress, of either British or Canadian pattern, was frequently older than the young militiaman who wore it! He bought his own boots, wore 1908-pattern web equipment, and carried the dependable Short-Magazine Lee-Enfield rifle.[1] When the Canadian Active Service Force was mobilized, even these obsolete uniforms were in short supply. Some militiamen wore their old uniforms, but most recruits remained in civilian clothes for several weeks. A pressing supply problem was the shortage of boots, which made training difficult during the brisk Canadian autumn. However, by the last week of October new clothing of all types began to reach the supply system.

A new khaki serge service uniform called "battledress," designed for utility and comfort, had been approved for use by the British army in March 1939.[2] The short blouse-style jacket had breast pockets, fly front, adjustable waistband, cuffs buttoning close to the wrist, and a stand-and-fall collar closed with two hooks. A large patch pocket with buttoned flap was set on the front of the left trouser leg, and a small pleated pocket high on the right leg was designed to take a first field dressing. Trousers were usually gathered at the ankle by a buttoned tab and tucked into short web anklets. The folding field-service cap of the late nineteenth century was reintroduced as a forage cap that could be folded and carried in the large pocket or pack when the steel helmet was worn. Black ammunition boots with plain toe-cap, steel heel plates, and hobnailed soles were standard wear with battledress.

Battledress was officially adopted by the Canadian Army in September 1939, and the first new uniforms arrived the last week of October.[3] Before embarkation, the troops of the 1st Canadian Division were completely clothed in Canadian-made battledress of excellent quality.

On arriving in England, all ranks were issued steel helmets and modern 1937-pattern web equipment, which consisted of two large web ammunition pouches supported by web braces crossing over the shoulders. The large haversack was carried on the back in battle order and suspended from the left side in full marching order; the water-bottle was carried on the right hip. A large web pack was carried in full marching order.

The plate depicts an infantry lance-corporal of the 2nd Canadian Division dressed for the bitter battle of the Rhineland in March 1945. A camouflage net cover with bits of coloured hessian breaks the outline of his helmet, and his personal shell dressing creates a bulge on the right side of his helmet net. The sleeveless leather jerkin gives some protection from the cold and rain without unduly hampering movement.

The basic ammunition pouches, designed to carry magazines for the Bren guns, are clearly detailed in the illustration. As the soldier is in battle order, he carries his rifle ammunition in a cotton disposable bandolier in which the clips of cartridges have been factory packed. Next to his rifle, the full-sized spade is the soldier's most essential piece of equipment.

The drab uniformity of battledress was broken by coloured cloth regimental shoulder badges and the rectangular cloth patches worn on the upper sleeve to designate the soldier's division. These coloured patches linked the men of First Canadian Army in the Second World War with their predecessors of the Canadian Corps in the earlier global struggle.

1914 to the present

History

In the autumn of 1914, a delegation of distinguished citizens from the Province of Quebec called on the Prime Minister to request that a French-Canadian battalion of infantry be enrolled for service overseas. The government was receptive to the idea, and proposed that the battalion form part of the Second Contingent then being recruited across Canada under district arrangement.[1]

Colonel F. M. Gaudet, a regular officer, was authorized to mobilize the new unit, designated the 22nd (French-Canadian) Battalion, at Saint-Jean, Quebec. Official authority to raise the battalion was given on 21 October, but actual recruiting began some time earlier.[2] The new battalion was assigned to the 5th Canadian Infantry Brigade of the 2nd Canadian Division. Thus the "Van Doos" became a part of Canada's military history.

The 22nd (French-Canadian) Battalion sailed for England in May 1915; after a period of intensive training, they proceeded to France on 15 September. Without the usual period of battle innoculation, the battalion immediately moved with the other units of the 5th Brigade to a sector of the front held by the newly formed Canadian Corps. The following spring, the 22nd (French-Canadian) Battalion took part in the bitter fighting for the Saint-Éloi Craters. Its first major battle was on the Somme front where, on 15 September, the battalion was one of two that stormed into Courcelette and held the town in the face of repeated German counter-attacks. Success cost the battalion dearly: the four rifle companies were reduced from a strength of 800 to 125 all ranks.[3]

In 1917, the battalion fought at Vimy Ridge, Hill 70, Lens, and in the grim battle for Passchendaele. The following year it was at Amiens and in the drive through the Hindenburg Line to Cambrai. During this battle, a battalion attack on Chérisy cost the "Van Doos" all their remaining officers, and reduced the unit to a fighting strength of forty men.[4]

The 22nd returned to Canada and demobilized in May 1919. In the course of the war, 244 officers and 5,675 other ranks had enlisted in the battalion, and 135 officers and 3,665 men had become casualties.[5] Two members of the battalion, Corporal Joseph Kaeble and Lieutenant Jean Brillant were posthumously awarded the Victoria Cross for their outstanding gallantry.

In the post-war reorganization of the Canadian Army, the number of permanent infantry regiments was increased to three. On 1 April 1920 a new French-Canadian regular infantry unit, the 22nd Regiment, perpetuated the memory of the battalion that distinguished itself in the costly battles of the Western Front. The home station of the new regiment was to be La Citadelle, Quebec, one of Canada's oldest military establishments. The regiment was granted the title Royal on 1 June 1921, and on 15 June 1928 it was redesignated the Royal 22ᵉ Régiment.[6] The regiment was greatly honoured when Maréchal Foch, Wartime Supreme Commander of the Allied Armies in France, became its first Honorary Colonel.

In 1927, the Royal 22ᵉ Régiment became affiliated with the Royal Welch Fusiliers of the British Army[7] – and acquired a goat as regimental mascot. The affiliation continued over the years, and the Fusiliers mounted guard over La Citadelle in 1962.[8] On 15 February 1975 the regiment also became affiliated with the 27ᵉ Brigade de Chasseurs Alpins Français of the French army.[9]

In September 1939, the Royal 22ᵉ Régiment mobilized to full war establishment and proceeded to England in December as part of the 3rd Infantry Brigade of the 1st Canadian Division. On 17 April 1940, a detachment of the regiment mounted guard for the Royal Household at Buckingham Palace – the first time that a regiment of the Commonwealth, rather than a British unit, had performed this duty.[10]

The regiment took part in the assault-landings on Sicily in July 1943 and in the subsequent invasion of Italy. During the vicious December battle for Ortona, Captain Paul Triquet of the "Van Doos" won the Victoria Cross for his part in the capture and retention of the key position of Casa Berardi.

In 1944, the unit moved to the Liri Valley for attacks on the Gustav and Hitler Lines followed by a shift to the Adriatic coast for the assault on the Gothic Line. Early in 1945, the regiment moved to North-West Europe to take part in the final weeks of the campaign. By October 1945, the Royal 22ᵉ was back home at La Citadelle.

Hardly had the regiment adjusted to peace-time soldiering when, in 1951, it was called for overseas service in Korea. During the brief but bitter campaign, the regiment won its most recent battle honour, *Korea 1951-53*, as well as forty decorations and forty-one mentions in dispatches – but at a cost of 10 officers and men killed and several hundred wounded. Two additional battalions of the regiment, raised for service in Korea, remained part of the regiment's expanded establishment when it furnished units for Canada's NATO force in Europe and the United Nations' peace-keeping force in Cyprus.

This magnificent regiment, with battle honours commemorating distinguished service in three major overseas conflicts, perpetuates the reputation of a battalion raised to demonstrate the desire of French Canadians to fully participate in Canada's commitments. But it does more than this – it perpetuates the military heritage that French-speaking Canadians have woven into the fabric of this country for more than 300 years.

1914 to the present

Uniform

When the 22nd Regiment became an infantry unit of Canada's Permanent Active Militia in 1920, the basic militia uniform was the British-pattern drab serge service dress of 1914-18. However, after a change of title to the Royal 22ᵉ Régiment and several years' experience in peace-time soldiering, a full-dress uniform was adopted, which added some colour to the round of ceremonial duties.

Initially, regimental full dress included the white Wolseley helmet with brass spike and chin chain, and red puggree with regimental badge.[1] When the regiment became affiliated with the Royal Welch Fusiliers, the helmet was replaced by a black bearskin with a red hackle on the left side and brass chin chain. The other ranks' bearskin cap resembled that of the foot guards, rather than the low smooth fur cap of the fusiliers. However, like fusilier regiments, the Royal 22ᵉ wore a regimental cap badge on the front of the bearskin.[2]

The other ranks' full-dress scarlet tunic was the standard seven-button infantry pattern, which had remained unchanged since first issued to the Canadian militia in the early 1880s. The dark-blue collar was piped with white along the base, and the blue shoulder-straps were edged in white. The dark-blue pointed cuffs were trimmed with white lace forming a crow's-foot at the point. The tunic front was edged with white cloth, and the skirt back was trimmed with white braid down each back seam from the waist to the hem of the skirt. The dark-blue trousers with a scarlet welt down the outside seam were worn over laced black boots.[3] The original waist-belts were of white buff leather with brass snake fastener; a regimental belt-plate was introduced later. White gloves were worn on ceremonial parades.[4]

Bandsmen and drummers wore the same scarlet tunic as the other ranks, but added white-edged scarlet wings with five bars of white braid. The original bandsmen's tunics were trimmed with white cloth along the front and back sleeve seams and the entire length of the back seam.[5]

The officer's scarlet tunic was closed with eight regimental buttons. The skirt back had three-pointed slashes edged in white cloth, with buttons at the points. The dark blue collar was ornamented with ⅝-in. gold lace along the edge and gold Russia braid along the base. The dark-blue pointed cuffs were edged with ⅝-in. gold lace with a tracing in gold Russia braid forming an Austrian knot above the braid and a small eye below. The twisted round gold shoulder cords were lined with scarlet and fastened with a small regimental button.[6]

The dark-blue cloth trousers, trimmed with scarlet welts, were worn with black Wellington boots. Officers wore a crimson sash about the waist. Sword slings were of gold lace on red morocco leather with gilt buckles.

The full-dress scarlets were packed away when the regiment donned battledress and moved to England in 1939. However, full dress was resumed after the war by ceremonial detachments, and could be seen at the daily guard-mounting ceremony at La Citadelle in Quebec City. The officer in the illustration is dressed in the full dress worn after the Second World War. The forage cap worn with this uniform (not seen in the illustration) was the peaked dark-blue service-dress cap with scarlet band and black leather strap. The black peak was trimmed with a band of heavy gold lace to designate field officers, but left plain on the caps of subaltern officers.

A detachment of the Royal 22ᵉ Régiment was the first corps of the Canadian Forces to wear the new green uniform, in 1967. Nonetheless, the regiment's full-dress scarlet uniform, bearskin cap, and badge bearing the motto, *Je me souviens* (I remember), preserve the regiment's glorious history.

1903-1972
History

The care and maintenance of military stores and properties has been part of the Canadian scene since the first settlers and soldiers arrived from France. When British forces arrived, they were accompanied by representatives of the Board of Ordnance to supervise the construction of forts and military buildings, and to establish stores depots at Halifax and in New Brunswick, Quebec, and Ontario. By 1829, there were nine such stores depots in Canada.[1]

The Canadian Active Militia, created in 1855, was supplied through the British military stores depots established in Canada. When the British troops were withdrawn in 1871, the Canadian authorities were faced with the problem of establishing a replacement system for procuring and distributing military stores.

To meet this need, a Canadian Stores Department, a civil department of the Canadian government, was organized.[2] One of its first tasks was to supply the Red River Expedition sent to Manitoba in 1870 to suppress the First Riel Rebellion. A few years later, the department was called on to outfit the newly created North West Mounted Police for its march into Canada's Northwest.

Equipping and continuously supplying the North West Field Force during the Northwest Rebellion of 1885 placed a heavy strain on the Stores Department, and considerable aid was provided by the Hudson's Bay Company network of stores and posts throughout the region. An even more demanding test came in 1899, when contingents for service in South Africa had to be equipped for an overseas campaign.

In 1898, Major-General E.T.H. Hutton, General Officer Commanding the Canadian Militia, observed that the militia "is but a collection of military units without cohesion, without staff, and without those military departments by which an army is moved, fed, or ministered to in sickness."[3] He criticized civilian control of the stores, and recommended the formation of an Ordnance Stores Corps to adopt and implement standardized procedures for the procurement, storage, maintenance, and issue of military stores and equipment.[4]

On 1 July 1903, the Ordnance Stores Corps was formed and a Director General of Ordnance appointed. The Director was charged with the responsibility of supplying the militia with war-like stores except engineer stores, with the issue of equipment, clothing, and necessaries, with supplying armaments and dealing with armament pattern and design, and with the inspection of all stores. In addition, he was also to administer the Ordnance Branch and the Ordnance Stores Corps, and to ensure that the militia units were properly supplied to take to the field.[5]

The Ordnance Stores Corps was redesignated the Canadian Ordnance Corps in 1907.[6] At the outbreak of war in 1914, the tiny corps struggled with the staggering task of providing clothing, equipment, and stores of every conceivable description for the 30,000 men assembled at Valcartier. When the First Contingent sailed for England in September, it was accompanied by an ordnance unit of thirty-two all ranks.[7]

As the Canadian army expanded, the corps also grew; by the end of the First World War it numbered 1,315 all ranks.[8] Detachments of the Canadian Ordnance Corps served in Russia and the West Indies as well as in Europe. In recognition of its outstanding wartime service, the regular component of the corps was granted the prefix Royal in 1919, an honour that was extended to the militia component in 1936.[9]

During the Second World War, the Corps grew from a strength of 300 to some 25,000 all ranks, and its ordnance installations in Canada employed 30,000 civilians.[10] Full combatant status was granted to the Corps in 1941.[11] Subsequently, Ordnance personnel were present in every Canadian theatre of operations from Dieppe and Hong Kong to the assault-landings on the beaches of Normandy. Repair services needed for the mass of motor transport and complicated weapons and equipment became so specialized that, in February 1944, the Corps of Royal Canadian Electrical and Mechanical Engineers was formed from elements of the RCOC.[12]

After the Second World War, the corps continued to support elements of the Canadian Army in Korea, the NATO forces in North-West Europe, and a variety of United Nations' peace-keeping operations. On the unification of the Canadian Forces, Ordnance was amalgamated with the Service Corps and Pay Corps to form a Logistics Branch. The title of The Royal Canadian Ordnance Corps has been deleted from the roll of corps and regiments of the Canadian Army, but its function, supplying the soldier with his stores and weapons, remains unchanged.

Uniform

When the Ordnance Stores Corps was formed in 1903, the distinctive Corps uniform prescribed included the universal-pattern white helmet with brass spike and curb chain.[1] Officers of the Corps with the rank of colonel wore a cocked hat with a plume of black and white swan feathers in full dress.

The dark-blue tunic had eight buttons in front and two at the waist behind. The jacket front and skirt plaits were edged with scarlet cloth; the scarlet collar was edged with lace and trimmed around the base with gold braid. Pointed scarlet cuffs were trimmed with a bar of gold lace; gold braid formed an Austrian knot above the point and a double crow's-foot below. Badges of ranks were attached to twisted gold braid shoulder cords lined with blue cloth.

Trousers and pantaloons were of blue cloth with two scarlet stripes 1/8-in. apart down each outside seam. Black Wellington boots and steel box spurs were worn with trousers, and black butcher boots and jack spurs with pantaloons.

A crimson net sash was worn around the waist with the tassels hanging over the left hip. The sword was attached to a web sword-belt worn under the tunic. Sword slings and shoulder-belt were of gold lace with a red centre stripe. The shoulder-belt supported a black patent-leather binocular case.

The officers' undress uniform consisted of a blue serge patrol jacket of universal pattern with scarlet shoulder-straps, dark-blue serge pantaloons or overalls with a double red stripe, and a dark-blue peaked forage cap with a scarlet band and welt around the crown.[2]

The officers' mess jacket was dark blue with scarlet roll collar and cuffs. The shoulder-straps were scarlet with a blue light, and the waistcoat was dark blue with four small regimental buttons.[3]

Between the wars The Royal Canadian Ordnance Corps, like all units of the Canadian army, usually wore drab serge service dress. Full dress was similar to that originally prescribed for the Corps except for the new white Wolseley helmet with spike, curb chain, and white puggree. The sash was discarded in favour of a waist-belt of gold lace with red centre stripe. The rear skirts of the tunic were ornamented with a two-pointed slash edged with gold braid, and three buttons and a narrow edging of scarlet cloth down the centre of the back skirts.[4]

After the Second World War, full dress was retained by all regimental bandsmen for ceremonial duties. Officers' full dress worn by the Director of Music was slightly altered from the pre-war pattern: the helmet puggree was changed from white to scarlet, and the scarlet centre stripe was removed from the waist-belt, pouch belt, and sword slings.[5]

The drum major, illustrated in the plate, wears shoulder-straps of blue cloth edged with scarlet. His cuffs are trimmed with gold lace and braid in the same pattern as the officer's tunic. The drum major's scarlet sash, heavily embellished with gold lace, is mounted with the Queen's Cypher, an embroidered badge of the corps, and a pair of gilt-tipped ebony drum sticks.[6]

The bandsmen's uniform was similar to that of the drum major except that the cuffs were trimmed with a single row of gold braid that formed a crow's-foot at the point.[7] The three-pointed slashes on the rear of the skirt were edged in red cloth; waist-belt and pouch belt were of white leather, and the pouch was of black patent leather.[8]

Since the amalgamation of the forces, a common uniform of green embellished with worsted gold cord is worn by all regular bandsmen. On special occasions, however, regimental drummers appear in the old full dress to remind us that the colourful blue, scarlet or green uniforms once were the everyday work dress of the Canadian soldier.

1871 to the present

History

In November 1871, all British soldiers except the Halifax and Esquimalt garrisons withdrew from Canada, and Canada's most urgent defence priority became the maintenance of permanent fortifications. On 20 October 1871, the formation of two regular batteries of artillery was authorized for the "care, protection, and maintenance of Forts, Magazines, Armament and Warlike Stores recently, or about to be handed over to the Canadian Government in the Provinces of Ontario and Quebec."[1] The Royal Canadian Horse Artillery is the direct descendant of these two regular batteries.

The two units were soon raised; A Battery was stationed at Kingston and B Battery at Quebec. Each battery was formed into two divisions: a mounted division serving as field gunners, and a dismounted division acting as garrison artillery. In addition to the heavy ordnance of the fixed fortifications, each battery was equipped with four 9-pounder smooth-bore muzzle-loading guns and two 24-pounder howitzers. The ancient 9-pounders were replaced in 1873 by new 9-pounder muzzle-loading rifled field guns.

In addition to performing normal garrison duties, the regular batteries functioned as schools of gunnery for the militia artillery. In February 1880, both schools were designated Royal Schools of Gunnery; three years later they were retitled Royal Schools of Artillery. A third battery of regulars was authorized; and, although C Battery was not formed until 1887, the three regular batteries were designated the Regiment of Canadian Artillery in 1883.[2]

Both A and B batteries were sent West in 1885 on the outbreak of the Northwest Rebellion. A Battery, marching with General Middleton's main column, went into action at Fish Creek on 24 April, thereby becoming the first Canadian artillery unit since Confederation to fire at the enemy.[3]

The Regiment was granted the coveted prefix Royal and titled The Royal Canadian Artillery in 1893.[4] At the same time, it was also reorganized: the mounted divisions of the original units were formed into A and B batteries, Royal Canadian Field Artillery; the dismounted divisions and C Battery were organized as Nos. 1 and 2 companies, Royal Canadian Garrison Artillery.[5]

The second Canadian contingent for South Africa, approved in December 1899, included a field-artillery brigade of three batteries, each armed with six 12-pounder breech-loading guns. One section of each battery was drawn from the regular gunners; the remainder was recruited from militia artillery units.[6] The Canadian artillery gained a considerable measure of experience, prestige, and self-confidence from its very creditable performance in South Africa.[7]

At the turn of the century, an effort was made to convert the militia into a cohesive fighting formation. Units were grouped into brigades with supporting arms and services. A and B batteries were ordered to train as horse artillery to act with cavalry brigades.[8] In 1905, these batteries became horse artillery in name as well as function. They were designated A and B batteries, Royal Canadian Horse Artillery, and rearmed with the new 13-pounder quick-firing gun adopted by the Royal Horse Artillery of the British Army.[9]

The reorganization, rearming, and retraining of the gunners came just in time to prepare them for the stern test of the First World War. The Royal Canadian Horse Artillery Brigade was formed in late August and attached to the Canadian Cavalry Brigade.[10] As the cavalry formed part of the British Cavalry Corps, the RCHA Brigade supported various British formations as well as Canadian units.

The RCHA returned to peace-time soldiering in fine style when C Battery was reconstituted and stationed at Winnipeg; but in 1922, disaster loomed when it was proposed that all horse artillery units be converted and redesignated as field artillery. Ultimately sentiment prevailed and the horse gunners were permitted to retain their traditional designation, although it lost all practical significance when the regiment was mechanized in 1930.[11]

On the outbreak of the Second World War, the three batteries of the RCHA were formed into the 1st Field Brigade, RCHA, of the 1st Canadian Division.[12] Shortly after their arrival in England, the artillery brigades were reorganized into field regiments, and the 1st Field Brigade became the 1st Field Regiment, RCHA. The regiment remained with the 1st Canadian Division for the duration of the war, supporting operations in Sicily, Italy, and North-West Europe.

When the regular force was reorganized after the war, the 1st Field Regiment, RCHA was formed at Camp Shilo, Manitoba. In August 1950, the Canadian government authorized the formation of an infantry brigade group to serve with the United Nations force in Korea; and a new artillery unit, the 2nd Field Regiment, RCHA was formed.[13] Two additional regiments of field artillery were raised in 1951, when Canada recruited the 27th Canadian Infantry Brigade Group for service with the NATO force in Europe. The new regiments, the 79th and 81st field regiments, were subsequently redesignated the 3rd and 4th field regiments, RCHA.[14]

In 1971, The Royal Canadian Horse Artillery celebrated 100 years of unbroken service since the raising of A and B batteries in 1871. Today the regiment continues to serve in Canada, in Europe with Canada's NATO force, and as part of Canada's continuing contribution to UN peace-keeping operations.

1871 to the present

Uniform

When the first regular batteries of Canadian artillery were formed in 1871, their commanding officers were faced with the task of clothing the new units on short notice. The commander of B Battery solved the problem by borrowing the uniforms of the Quebec Volunteer Artillery.[1]

The dress prescribed for the Quebec corps was like that of the Royal Artillery. The dark sable busby with black leather chin-strap and brass buckle had a scarlet bag on the right side and a white hair plume with grenade and socket on the left.[2] The skirts of the dark-blue cloth tunic were rounded in front and closed behind with a plait on each side. The front, skirts, and rear plaits were edged with scarlet cloth. There were eight brass buttons in front and two behind at the waist. Officers and senior NCOs had scarlet collars trimmed all around with gold cord; those of the remainder of the men were similarly trimmed with yellow cord. Field officers' collars were trimmed all around with gold lace; subaltern officers had gold lace only on the collar edge.[3] Officers' badges of rank were worn on the collar.

The men's tunic cuffs were trimmed with an Austrian knot of yellow cord, while those of the officers were trimmed with gold cord and lace according to rank: field officers had a gold lace chevron with figured lace above and below; subaltern officers had a gold lace Austrian knot, laced in gold for captains and plain for lieutenants. Officers wore a gold cord loop on the shoulders. The men had blue cloth shoulder-straps edged with scarlet cloth.[4]

Blue cloth trousers with a 2-in. scarlet stripe were worn over Wellington boots by all ranks; blue pantaloons were worn with riding boots and jack spurs for mounted duties. Officers' full-dress trousers were trimmed with a stripe of gold lace.

The full-dress officers' sword-belt and slings were of gold lace; the sword-knot was of gold cord with a gold acorn. A gold-lace pouch belt held a blue leather pouch with blue cloth-covered flap. In undress, all these accoutrements were of white leather, except for the pouch, which was of black patent leather.

All ranks wore the round blue pillbox forage cap with black chin-strap. Those of officers, staff sergeants, and sergeants had a band of gold lace and gold button; the band and button on the men's caps were yellow. Corporals and bombardiers wore miniature rank badges in yellow on the front of the cap above the band.[5]

By 1886, the busby had been replaced by the white helmet with gilt or brass ball.[6] With other relatively minor changes, this uniform remained the full dress of the regular Canadian artillery for almost forty years.

When A and B batteries were converted to horse artillery in 1905, a uniform similar to that of the British RHA was adopted. The cap was a black sable busby with red bag, black chin strap, and cap lines: gold cord for officers and yellow for other ranks. The plume worn on the front of the busby was white with a red base. Officers' plumes were made of feathers, and those of the men were of hair. The red base of the plume was the only feature that distinguished the dress of the RCHA from that of the RHA.

All ranks wore a dark-blue shell-jacket edged all around with gold or yellow cord, depending on rank, that formed a figure eight at the bottom of each back seam. The jacket front was ornamented with yellow or gold cord in fifteen to eighteen loops depending on the height of the wearer. The back seams were trimmed with similar cord in a crow's-foot at the top and an Austrian knot at the side of the waist. The scarlet collar was trimmed all around with gold or yellow cord. Officers' collars were trimmed with lace along the top, and were embroidered with a silver grenade and the word Canada in gold on the flame. Other ranks had loops of yellow cord at the shoulders, and officers wore braided gold-wire shoulder cords. Officers' cuffs were edged with an Austrian knot of gold lace; those of staff sergeants and sergeants were of gold cord, while the cuffs of the men had knots of yellow worsted cord.[7]

For mounted duties all ranks wore blue cloth pantaloons with scarlet stripes, black riding boots, and steel jack spurs. At other times, dark-blue overalls were worn over black Wellingtons with box spurs.[8]

Officers wore a gold lace pouch belt with black patent-leather pouch. The sword-belt, worn under the jacket, was supported by sword slings of gold lace; the sword-knot was of gold cord with gold acorn. Other ranks wore white slings and sword-knots.[9]

Full dress was worn by all three batteries of The Royal Canadian Horse Artillery when performing the musical drive in the 1920s. The last performance of this spectacular ceremony was given by C Battery at Winnipeg in 1933.[10]

After the Second World War, the striking full dress was again worn when four officers of the regiment were assigned to the Sovereign's Mounted Escort at Her Majesty's coronation in 1953.[11] Full dress also was worn regularly by the RCHA band.

The plate depicts the commanding officer's trumpeter in dismounted review order.[12] He carries both trumpet and bugle on the red, blue, and yellow cords of Royal corps. It was fitting that this trumpeter representing "the right of the line," i.e., Canada's senior regular regiment, appeared in full dress at numerous functions during the celebration of Canada's Centennial in 1967.

1968 to the present

History

On 1 February 1968, the Canadian Army ceased to exist when it was unified with the Royal Canadian Navy and the Royal Canadian Air Force in a single service, the Canadian Forces.

The concept of integration and eventual unification of the armed services dates back to the reorganization of the Canadian forces after the First World War. In 1920, General Sir Arthur Currie recommended that the Department of Militia and Defence and the Department of Naval Services be replaced by a single Department of Defence.[1] Acting on Currie's proposal and supporting opinions, the government passed the necessary legislation to create a Department of Defence, effective 1 January 1923.[2]

However, even before the new bill became law, senior navy and air force officers began to have second thoughts about the proposals they had endorsed. Their apprehension proved well founded for, in March 1922, the Canadian air force was reduced to a directorate of the General Staff, and its estimates were slashed by sixty per cent.[3] The worst fears of the navy were confirmed in November, when by Order-in-Council the senior army officer was appointed to the newly created position of Chief of Staff of the Department of National Defence. The Director of Naval Services was to report to him rather than directly to the Minister.[4] This touched off a first-class row between the senior officers of the two services; it subsided only when the position of Chief of Staff of the Department was abolished in 1927 and the Director of Naval Services was appointed Chief of the Naval Staff of Canada.

There were further attempts to integrate the command structure. In 1932, Major-General A.G.L. McNaughton, Chief of the General Staff of the Army proposed a reintroduction of a single Chief of Staff for the Department of National Defence.[5] Again the navy objected. Having achieved equality, the sailors were not about to surrender their hard-won independence. During the years that followed, as ministers and service chiefs changed, integration dropped from sight.

During the Second World War, Canada's naval and air services each reported to its own minister; however, at the end of the war, the armed services came under the centralized control of a single Minister of National Defence. Obviously, a unified defence policy was essential to Canada's post-war development, and the services could not be allowed to go their separate ways. To achieve some degree of co-ordination, an inter-service Chiefs-of-Staff Committee was established in 1950, with the collective responsibility of advising the government on matters of defence policy, and of directing joint service organizations and operations. As the chairman had no executive authority, decisions required unanimous agreement.[6] At best the committee was cumbersome, at worst ineffective.

Singularly unimpressed by the command structure of the armed services, the Royal Commission on Government Organization (the Glassco Commission) recommended that the chairman of the Chiefs-of-Staff Committee be given some executive powers.[7] However, the government decided that the basic issue could be resolved only by the establishment of a single defence staff under a single chief.[8] On 1 August 1964, the Chief-of-Staff positions of the separate services were abolished, and Air Chief Marshal F. R. Miller was appointed Chief of the Defence Staff.

The government had warned that the integration of the defence staff was only the first step toward a unified defence force. The Canadian Forces Reorganization Act was passed in 1967, stating that "the Canadian Forces are the armed forces of Her Majesty raised by Canada and consist of one Service called the Canadian Armed Forces."[9] Unification had become a fact of Canadian military life. On 1 February 1968, the Royal Canadian Navy, the Canadian Army, and the Royal Canadian Air Force ceased to exist as separate services. Army ranks were used as the standard in the main, although this has since been modified.

While it has produced some profound changes in the structure of Canada's armed forces, a decade of unification has left the average Canadian soldier remarkably unaffected. Although his uniform has changed in style and colour, his regiment has retained its title, badges, and honours. Moreover, his primary task remains the same as it has been for centuries: to engage the enemy.

1968 to the present

Uniform

The visible symbol of unification is the new Canadian Forces uniform of dark green, which is worn by all ranks of sea, land, and air personnel. The new dress made its first formal public appearance on Canada Day, 1 July 1967. The Honourable Lionel Chevrier, Commissioner General of Expo, inspected a fifty-man guard-of-honour of the Royal 22e Régiment at the Place des Nations during the World's Fair in Montreal.[1]

Preliminary trials brought about a number of minor modifications, and issue of the CF uniform to the regular force began in 1969. For some months it was possible to see four distinctive service dress uniforms at some bases; however, by 1971, issue of the new uniform was completed.[2]

The CF service cap is a dark-green peaked cap with rolled edge, green woven cap band, and black chin-strap with two small CF buttons. The black peak is plain for the men; that of the officers is trimmed with gold braid or oak leaves, depending on rank.[3]

The dark-green single-breasted jacket has a rear-vented skirt; the front closes with four large CF buttons. Two breast patch pockets are centre pleated and have pointed flaps fastened with medium buttons; the inset side pockets have plain flaps. Only general officers have shoulder-straps on their jackets.

The dark-green trousers are cuffless with a single side pleat. Both jacket and trousers are of a light-weight crease-resistant wool-polyester fabric. The linden (a very light green) shirt of polyester-cotton fibre has shoulder-straps and centre-pleated patch breast pockets with buttoned flaps. It is worn with a dark-green tie. Black socks and shoes complete the basic service dress.

A national badge, Canada, in 1/4-in. gold-coloured embroidery on a dark-green background is worn on each sleeve one inch below the shoulder seam. Rank badges for NCOs, warrant officers, and men are of gold-coloured embroidery on a dark-green background. Officers' rank is denoted by narrow rings of gold braid around each cuff. General officers wear a single ring of wide gold braid around each cuff and appropriate rank badges of gold-coloured embroidery on the shoulder-straps. A small gold maple leaf has replaced the traditional star, but the crown has remained.

Canadian Forces buttons are worn by all ranks, regardless of service element or regiment. These buttons are gold plated, rimmed, and horizontally striated; they bear the crest from Canada's armorial bearings: a crowned lion, passant guardant,

standing on a heraldic wreath, and holding in the outstretched dexter forepaw a maple leaf.

Winter dress includes a dark-green, double-breasted beltless greatcoat with narrow notched lapels, shoulder-straps, and black buttons. The side pockets have plain flaps. The length of the greatcoat may vary from mid-knee to one inch below the kneecap. A dark-green woollen scarf and black leather gloves are worn with the greatcoat. The winter cap of black orlon imitation fur is wedge shaped with a small green bag on the left side.

Additional items are worn with the various orders of dress. A light-weight open-collar shirt is worn in shirt-sleeve order in hot weather, and dark-green Bermuda-style shorts and knee-length socks are issued for hot climate areas.

In addition to service dress, the soldier is issued a combat uniform for field service and a working dress of dark-green denim trousers and jacket, and shirts of a darker blue-green. A dark-green beret is worn as a forage cap with both working dress and combat uniform. Armoured and airborne personnel wear black and maroon berets respectively with combat uniforms, while the air element prefers the traditional folding field-service cap in dark green.

The sergeant of the Princess Patricia's Canadian Light Infantry illustrated in the plate is in S-1 or ceremonial order of dress. He wears his medals, the red sash of infantry sergeants and warrant officers, and a white web waist-belt to which the bayonet frog is attached.

Regiments retain a number of distinctive items of dress such as collar and cap badges, and regimental belt buckles. The sergeant belongs to the 2nd Battalion, PPCLI, and wears the watered blue gold-edged rectangle of ribbon on each sleeve immediately below the national shoulder title. The ribbon denotes the United States Distinguished Unit Citation which was awarded to the battalion for its action at Kap'yong, Korea in 1951.[4]

The purpose of the common CF uniform is to give the Canadian Forces a unified appearance. With their love of tradition, however, soldiers have managed to preserve some of the unique bits of cloth and metal that set them apart as members of a specific unit. Though the colourful scarlet, blue, and rifle-green uniforms of the past have long since disappeared, the spirit of the regiments remains to provide that intangible force that binds men together in the face of adversity.

Notes

In order to simplify the presentation of the notes, we have abbreviated the names of various government organizations and the titles of military publications as set out below. A complete description of all sources appears in the bibliography.

AC	Archives des Colonies, Archives nationales, Paris
AG	Archives de la Guerre, Service historique de l'armée, Vincennes
AM	Archives de la Marine, Archives nationales, Paris
ANQM	Archives nationales du Québec, Montreal
BMA	Bibliothèque du ministère des Armées, Paris
BN	Bibliothèque nationale, Paris
DMD	Department of Militia and Defence, Ottawa
DND	Department of National Defence, Ottawa
GO	General Orders
MGO	Militia General Orders
MND	Ministry of National Defence, Ottawa
MO	Militia Orders
MR	*Report of the State of Militia of the Dominion of Canada*
PAC	Public Archives of Canada, Ottawa
PRO	Public Records Office, London
WO	War Office, Public Records Office, London

LE RÉGIMENT DE CARIGNAN-SALIÈRES

History

1 *Gazette de France*, 15 May 1665, no. 62, pp. 510-11.

2 Daniel, *Histoire de la milice françoise*, vol. 2, p. 422.

3 De La Chesnaye-Desbois and Badier, *Dictionnaire de la noblesse*, vol. 18, p. 358.

4 BN, vol. 4237, fol. 45v.

5 Louvois, Les Tiroirs de Louis XIV, BMA, fol. 39-46.

6 Mercier, "Relation de ce qui," *Relations des Jésuites*, vol. 3, Relation 1665, p. 10.

7 *Ibid.*, Relation 1666, pp. 7-9.

8 Colbert to Talon, 20 February 1668, *Rapport de l'archiviste de la province de Québec, 1930-1931*, p. 91.

9 Roy and Malchelosse, *Le régiment de Carignan*. This work lists the officers and men of the regiment who remained in Canada, and also reproduces the "Mémoire de Mr De Salières des choses qui se sont passées en Canada les plus considérables depuis qu'il est arrivé," for 1665 and 1666.

Uniform

1 AC, C11A, vol. 2, fol. 273-80. This uniform is reconstructed largely from a long statement of clothing, equipment, and weapons for the twenty-four companies in Canada, dated 1666.

2 Peyrins, *Traité des marques nationales*, p. 134. The livery of Salières is unknown.

3 Milleville, *Armorial historique de la noblesse de France*, p. 233.

4 Roy, ed., *Inventaire des testaments*, vol. 3, pp. 272-78 . This work reproduces inventories of the belongings of two officers of the regiment killed in July 1666.

5 Casson, *Histoire du Montréal*, p. 180.

6 AC, C11A, vol. 2, fol. 274.

LES COMPAGNIES FRANCHES DE LA MARINE

History

1 La Hontan, *New Voyages to North America*, vol. 1, p. 32; AC, F1A, vol. 2, fol. 243.

2 AC, B, vol. 11, fol. 18.

3 La Hontan, *New Voyages to North America*, vol. 1, *passim*; AC, F1A, vols. 3, 4, *passim*.

4 AC, B, vol. 15, fol. 17; vol. 105, fol. 6.

5 AC, C11A, vol. 102, fol. 240; Journal du marquis de Montcalm (20 July 1757), PAC, MG18, K8, vol. 1.

6 *Lettres et mémoires*, pp. 141-45; AC, C11G, vol. 12, fol. 492.

7 AC, D2C, vol. 48, fol. 129.

8 O'Callaghan, *Documents Relative*, vol. 10, p. 606; Aleyrac, *Aventures militaires*, p. 32.

9 J.C.B., *Voyage au Canada*, pp. 45-105; O'Callaghan, *Documents Relative*, vol. 10, pp. 303-04.

10 J.C.B., *Voyage au Canada*, pp. 39-45; AC, B, vol. 22, fols. 243-44.

11 AC, C11A, vol. 31, fol. 80; C11G, vol. 12, fol. 302; B, vol. 55, fol. 536.

12 AC, C11A, vol. 87, fol. 214; Salone, *La colonisation*, pp. 344-47.

Uniform

1 AC, C11A, vol. 93, fols. 342-43; C11B, vol. 32, fol. 183; C11B, vol. 37, fol. 117; B, vol. 92, fol. 5; B, vol. 96, fol. 172; C11A, vol. 37, fol. 131.

2 Peyrins, *Traité des marques nationales*, pp. 303-04; AC, C11A, vol. 93, fol. 343; C11B, vol. 27, fol. 275; C11B, vol. 37, fols. 117, 201; F1A, vol. 35, fol. 10; F1A, vol. 88, fol. 239.

3 AC, C11A, vol. 54, fol. 201; C11B, vol. 37, fol. 237; ANQM, greffe Foucher, no. 6573; greffe J.-B. Adhémar, no. 10737.

4 AC, B, vol. 55, fols. 96, 214.

5 Margérand, *Armement et équipement, passim*; AC, C11A, vol. 98, fol. 73; C11B, vol. 37, fols. 117, 205.

6 Aubert de Gaspé, *Les anciens Canadiens*, pp. 343-44; Fortescue, *History of the British Army*, vol. 2, p. 281.

7 Journal du marquis de Montcalm (21-25 February 1757), PAC, MG18, K8, vol. 1.

8 AC, B, vol. 27, fol. 28; B, vol. 86, fol. 395; C11A, vol. 98, fols. 61, 73; F1A, vol. 2, fol. 308; AM, B1, vol. 5, fol. 20; Parks Canada, Ottawa. See reserve collection for the 1728-model French army musket.

LE RÉGIMENT DE LANGUEDOC

History

1 AG, A1, vol. 3404, nos. 116, 178

2 AC, A1, vol. 3404, no. 178; O'Callaghan, *Documents Relative*, vol. 10, pp. 297-99.

3 Journal du marquis de Montcalm (9-26 September 1757), PAC, MG18, K8, vol. 1.

4 Parkman, *Montcalm and Wolfe*, pp. 207-27.

5 Journal du marquis de Montcalm, PAC, MG18, K8, vol. 1, *passim*.

6 Journal de campagne de Lévis au Canada (12 September 1759 – 14 September 1760), PAC, MG18, K8, vol. 12.

Uniform

1 Briquet, *Code militaire*, vol. 4, pp. 317-20.

2 Instruction sur la façon et traitement d'un justaucorps de soldat (29 January 1747); Waugh, *The Cut of Men's Clothes*, pp. 86-99; *État général des troupes françoises*, p. 104; Rousselot, "Manuscrit de Tarascon," *Carnet de la Sabretache* (1972), no. 12, pp. 35-36.

3 AC, C11A, vol. 100, fol. 268.

4 Collection des uniformes des troupes du roi, infanterie française et étrangère, 1757, BMA, ms. A1 J12; Montandre-Lonchamps et Montandre, *État militaire de France*, 1758, p. 159; *ibid.*, 1759, p. 260; *ibid.*, 1760, p. 245.

5 La Chesnaye-Desbois, *Dictionnaire militaire*, vol. 1, p. 973; *ibid.*, vol. 2, p. 22; Guignard, *École de Mars*, pp. 606, 614-15.

LE RÉGIMENT DE BÉARN

History

1 Susane, *Histoire de l'ancienne*, vol. 8, pp. 209-11; Pouchot, *Memoir Upon*, vol. 1, pp. 34, 38-53.

2 Journal du marquis de Montcalm (30-31 May and 2, 20-21 June 1756), PAC, MG18, K8, vol. 1.

3 Parkman, *Montcalm and Wolfe*, p. 287.

4 Pouchot, *Memoir Upon*, vol. 1, pp. 62-72; Journal du marquis de Montcalm (10-24 July 1756), PAC, MG18, K8, vol. 1.; Stanley, *New France*, pp. 143-47.

5 Journal du marquis de Montcalm (29 July–9 August 1757), PAC, MG18, K8, vol. 1.

6 *Ibid.* (8 July 1758).

7 Journal de campagne de Lévis au Canada (May and September 1759 and 16 September 1760), PAC, MG18, K8, vol. 12.

Uniform

1 AC, C11A, vol. 100, fol. 268..

2 Collection des uniformes des troupes du roi, infanterie française et étrangère, 1757, BMA, ms. A1 J12; Montandre-Lonchamps et Montandre, *État militaire de France* (1758), p. 167.

3 Briquet, *Code militaire*, vol. 4, pp. 317-27.

LE RÉGIMENT DE LA REINE

History

1 O'Callaghan, *Documents Relative*, vol. 10, pp. 297-99.

2 Pouchot, *Memoir Upon*, vol. 1, pp. 46-51.

3 *Ibid.*, p. 6.

4 Journal du marquis de Montcalm (28 July 1757), PAC, MG18, K8, vol. 1.

5 Fortescue, *A History of the British Army*, vol. 2, p. 312.

6 Parkman, *Montcalm and Wolfe*, p. 339; Stanley, *New France*, pp. 159-61; Hamilton, *Adventure in the Wilderness*, pp. 165-71.

7 Journal du marquis de Montcalm (8 July 1758), PAC, MG18, K8, vol. 1.

8 *Ibid.*, (10 May 1759).

9 Journal de campagne de Lévis au Canada (October 1759 – September 1760), PAC, MG18, K8, vol. 12.

Uniform

1 AC, C11A, vol. 100, fol. 268.

2 Collection des uniformes des troupes du roi, infanterie française et étrangère, 1757, BMA, ms. A1 J12; Montandre-Lonchamps et Montandre, *État militaire*, 1758, p. 136.

3 Peyrins, *Traité des marques nationales*, p. 303.

4 AC, C11A, vol. 100, fol. 268.

LE RÉGIMENT DE GUYENNE

History

1 Unless otherwise indicated, the history of the Régiment de Guyenne is based on the papers of the Chevalier de La Pause, a captain of the regiment, who served in Canada from 1755 to 1760. See PAC, MG18, J9, vols. 1-4 and the *Rapport de l'archiviste de la province de Québec* for the years 1931-1934.

2 Fortescue, *A History of the British Army*, vol. 2, p. 337.

3 Stacey, *Québec 1759*, pp. 113-15.

Uniform

1 AC, C11A, vol. 100, fol. 268.

2 Collection des uniformes des troupes du roi, infanterie française et étrangère 1757, BMA, ms. A1 J12; Montandre-Lonchamps et Montandre, *État militaire*, 1758, p. 166.

3 Briquet, *Code militaire*, vol. 4, pp. 321-23.

LE RÉGIMENT ROYAL-ROUSSILLON

History

1 Journal du marquis de Montcalm (1756, 1757, 1758), PAC, MG18, K8, vol. 1.

2 *Ibid.* (May, June, July 1759); Stacey, *Quebec, 1759*, pp. 42, 43.

3 Stacey, *Quebec, 1759*, pp. 138-55.

4 Journal de campagne de Lévis au Canada (September 1759 – September 1760), PAC, MG18, K8, vol. 12.

Uniform

1 Collection des uniformes des troupes du roi, infanterie française et étrangère, 1757, BMA, ms. A1 J12; Briquet, *Code militaire*, vol. 4, pp. 317-27.

2 Rousselot, *L'armée française*, plate 19; Boudriot, "Le port d'Antibes peint par Joseph Vernet en 1756," *Neptunia* (1973), no. 111, pp. 8-20.

3 Musée de l'armée, Château de l'Empéri, Salon-de-Provence, France. See the 1756 drum of the regiment.

LE RÉGIMENT DE LA SARRE

History

1 Journal du marquis de Montcalm (1756 – August 1759), PAC, MG18, K8, vol. 1.

2 Journal de campagne de Lévis au Canada (September 1759 – September 1760), PAC, MG18, K8, vol. 12; O'Callaghan, *Documents relative*, vol. 10, pp. 1014-16, 1075-89, 1106-27.

Uniform

1 Collection des uniformes des troupes du roi, infanterie française et étrangère, 1757, BMA, ms. A1 J12.

2 AC, C11A, vol. 100, fol. 268.

3 Margerand, *Armement et équipement*, pp. 76-79.

LE RÉGIMENT DE BERRY

History

1 AG, A1, 3457, no. 100 *bis.*

2 Journal du marquis de Montcalm (9-27 September 1757), PAC, MG18, K8, vol. 1.

3 *Ibid.* (30 June – 9 July 1758); Hamilton, *Adventure in the Wilderness,* pp. 229-34.

4 O'Callaghan, *Documents Relative,* vol. 10, pp. 1054-55.

5 Journal de campagne de Lévis au Canada (1760); PAC, MG18, K8, vol. 12; Webster, *The Journal of Jeffrey Amherst,* p. 248.

Uniform

1 Collection des uniformes des troupes du roi, infanterie française et étrangère, 1757, BMA, ms. A1 J12.

2 Hamilton, *Adventure in the Wilderness,* p. 87, 92.

3 *État général des troupes françoises, passim.* This work describes the colours; Collection des drapeaux de l'infanterie française, 1741-1776, BMA, ms. A1 J19. This work is the official pattern book. Time has altered some of the hues illustrated; therefore, this work should be used with the contemporary 1753 descriptions in *État général des troupes françoises,* above.

THE 60TH (ROYAL AMERICAN) REGIMENT OF FOOT

History

1 Chichester and Burgess-Short, *The Records and Badges,* p. 666.

2 Pargellis, *Military Affairs,* p. 292. Includes a reproduction of a letter, Loudoun to Cumberland, 5 January 1757.

3 Instructions, Loudoun to the Commanding Officers of the 62nd or Royal American Regiment, 28 December 1756, quoted in Pargellis, *Lord Loudoun in North America,* pp. 299-300.

4 *A Brief History of the King's,* p. 5.

5 Chichester and Burgess-Short, *The Records and Badges,* p. 668.

6 Stewart, *The Service of British Regiments,* pp. 258-59.

Uniform

1 Butler, *The Annals of the King's,* vol. 6, pp. 1-2.

2 Haswell Miller and Dawnay, *Military Drawings,* vol. 1, pp. 55-72; *ibid.,* vol. 2, pp. 15-17. Reproductions and descriptions of Morier's paintings of grenadiers of British regiments of 1751; General Orders 1717-1764 (May 1755), War Office Library, London.

3 Anderson *et al., The Military Arms of Canada,* pp. 11-13.

4 Wallace, *A Regimental Chronicle,* p. 44.

5 Knox, *A Historical Journal,* vol. 1, p. 352. Major-General Wolfe's order (May 1759) for the dress of the light infantry is quoted.

6 *A Brief History of the King's,* p. 9.

THE 78TH (HIGHLAND) REGIMENT OF FOOT (FRASER'S HIGHLANDERS)

History

1 Roy, Lieutenant-General Simon Fraser, National Library of Scotland, Ms-Acc. 406A, pp. 40-43.

2 *Ibid.,* p. 84.

Uniform

1 *A List of His Majesty's,* p. 27

2 Stewart, *Sketches of the Character,* vol. 2, p. 68.

3 *Ibid.,* p. 66.

4 Hesketh, *Tartans,* p. 70.

5 W. Thorburn, Scottish United Services Museum, to Commander Ian Hamilton, R.N., January and February 1964.

6 Haswell Miller and Dawnay, *Military Drawings,* vol. 1, plate 70. See Morier's painting of a grenadier of the 42nd Highland Regiment of Foot, 1751.

7 Lawson, *A History of the Uniforms,* vol. 2, p. 46.

THE LOUISBOURG GRENADIERS

History

1 Lawson, *History of the Uniforms,* vol. 1, p. 28. Quotes order (19 May 1677).

2 Fortescue, *History of the British Army,* vol. 1, p. 327.

3 Rogers, *Weapons of the British Soldier,* p. 80.

4 Fortescue, *History of the British Army,* vol. 2, p. 367.

5 Stacey, *Québec, 1759,* pp. 184-91. Reproduction of Wolfe's dispatch to Pitt. Récher, *Journal du siège de Québec,* p. 27.

6 *A Brief History of the King's,* p. 5.

7 Thompson, *A Short Authentic Account,* pp. 28-36.

8 Stacey, *Québec, 1759,* pp. 160-61.

Uniform

1 Haswell Miller and Dawnay, *Military Drawings,* vol. 1, plates 55-72; *ibid.,* vol. 2, pp. 15-17. See Morier's paintings of grenadiers of the British Army, 1751. The text on the dress of the Louisbourg Grenadiers is based on this collection of contemporary information. Undoubtedly, modifications of dress and equipment were made as the campaign progressed.

2 Rogers, *Weapons of the British Soldier,* p. 82.

THE 84TH REGIMENT OF FOOT (ROYAL HIGHLAND EMIGRANTS)

History

1 Stanley, *Canada Invaded, 1775-1776*, p. 31.

2 British H.Q. Papers in America, vol. 7, 15(1) 85, PAC (microfilm M343). Gage to Maclean, 12 June 1775.

3 Cohen, *Canada Preserved*, p. 23

4 *Ibid.*, p. 101.

5 British H.Q. Papers in America, vol. 16, no. 1874, 113, PAC (microfilm M348). Germain to Clinton, 1 April 1779.

6 Atkinson, "British Forces in North America 1775-1781," *Journal of the Society for Army Historical Research* (1937), vol. 16, no. 61, pp. 3-23.

Uniform

1 British H.Q. Papers in America, vol. 7, 15(1), 85, PAC (microfilm M343). Gage to Maclean, 12 June 1775.

2 Stanley, *Canada Invaded, 1775-1776*, plate 21. Reproduction of a miniature of Colonel Maclean; *Military Collector and Historian* (1961), vol. 13, no. 3, p. 93. Reproduction of a miniature of Major John Small. These miniatures illustrate the development of the Highland bonnet from the flat beret style to the more rigid Kilmarnock pattern.

3 Hearman and Holst, "The Frederick von German Drawings," *Military Collector and Historian*, vol. 16 (1964), no. 1, p. 1.

4 McBarron and Todd, "British 84th Regiment of Foot (Royal Highland Emigrants), 1775-1783," *Military Collector and Historian*, vol. 11 (1959), no. 4, p. 109, plate 165. Reproduction of the account of Major John Small in "A Regimental Ledger, Royal Highland Emigrants, 1775-1783."

5 Order Book, Royal Highland Emigrants (10 August 1777), PAC, MG23, K1, vol. 21.

6 Haarman and Holst, "The Frederick von German Drawings," *Military Collector and Historian*, vol. 16 (1964), no. 1, pp. 1-9.

7 McBarron and Todd, "British 84th Regiment of Foot (Royal Highland Emigrants), 1775-1783," *Military Collector and Historian*, vol. 11 (1959), no. 4, p. 109.

8 PRO, WO 1/2, pt. 2, p. 334. "Royal Highland Emigrants," Maclean to Barrington, 11 May 1776.

9 Lindsay, "Narrative of the Invasion," *The Canadian Review and Magazine* (1826), no. 5, p. 94; Order Book, Royal Highland Emigrants (5 May 1776), PAC.

10 Order Book, Royal Highland Emigrants (17 December 1775), PAC.

11 Order Book, Royal Highland Emigrants (14 May 1781 and 20 May 1782), PAC.

12 Strachan, *British Military Uniforms 1768-96*, p. 273; PRO, WO 28/3, p. 185. Maclean to Haldimand, 19 October 1781.

13 Rogers, *Weapons of the British Soldier*, p. 104.

THE ROYAL NEWFOUNDLAND REGIMENT OF FENCIBLE INFANTRY

History

1 Webber, *Skinner's Fencibles*, p. 68. Windham to Skinner, 25 April 1795.

2 PRO, WO 40/18. "Memorial," Skerrett to War Minister, 16 June 1806.

3 Hunter to Brock, 25 September 1807, PAC, RG8, C1009, p. 55.

4 PAC, RG8, C1218, p. 207; C1168; C1707, p. 14.

5 PAC, RG8, C730, p. 147.

6 Nicholson, *The Fighting Newfoundlander*, p. 85.

Uniform

1 PRO, WO 40/18. "Memorial," Skerrett to War Minister, 16 June 1806.

2 Cattley, "The British Infantry Shako," *Journal of the Society for Army Historical Research*, vol. 15 (1936), no. 60, pp. 188-91.

3 Smith, *Costumes of the Army, passim*.

THE 104TH (NEW BRUNSWICK) REGIMENT OF FOOT

History

1 Howe, "The King's New Brunswick Regiment, 1793-1802," *Collection of New Brunswick Historical Society*, vol. 1 (1894), pp. 13-62.

2 Stanley, "The New Brunswick Fencibles," *Canadian Defence Quarterly*, vol. 16 (1935), no. 1, p. 39.

3 Letter of service, War Office to Brigadier-General Hunter, 1 August 1803, PAC, RG8, C718, p. 20.

4 *Ibid.*, p. 185. Calvert to Craig, 20 September 1810.

5 Le Couteur, "A Winter March in Canada in 1813," *United States Journal* (1831), pt. 3, pp. 177-87.

6 Squires, *The 104th Regiment of Foot, passim*.

Uniform

1 Letter of service, War Office to Brigadier-General Hunter, 1 August 1803, PAC, RG8, C718, p. 20.

2 Cattley, "The British Infantry Shako," *Journal of the Society*, vol. 15 (1936), no. 60, p. 188-208.

3 *Ibid.*

4 Squires, *The 104th Regiment of Foot*, p. 68. Photograph of actual buttons of the regiment.

5 Smith, *Costumes of the Army*. Schematic charts of uniforms.

6 Squires, *The 104th Regiment of Foot*, p. 66.

7 Smith, *Costumes of the Army*. Plate of a pioneer of infantry of the line.

8 See the belt-plate of the regiment. New Brunswick Museum, Saint John.

THE PROVINCIAL CORPS OF LIGHT INFANTRY (CANADIAN VOLTIGEURS)

History

1 Conditions for raising (15 April 1812), Prevost, PAC, RG8, C1218, p. 210.

2 Johnson to de Monviel, 2 July 1813, PAC, RG8, C703, p. 106. General Order, HQ Kingston, 13 August 1813, C1171, p. 6.

3 Hitsman, *The Incredible War of 1812*, p. 133.

4 Salaberry to de Watteville, 26 October 1813, PAC, RG8, C680, p. 331.

5 *Québec Gazette*, 4 November 1813.

6 Prevost to Torrens, 15 March 1814, PAC, RG8, C1227, p. 29.

7 General Order, Quebec, 1 March 1815, PAC, RG8, C1172, p. 128A.

Uniform

1 PAC, RG8, C796, pp. 65-66.

2 PAC, RG8, C796, pp. 134, 187; RG8, C797, p. 31; RG8, C1120, pp. 92, 102, 240.

3 PAC, MG11, Q130, pt. 1, p. 39.

4 Collection Baby, Université de Montréal. See the black and white portrait of Capitain Viger, Canadian Voltigeurs, wearing a visored fur cap.

5 Portraits of Lieutenant-Colonel de Salaberry and Lieutenant Globensky in the uniform of the Canadian Voltigeurs, Château de Ramezay Museum, Montreal.

6 See the colour reproduction of the portrait of John Hebden, Adjutant of the Canadian Voltigeurs, *c.* 1814, PAC.

THE GLENGARRY LIGHT INFANTRY FENCIBLE REGIMENT

History

1 Prevost to Liverpool, 4 March 1812, PAC, MG11, Q117-1, p. 85.

2 Stewart, *Sketches of the Character*, vol. 2, pp. 426-27.

3 Returns of the Glengarry Light Infantry, 12 November 1812, PAC, RG8, C1707, pp. 47-48.

4 Macdonell to Harvey, 25 February 1813, PAC, RG8, C678, p. 100.

5 Sheaffe to Prevost, 5 May 1813, PAC, RG8, C1219, pp. 40-49.

6 "Commendation for behaviour," 30 May 1813, PAC, RG8, C1170, p. 218.

7 Vincent to Prevost, 6 June 1813, PAC, RG8, C1219, p. 60.

8 "How to Fight Brother Jonathan," *The Museum of Foreign Literature, Science and Art*, vol. 42 (May-August 1841), pp. 210-14.

9 Drummond to Prevost, 7 May 1814, PAC, RG8, C1219, pp. 222-26.

10 Drummond to Prevost, 28 June 1814, PAC, RG8, C683, p. 307.

11 Drummond to Prevost, 27 July 1814, PAC, RG8, C684, p. 243.

12 Drummond to Prevost, 19 September 1814, PAC, RG8, C1219, pp. 290-91; District General Order, Niagara Falls, 20 October 1814, PAC, RG8, C686, p. 73.

13 Drummond to Prevost, 24 November 1814, PAC, RG8, C686, p. 195; General Order, Quebec, 19 May 1815, PAC, RG8, C1203 1/2, p. 178.

14 Boss, *The Stormont, Dundas*, p. 40.

Uniform

1 PAC, RG8, C1218, pp. 92-100.

2 Hitsman, *The Incredible War of 1812*, p. 20.

3 *Ibid.*, pp. 34-35.

4 Lieutenant-General George Prevost to Field-Marshal, HRH The Duke of York, 17 July 1812, PAC, RG8, C1218, p. 319.

5 Summer, "Uniforms of the Rifle Brigade, circa 1804," *Journal of the Society for Army Historical Research*, vol. 20 (Spring 1941), p. 38.

6 *Ibid.*, p. 41.

7 See original cap badge recovered at Coteau-du-Lac, Parks Canada, Ottawa.

8 PAC, MG11, Q118, p. 305. There is no mention of rifles among the arms sent from England.

9 See the reproduction of the portrait of Lieutenant-Colonel "Red George" Macdonell of the Glengarry Light Infantry, PAC. The description of the officer's jacket is based on this portrait.

10 Stewart, "Glengarry Light Infantry Regiment 1812-1816," *Military Collector and Historian*, vol. 16 (1964), no. 2, pp. 53-56.

11 PAC, RG9, 1B1, vol. 73, n.p.

THE CHEBUCTO GREYS

History

1 Edwards, "The Militia of Nova Scotia, 1749-1867," *Collections of the Nova Scotia Historical Society*, vol. 17 (1913), pp. 63-109.

2 Grierson, *Records of the Scottish*, p. 6.

3 Egan, *History of the Halifax*, p. 98.

4 *Ibid.*, p. 5.

Uniform

1 Grierson, *Records of the Scottish*, p. 9.

2 Robson, *The Uniform of the London Scottish*, p. 7.

3 Egan, *History of the Halifax*, p. 98.

4 See specimen of the Chebucto Grey's shako, Army Museum, The Citadel, Halifax.

5 Edwards, "The Militia of Nova Scotia, 1749-1867," *Collections of the Nova Scotia Historical Society*, vol. 17 (1913), p. 107. Photograph of a private of the Chebucto Greys in full dress.

6 Egan, *History of the Halifax*, p. ii. Photograph of a private of the Chebucto Greys in full dress.

7 Edwards, "The Militia of Nova Scotia, 1749-1867," *Collections of the Nova Scotia Historical Society*, vol. 17 (1913), p. 107. Photograph of a private of the Chebucto Greys in undress.

8 Egan, *History of the Halifax*, p. 24.

9 Edwards, "The Militia of Nova Scotia, 1749-1867," *Collections of the Nova Scotia Historical Society*, vol. 17 (1913), p. 96.

10 *Ibid.*, p. 96. Photograph of officers of the Halifax Volunteer Battalion, *c.* 1868.

THE ROYAL REGIMENT OF CANADA

History

1 Goodspeed, *Battle Royal*, p. 7.

2 Chambers, *History of the Royal Grenadiers*, p. 16.

3 Goodspeed, *Battle Royal*, p. 25.

4 *Ibid.*, p. 313.

5 Dornbusch, *The Canadian Army, 1855-1965*, p. 109.

Uniform

1 Circular letter, Adjutant-General's Office, Quebec, 19 May 1860.

2 Champion, *History of the 10th Royals*, p. 36.

3 Chambers, *History of the Royal Grenadiers*. See photograph, p. 29.

4 See specimen of Canadian Militia tunic, *c.* 1860, Royal Canadian Mounted Police Museum, Regina.

5 Canada, DMD, *Regulations Relating to the Issue*, p. 11.

6 Chambers, *History of the Royal Grenadiers*, p. 31. Photograph of Lieutenant-Colonel Brunel in undress.

7 *Ibid.*, p. 28.

8 *Ibid.*, p. 118.

9 *Ibid.*, p. 88.

TORONTO ENGINEER COMPANY

History

1 MGO, 14 January 1876.

2 Kerry and McDill, *The History of the Corps*, p. 30.

3 MR 1878, app. 1, p. 15.

4 MR 1879, app. 1, p. 234. Report of Major G.R. Walker, R.E.

5 MR 1878, p. xxx. Report of the General Officer Commanding the Militia.

6 Canada, DND, *The Regiments and Corps*, p. 16.

Uniform

1 MR 1878, p. 323. Report of the Director of Stores.

2 Contemporary photograph of sappers, Royal Engineers. David Ross Collection, Saint John; Christopher-Latham, *Infantry Uniforms*, plate 17.

3 Print of dress and equipment of Royal Engineers, *c.* 1870, PAC, photo C-17282.

4 *Ibid.*

5 MR 1879, p. 234.

6 MGO, no. 2, 30 July 1880.

7 MR 1878, p. 15.

8 MR 1880, p. 397.

9 Contemporary photograph of Lieutenant-Colonel Scoble in full dress, *c.* 1876. David Ross Collection.

10 *Canada Gazette*, 4 March 1876. Militia Dress Regulations, 1876.

11 *Ibid.*

THE QUEEN'S OWN RIFLES OF CANADA

History

1 MGO, 17 November 1859.

2 MGO, 26 April 1860.

3 MGO, 21 November 1862.

4 MGO, 18 March 1863.

5 Chambers, *The Queen's Own Rifles*, p. 59.

6 MGO, 13 January 1882.

7 Chambers, *The Queen's Own Rifles*, p. 107.

8 Goodspeed, *Battle Royal*, pp. 72-73.

9 Canada, DND, *The Regiments and Corps*, p. 121.

Uniform

1 Chambers, *The Queen's Own Rifles*, p. 43. Quotes regimental orders, 2nd Battalion Volunteer Rifles, 14 May 1860.

2 Fraser, *The 48th Highlanders*, p. 25; contemporary photograph, J.L. Summers Collection; "Commanding Officer's Reports," 13 October 1862, PAC, RG9, 1C8, vol. 4, p. 127. This circular deals with the clothing and equipment of Volunteers, Upper Canada.

3 Fraser, *The 48th Highlanders*, p. 25.

4 Chambers, *The Queen's Own Rifles*, p. 49.

5 Chambers, *The Queen's Own Rifles*, p. 48. Regimental Orders, 2nd Battalion Volunteer Militia, 18 December 1862.

6 Chambers, *The Queen's Own Rifles*, p. 70.

7 *Ibid.*, p. 83.

8 Contemporary Photograph. J.L. Summers Collection.

9 "Surrender of Poundmaker," painting by Captain Rutherford, PAC.

10 Chambers, *The Queen's Own Rifles*, p. 108; contemporary photograph. J.L. Summers Collection.

11 Canada, DMD, "Report upon the Suppression," app. 3, p. 65.

THE NORTH WEST MOUNTED POLICE

History

1 Chambers, *The Royal North-West*, p. 16.

2 Canada, Royal North-West Mounted Police, *Report of the Commissioner, 1874*, p. 32.

3 Chambers, *The Royal North-West*, p. 140.

Uniform

1 Chambers, *The Royal North-West*, p. 18.

2 Canada, Royal North-West Mounted Police, *Report of the Commissioner, 1874*, p. 26.

3 Chambers, *The Royal North-West*, p. 151.

4 "Tailor's Bill," Personal correspondence, Superintendent J.M. Walsh, 1876. RCMP Museum, Regina.

5 Photograph of superintendent William Winder. Glenbow-Alberta Institute, Calgary.

6 Photographs of 1876-pattern officer's undress jacket. Glenbow-Alberta Institute, Calgary.

7 Specimens of officer's undress pouch belt, binocular case, and sword slings. RCMP Museum, Regina.

8 Specimen of constable's full-dress tunic. RCMP Museum, Regina; Phillips and Kirby, *Small Arms*, p. 13. Photograph of constable in full dress, 1880.

9 Canada, Royal North-West Mounted Police, *Report of the Commissioner, 1879*, p. 5.

10 *Ibid.*

11 Phillips and Kirby, *Small Arms*, pp. 5-13, 24-25.

12 Canada, Royal North-West Mounted Police, *Report of the Commissioner, 1880*, p. 12.

THE BLACK WATCH (ROYAL HIGHLAND REGIMENT) OF CANADA

History

1 MGO, 31 January 1862.

2 MGO, 7 November 1862.

3 MGO, 9 October 1863.

4 MGO, 2 June 1871.

5 Hutchinson, *Canada's Black Watch*, p. 17.

6 MGO, 12 April 1872.

7 MGO, 14 January 1876.

8 MGO, 27 February 1880.

9 MGO, 29 February 1884.

10 GO, 71, May 1904.

11 GO, 147, October 1906.

12 Hutchinson, *Canada's Black Watch*, p. 66.

13 GO, 1 July 1935.

14 Hutchinson, *Canada's Black Watch*, p. 244.

15 Canada, DND, *The Regiments and Corps*, p. 124.

16 Reid, *The Scottish Traditions*, p. 154.

Uniform

1 Chambers, *The 5th Regiment*, p. 30.

2 *Ibid.*, p. 36.

3 Hutchinson, *Canada's Black Watch*, p. 24: Photograph *c.* 1866.

4 *Ibid.*, p. 10.

5 *Ibid.*, facing p. 25: photograph *c.* 1876.

6 *Ibid.*, facing p. 40: photograph *c.* 1876.

7 Chambers, *The 5th Regiment*, p. 67.

8 *Ibid.*, p. 68.

9 GO, 26 May 1895.

10 Contemporary photograph. Benson-Freeman Papers, Army Museums, Ogilby Trust, London.

11 GO, 18, February 1899.

12 Hutchinson, *Canada's Black Watch*, p. 41: photograph *c.* 1891.

THE ROYAL CANADIAN DRAGOONS

History

1 Canada, Parliament, *Acts of the Parliament of the Dominion of Canada, 1883*, p. 67.

2 MR 1884, p. 173.

3 MGO, 15 July 1897.

4 *Ibid.*, 24 May 1892.

5 *Ibid.*, 11 August 1893.

6 Canada, DMD, *Supplementary Report, Organization, Equipment, Dispatch and Service of the Canadian Contingent During the War in South Africa, 1899-1900*, p. 91.

7 *Ibid.*, p. 99.

8 Fetherstonhaugh, *A Short History*, p. 20.

9 Nicholson, *Canadian Expeditionary Force*, p. 163, n.

Uniform

1 Contemporary photograph of sergeants and senior NCOs. CFB Military Museum, Gagetown.

2 MGO, 3 September 1880.

3 Canada DMD, *Regulations and Orders*, p. 46.

4 Contemporary photograph, Cavalry School Corps. CFB Military Museum, Gagetown.

5 MR 1885, p. xxi. Report of the General Officer Commanding the Canadian Militia, 30 December 1885.

6 MR 1883, p. 3. Report of the General Officer Commanding the Militia, 1 December 1883.

7 Photograph, sergeants and senior NCOs. CFB Military Museum, Gagetown.

8 MR 1884, p. 174. Annual report of A Troop, Cavalry School Corps and School of Cavalry, 1 December 1884.

9 *Navy and Army Illustrated*, vol. 6, no. 61, p. 48. Contemporary photograph.

10 MGO, 11 August 1893.

11 *Navy and Army Illustrated*, vol. 6, no. 61, p. 48; no. 63, p. 96; no. 73, pp. 334-35. Contemporary photographs.

12 Captain A. Benoit to manufacturer, with special instructions regarding specifications for serge frock for Royal Canadian Dragoons, 2 June 1896. PAC, RG9, II, D1, vol 6A, p. 374.

13 Worthington, *The Spur and the Sprocket*, p. 12.

14 *Navy and Army Illustrated*, vol. 6, no. 61, p. 48. Contemporary photograph. At this time it was the practice in some British Army regiments of dragoons to arm the front rank with lances.

15 Fetherstonhaugh, *A Short History*, p. 14.

16 GO, 50, April 1908.

17 Photograph, musical ride in full dress, 1913. CFB Military Museum, Gagetown.

8TH CANADIAN HUSSARS (PRINCESS LOUISE'S)

History

1 Crook and Marteinson, *A Pictorial History*, p. 8. Excerpts from the Militia Act of 1825, Province of New Brunswick.

2 *Ibid.*, p. 12. Original Order Book of the Adjutant General of the Province of New Brunswick; MGO, 4 April 1848.

3 How, *The 8th Hussars*, pp. 23-24.

4 MGO, 30 April 1869.

5 *MR 1873*. Report of the Inspecting Officer.

6 How, *The 8th Hussars*, pp. 36-38.

7 MGO, 18 July 1884.

8 Crook and Marteinson, *A Pictorial History*, p. 35. According to contemporary newspaper reports, the offer and rejection were repeated for the Sudan campaign of 1896.

9 How, *The 8th Hussars*, pp. 96-99.

10 Crook and Marteinson, *A Pictorial History*, p. 334. Photograph of march past, 18 June 1973.

Uniform

1 How, *The 8th Hussars*, p. 14.

2 *Ibid.*, p. 21.

3 *MR 1870*, pp. 84-87.

4 Crook and Marteinson, *A Pictorial History*, p. 31. Engraving showing members of the vice-regal escort, 8th Regiment of Cavalry, wearing busbies, August 1879.

5 How, *The 8th Hussars*, p. 29. Inspection report of Lieutenant-Colonel Maunsell.

6 How, *The 8th Hussars*, p. 34.

7 Crook and Marteinson, *A Pictorial History*, pp. 36-37: Photographs, late 1880s.

8 *Ibid.*, p. 54. Photograph, officer in full dress.

9 Lieutenant-Colonel Beveridge to Rear-Admiral Dillon, 5 July 1972. Canadian War Museum, Ottawa.

10 Crook and Marteinson, *A Pictorial History*, pp. 50-54. Photographs of officers in undress.

11 Letter from Captain A. Benoit, 2 June 1896, giving specifications for new pattern serge jackets. PAC, RG9, II, D1, vol. 6A, p. 374.

12 Crook and Marteinson, *A Pictorial History*, p. 60. Photograph of NCOs, 1903.

13 *Ibid.*, p. 61. Photograph of mounted squadron, 1910.

14 How, *8th Hussars*, p. 67.

THE GOVERNOR GENERAL'S HORSE GUARDS

History

1 Denison, *Historical Records*, p. 2.

2 PAC, RG9, 1B1, vol. 76. Adjutant-General's Office, Upper Canada, record of issue of swords and pistols to 1st West York Militia Cavalry Troop, 5 May 1831.

3 Denison, *Historical Records*, p. 6.

4 *Ibid.*, p. 13.

5 *Ibid.*, p. 17; MGO, 12 March 1853.

6 Denison, *Historical Records*, p. 18.

7 *Ibid.*, p. 22.

8 MGO, 27 April 1866.

9 Denison, *Soldiering in Canada*, p. 98.

10 Chambers, *The Governor General's*, p. 81.

11 Canada, DND, *The Regiments and Corps*, p. 52.

12 *Ibid.*

13 *Ibid.*

Uniform

1 Denison, *Historical Records*, p. 3.

2 *Ibid.*, p. 4.

3 *Ibid.*, p. 12.

4 *Ibid.*, p. 11.

5 "Commanding Officer's Report," on circular, 13 October 1862, PAC, RG9, 1C8, vol. 4, concerning clothing and equipment of volunteers, Upper Canada. It is reported that the 1st York Troop of Cavalry wore "the old bell-crown shako in use about thirty years ago, with silver-plate trimming and white horsehair plume."

6 Denison, *Historical Records*, p. 18.

7 "Commanding Officer's Report," on circular, 13 October 1862, PAC, RG9, 1C8, vol. 4. (See note 5 above.)

8 Chambers, *The Governor General's*, pp. 78-79. Regimental Standing Orders, 1898; Canada, DMD, *Dress Regulations*, 4 March 1876.

9 Chambers, *The Governor General's*, pp. 118-19. Contemporary photographs.

10 *Ibid.*, p. 79.

11 Barnes, *Military Uniforms*, p. 200.

12 Chambers, *The Governor General's*, pp. 107, 110. Contemporary photographs.

3RD "MONTREAL" FIELD BATTERY

History

1 AC, C11A, vol. 50, fol. 168.

2 Baxter, *Historical Records*, p. 4.

3 Chambers, *The Origin and Services*, p. 17.

4 Irving, *Officers of the British Forces*, pp. 39, 40, 75, 76, 113.

5 "The Regulations to which every officer is bound to subscribe on joining the Quebec Artillery," Quebec, November 1830, PAC, MG24, G26; Chambers, *Origin and Services*, pp. 17-18.

6 Nicholson, *The Gunners of Canada*, p. 76.

7 Canada (Province), Laws, Statutes, etc., "An Act to regulate the Militia of this Province (Militia Act 1855)," *Statutes of the Provinces of Canada, 1855*, pt. 2, p. 275.

8 Chambers, *The Origin and Services*, p. 27.

9 *Ibid.*, p. 28.

10 *Ibid.*

11 *Navy and Army Illustrated*, vol. 6, no. 67, p. 190.

12 Chambers, *The Origin and Services*, p. 40.

13 *Ibid.*, p. 56.

14 Chown, *The 9-Pdr Muzzle Loading Rifle*, p. 32.

15 Nicholson, *The Gunners of Canada*, vol. 1, p. 131.

16 Chambers, *The Origin and Services*, p. 73.

17 Nicholson, *The Gunners of Canada*, vol. 1, pp. 165-67.

18 *Ibid.*, pp. 199, 204.

19 *Ibid.*, vol. 2, p. 648.

Uniform

1 Chambers, *The Origin and Services*, p. 32. Photograph of Stevenson and Hogan.

2 *Ibid.*, p. 18. Photograph of Major Coffin.

3 *Illustrated London News*, Supplement, 10 March 1860. Illustration of Volunteer Forces of Montreal, 1860, based on a photograph by Notman; Chambers, *The Origin and Services*, p. 27.

4 "Commanding Officer's Report," on circular, 13 October 1867, PAC, RG9, 1C8, vol. 3, concerning clothing and equipment of volunteers.

5 Chambers, *The Origin and Services*, p. 23. Photograph of Major Hogan.

6 *Ibid.*, p. 51.

7 *Ibid.*, p. 70. Photograph of officers of the battery.

8 MGO, 1 December 1893.

9 Chambers, *The Origin and Services*, p. 72.

10 *Navy and Army Illustrated*, vol. 6, no. 67, p. 192. Photograph of a sergeant-major and trumpeter.

THE ROYAL CANADIAN REGIMENT

History

1 Stanley, *Canada's Soldiers*, p. 248.

2 MGO, 21 December 1883.

3 *MR 1884*, pp. 183-86. Report of the commandants of the School of Infantry.

4 Fetherstonhaugh, *The Royal Canadian Regiment*, p. 21.

5 Middleton, *Suppression of the Rebellion*, p. 44.

6 Fetherstonhaugh, *The Royal Canadian Regiment*, p. 43.

7 MGO, 15 July 1887.

8 *MR 1892*, p. 2. Report of the General Officer Commanding the Militia.

9 MGO, 11 August 1893.

10 Fetherstonhaugh, *The Royal Canadian Regiment*, p. 51.

11 *MR 1898*, p. 37.

12 Fetherstonhaugh, *The Royal Canadian Regiment*, p. 78.

13 Canada, DND, *The Regiments and Corps*, p. 113.

14 *Ibid.*

15 Fetherstonhaugh, *The Royal Canadian Regiment*, p. 138.

Uniform

1 Canada, DMD, *Regulations and Orders, 1883*, p. 75.

2 See specimen tunic, trousers, and forage cap of the period. The Royal Canadian Regiment Museum, London, Ontario.

3 Canada, DMD, *Regulations and Orders, 1879*. Dress Regulations.

4 MGO, 16 July 1880.

5 MGO, 12 December 1884.

6 *MR 1884*, pp. 183-86. Report of the Commandants of the School of Infantry.

7 Contemporary photograph. PAC, Peter Collection. Neg. C-18111.

8 Contemporary photograph. J.L. Summers Collection.

9 Contemporary photograph. The Royal Canadian Regiment Museum, London, Ontario.

10 Robertson, *Relentless Verity*, p. 56. Photograph.

11 Fetherstonhaugh, *The Royal Canadian Regiment*, p. 67.

12 Contemporary photograph. J.L. Summers Collection.

13 Disher, "The Long March of the Yukon Field Force," *The Beaver* (Fall 1962), p. 4.

LORD STRATHCONA'S HORSE (ROYAL CANADIANS)

History

1 Regimental Order no. 2, 3 November 1900.

2 R. Cunniffe, The History of the Strathcona Horse, 1963, p. 7. Unpublished typescript based on regimental documents. Lord Strathcona's Horse (Royal Canadians) Museum, Calgary.

3 Militia Council, *Annual Report, 1910.*

4 Canada, DND, *The Regiments and Corps*, p. 46.

5 *Ibid.*

6 "Regimental Establishments of the Active Militia, 1900-1901," GO, June 1900. Squadrons were designated by letter in regimental establishments, 1901-1902. See GO, July 1901.

7 GO, 153, October 1903.

Uniform

1 *MR 1900*, pp. 13-18. Appendix B to Supplementary Report on Canadian Contingents in South Africa.

2 GO, 26 February 1900.

3 Photograph of private in blue serge. Lord Strathcona's Horse (Royal Canadians) Museum, Calgary.

4 *MR 1900*, p. 18. Supplementary Report on Canadian Contingents in South Africa.

5 GO, 26, February 1900.

6 Photograph of Strathconas in service dress. Lord Strathcona's Horse (Royal Canadians) Museum, Calgary.

7 Regimental Order, no. 488, 2 May 1900.

8 *Ibid.*, no. 262, 5 April 1900.

9 Report of Lieutenant-Colonel F.L. Lessard, Royal Canadian Dragoons, to the Adjutant General, 2 January 1901, reproduced in *The Springbok* (Winter 1968), p. 53.

10 *MR 1900*, p. 112. Supplementary Report on Canadian Contingents in South Africa.

11 Photograph of a mounted private. Lord Strathcona's Horse (Royal Canadians) Museum, Calgary.

12 Regimental Order, no. 620, 22 May 1900.

13 Marquis, *Canada's Sons*, p. 45. Photograph of Lieutenant-Colonel S.B. Steele.

14 GO, 47, April 1906.

15 Canada, DMD, *Dress Regulations*, 1907, p. 24.

16 GO, 20, February 1904.

17 *Ibid.*, 2, January 1912.

18 McAvity, *Strathcona's 1939-'45*, p. 27.

THE CORPS OF GUIDES

History

1 GO, 61, April 1903.

2 Canada, DMD, *Dress Regulations*, 1907, p. 48.

3 GO, 91, April 1905.

4 Canada, DMD, *Report, 1903*, p. 38.

5 Canada, DMD, *Report, 1904*, p. 83.

6 GO, 23, February 1912, amended by 28, February 1913.

7 Hahn, *The Intelligence Service*, p. xiii.

Uniform

1 GO, 162, December 1906.

2 GO, 60, May 1904.

3 GO, 3, January 1910.

4 Canada, DMD, *Dress Regulations*, 1907, p. 36; specimen, officer's tunic, Corps of Guides. Glenbow-Alberta Institute, Calgary.

5 GO, 3, January 1910.

6 Canada, DMD, *Dress Regulations*, 1907, p. 36.

7 *Ibid.*, p. 18.

8 GO, 162, December 1906.

9 GO, 134, June 1908.

THE ROYAL CANADIAN ARMY SERVICE CORPS

History

1 Massé, *The Predecessors*, p. 115.

2 Middleton, *Suppression of the Rebellion*, p. 9.

3 GO, 141, November 1901.

4 Warren, *Wait for the Waggon*, p. 30.

5 Canada, DND, *The Regiments and Corps*, p. 21.

6 Canada, DMD, *Report, 1904*, p. 63. Report of the Quarter-Master General.

7 Warren, *Wait for the Waggon*, p. 38.

8 *Ibid.*, p. 46.

9 *Ibid.*, p. 115.

10 Canada, DND, *The Regiments and Corps*, p. 21.

11 Warren, *Wait for the Waggon*, pp. 182-83, illustration.

12 *Ibid.*, p. 359.

Uniform

1 Warren, *Wait for the Waggon*, p. xvii.

2 Canada, DMD, *Dress Regulations*, 1907, pp. 27-28.

3 Canada, DMD, *Dress Regulations*, 1932, pt. 16, p. 1.

4 Canada, DMD, *Dress Regulations*, 1907, p. 19.

5 Canada, DMD, *Dress Regulations*, 1907, p. 17; Photograph. J.L. Summers Collection.

6 Warren, *Wait for the Waggon*, pp. 182-83.

7 *Ibid.*

CANADIAN EXPEDITIONARY FORCE

History

1 Duguid, *Official History*, vol. 1, app. 10, pp. 10-11.

2 Nicholson, *The Canadian Expeditionary Force*, p. 124.

3 Stacey, *Military History for Canadian Students*, 1952, p. 33.

4 Swettenham, *To Seize the Victory*, p. viii. Preface of General A.G.L. McNaughton.

Uniform

1 GO, 73, May 1903.

2 Anderson, *et al.*, *The Military Arms of Canada*, p. 39.

3 Duguid, *Official History*, vol. 1, app. 106, p. 71.

4 Contemporary photographs. J.L. Summers Collection.

5 Corrigall, *History of the Twentieth*, p. 18.

6 MacPhail, *Official History*, p. 32.

7 Canada, Laws, Statutes, etc., *Sessional Papers, 1911*, paper no. 35, p. 117. Report of the Militia Council, 1910.

8 Duguid, *Official History*, vol. 1, app. 728, p. 365.

9 Corrigall, *History of the Twentieth*, p. 18.

10 Gould, *From B.C. to Baisieux*, p. 38.

11 Duguid, *Official History*, vol. 1, app. 111, p. 94. Letter, Major-General E.A.H. Alderson to Major General W.G. Gwatkin, 6 February 1916.

12 *Ibid.*, p. 97: Letter, General Sir Douglas Haig to Secretary, War Office, 21 June 1916.

13 Corrigall, *History of the Twentieth*, p. 42.

14 Personal correspondence with CEF Veterans; Photographs. J.L. Summers Collection.

15 Nicholson, *The Canadian Expeditionary Force*, p. 169.

16 *Ibid.*, app. G, facing p. 602.

PRINCESS PATRICIA'S CANADIAN LIGHT INFANTRY

History

1 Hodder-Williams, *Princess Patricia's*, vol. 1, p. 6.

2 *Ibid.*, p. 17.

3 *Ibid.*, p. 71.

4 Williams, *Princess Patricia's*, p. 33.

5 Regimental Executive Committee, *Princess Patricia's*, p. 16.

6 Wood, *Strange Battleground*, p. 183.

Uniform

1 Regimental Executive Committee, *Princess Patricia's*, p. 29.

2 Stevens, *Princess Patricia's*, p. 11.

3 Regimental Executive Committee, *Princess Patricia's*, p. 30.

4 Personal communication, J.L. Summers and Captain O. Gardner, ex-RSM.

5 Sketches of specimen garments, prepared by Captain V. Cole, Regimental Adjutant, 1970.

6 Specimen. PPCLI Regimental Museum, Currie Barracks, Calgary.

7 *Ibid.*

8 *Ibid.*

9 Photograph. Captain Gardner collection.

16TH CANADIAN LIGHT HORSE

History

1 Canada, DMD, *Report, 1903*, p. 36. Report of the General Officer Commanding.

2 GO, June 1900. "Regimental Establishments of the Active Militia, 1900-1901." Squadrons were designated by letter in regimental establishments, 1901-1902. See GO, July 1901.

3 Dornbusch, *The Canadian Army*, pp. 19-24.

4 GO, 154, July 1905; 127, August 1906.

5 GO, 186, October 1908.

6 Canada, DND, *The Regiments and Corps*, p. 210.

7 *Ibid.*

8 Canadian Cavalry Association, *Fifth Annual Report*, p. 16.

9 *Ibid.*, p. 11.

10 Canada, DMD, *Report, 1885*, p. xviii. Report of the General Officer Commanding.

11 Canada, DND, *The Regiments and Corps*, p. 209.

Uniform

1 Canada, DMD, *Report, 1903*, p. 42. Report of the General Officer Commanding.

2 Specimen uniform, 16th CLH and photograph. RCMP Museum, Regina.

3 Canada, DMD, *The Militia List, 1909*.

4 Photographs. J.L. Summers Collection.

5 Canadian Cavalry Association, *Proceedings, 1927*, pp. 62-64.

6 Photograph. J.L. Summers Collection.

7 Canadian Cavalry Association, *Proceedings, 1925*, p. 23.

THE ROYAL CANADIAN CORPS OF SIGNALS

History

1 Pratt, "Fifty Years of Canadian Military Communications," *Canadian Army Journal*, vol. 3, no. 3 (October 1953), p. 113.

2 Moir, *History of the Royal*, p. 1.

3 Canada, DMD, *Report, 1903*, pp. 38-39. Report of the General Officer Commanding.

4 GO, 96, June 1913.

5 GO, 98, June 1913.

6 Moir, *History of the Royal*, p. 46.

7 GO, 174, 15 June 1921.

8 Moir, *History of the Royal*, p. 280.

9 *Ibid.*, p. 284.

Uniform

1 Moir, *History of the Royal*, p. 5.

2 GO, 146, July 1908.

3 GO, 147, July 1908.

4 GO, 65, April 1912.

5 GO, 7, January 1914.

6 Moir, *History of the Royal*, p. 47.

7 Canada, DMD, *Dress Regulations, 1932*, pt. 10.

8 Moir, *History of the Royal*, p. 48.

9 Canada, DMD, *Regulations for the Clothing*, pt. 1, *Permanent Active Militia, 1935*.

10 Photograph. Canadian Forces Communications and Electronics Museum, Kingston, Ontario.

CANADIAN ARMY OVERSEAS 1939-1946

History

1 Stacey and Nicholson, *Official History of the Canadian Army*, Volumes 1, 2, and 3 have been used as a general reference for the history portion.

Uniform

1 Photographs of Canadian militiamen, 1939. J.L. Summers Collection.

2 Stacey, *Official History of the Canadian Army*, vol. 1, p. 55.

3 *Ibid.*

ROYAL 22e REGIMENT

History

1 Duguid, *Official History*, vol. 1, app. 711, p. 344.

2 *Ibid.*

3 Royal 22e Régiment, Historical Résumé. Typescript prepared for authors, 4 October 1976, La Citadelle, Quebec.

4 *Ibid.*

5 *Ibid.*

6 Canada, DND, *The Regiments and Corps*, p. 118.

7 GO, 92, 1 November 1927.

8 *The Royal Welch Fusiliers*, p. 17.

9 Royal 22e Régiment, Historical Résumé.

10 L. Turcotte, "The Royal 22e Régiment, 1914-1964," *Canadian Army Journal*, vol. 18, no. 2 (1964), p. 18.

Uniform

1 Photograph, *c.* 1927. J.L. Summers Collection.

2 GO, 193, 15 December 1928.

3 Colour photograph, *c.* 1965. J.L. Summers Collection.

4 Photograph, *c.* 1927. J.L. Summers Collection.

5 Photograph of regimental band, *c.* 1927. J.L. Summers Collection.

6 Canada Army, Royal 22e Régiment, *Standing Orders*, 1963.

THE ROYAL CANADIAN ORDNANCE CORPS

History

1 Baxter, "RCOC Diamond Jubilee," *Canadian Army Journal*, vol. 17, no. 1, p. 100.

2 Manuel, "Chart of Hereditary Descendancy, " *Canadian Army Journal*, vol. 18, no. 3, p. 112.

3 Canada, DMD, *Report, 1898*, p. 38. Report of the Major-General.

4 *Ibid.*, p. 39.

5 Canada, DMD, *Report, 1903*, p. 9. Report of the Deputy Minister.

6 GO, 194, December 1907.

7 Baxter, "RCOC Diamond Jubilee," *Canadian Army Journal*, vol. 17, no. 1, p. 101.

8 *Ibid.*

9 Canada, DND, *The Regiments and Corps*, p. 26.

10 Baxter, "RCOC Diamond Jubilee," *Canadian Army Journal*, vol. 17, no. 1, p. 103.

11 Canada, Army, The Royal Canadian Ordnance Corps, *Standing Orders*, 1965, p. 16.

12 Canada, DND, *The Regiments and Corps*, p. 28.

Uniform

1 Canada, DMD, *Dress Regulations, 1907*, pp. 29-30.

2 *Ibid.*, p. 17.

3 *Ibid.*, pp. 18-19.

4 Canada, DMD, *Dress Regulations, 1932*, pt. 17.

5 Canada, Army, The Royal Canadian Ordnance Corps, *Standing Orders*, 1965, p. 105.

6 Photograph. J.L. Summers Collection.

7 Canada, Army, The Royal Canadian Ordnance Corps, *Standing Orders*, 1965, p. 114.

8 Photograph. J.L. Summers Collection.

THE ROYAL CANADIAN HORSE ARTILLERY

History

1 MGO, 20 October 1871.

2 Canada, DND, *The Regiments and Corps*, p. 14.

3 Chambers, *The Royal Grenadiers*, p. 51.

4 Canada, DND, *The Regiments and Corps*, p. 15.

5 MGO, 18 August 1893.

6 Canada, DMD, *Report*, Sessional Papers, 35(a), 1901, p. 75.

7 Nicholson, *Gunners of Canada*, vol. 1, p. 160. Extract from *Report of the Dominion of Canada Artillery Association, 1899-1900*, p. 44.

8 MO, 16 (1), 20 February 1899.

9 GO, 200, September 1905.

10 Duguid, *Official History*, vol. 1, p. 158.

11 Nicholson, *The Gunners of Canada*, vol. 2, pp. 8-11.

12 Stacey, *Official History of the Canadian Army*, vol. 1, p. 43.

13 Wood, *Strange Battleground*, p. 37.

14 Canada, DND, *Report, 1953-1954*, p. 41.

Uniform

1 Strange, *Gunner Jingo's Jubilee*, p. 353.

2 *Standing Orders of the Provisional Brigade of Quebec Garrison Artillery, Volunteer Militia of Lower Canada, 1866*, pp. 4-7.

3 *Canada Gazette*, 4 March 1876, pp. 4-5. "Militia Dress Regulations."

4 Macdonald, *The History of the Dress*, plate 22.

5 Campbell, *The Dress of the Royal Artillery*, p. 24.

6 Canada, DMD, *Dress Regulations*, 1886, p. 6.

7 GO, 175(A), October 1912.

8 Canada, DMD, *Dress Regulations*, 1907, p. 25.

9 Nicholson, *The Gunners of Canada*, vol. 2, p. 144. Second photograph.

10 *Ibid.*, p. 22.

11 "Gunner Centennial," *Canadian Army Journal*, vol. 9, no. 3 (July 1955). Photograph.

12 Canada, Army, The Royal Regiment of Canadian Artillery, *Standing Orders*, 1963, p. 61.

THE CANADIAN FORCES

History

1 Eayrs, *In Defence of Canada*, vol. 1, p. 224. Currie to Meighen, 5 August 1920.

2 Canada, Laws, Statutes, etc., *Statutes of Canada, 1922*, p. 135. The National Defence Act, 1922.

3 Eayrs, *In Defence of Canada*, p. 231.

4 Order in Council, P.C. 2446, 24 November 1922.

5 Eayrs, *In Defence of Canada*, vol. 1, p. 335. Draft Order-in-Council, 24 October 1932.

6 Canada, DND, *White Paper on Defence*, March 1964, pp. 17-18.

7 *Ibid.*, p. 18.

8 *Ibid.*, p. 19.

9 Canada, Laws, Statutes, etc., *Statutes of Canada, 1966-1967*, p. 1283. Canadian Forces Reorganization Act, 1967.

Uniform

1 Lieutenant-Colonel N.A. Buckingham, Director of Ceremonial, for Chief of the Defence Staff, Ottawa, to J.L. Summers.

2 Canada, DND, *Provisional Dress Policy*, p. 1.

3 Canada, MND, *Dress Manual*, ss. 205, 206.

4 Wood, *Strange Battleground*, pp. 164-65.

Glossary

Aiguillette: a braided cord worn at the shoulder. During the seventeenth and eighteenth centuries, aiguillettes were worn, particularly by the cavalry. Beginning in 1731, cadets in the Compagnies franches de la Marine serving in Canada wore a blue and white aiguillette to distinguish them from the other ranks. British infantry officers wore an aiguillette of gold or silver (depending on the regiment) until 1768, when it was replaced by the epaulette. However, general and staff officers continued to wear the aiguillette well into the nineteenth century.

Busby: a fur cap worn by hussars, artillery, and engineers in the British service. The name derives from that of a firm of nineteenth-century military suppliers, "W. Busby, The Strand, London."

Cockade: a piece of cloth or leather attached to the headgear as a mark of national identification. The cockade came into wide use in the middle of the eighteenth century. That of France was either white or black until 1767, when white became mandatory. The cockade of Britain was black, that of Spain was red, and that of Holland was orange. Towards the end of the eighteenth century the troops of the United States adopted a black cockade with a small metal eagle. Although Canada has no national cockade, Canadian troops have worn those of Britain and France.

Dragoons: "a kind of cavalry, who serve both on horseback and on foot." (James, C., *A Universal Military Dictionary*, 1816). Originally a sort of mounted infantry, dragoons had become heavy cavalry by the eighteenth century. During the Seven Years' War, "light dragoon" regiments were raised by the British Army. From the beginning of the nineteenth century, light dragoon units made up of militia were authorized in Canada. For the first regular dragoon unit, see The Royal Canadian Dragoons.

Epaulette: fringed shoulder-piece, usually of gold or silver, worn to denote rank. French infantry officers wore epaulettes beginning in 1762; the British infantry adopted the epaulette in 1768. Epaulettes were sometimes worn by non-commissioned officers and other ranks in certain corps. For example, those of light dragoon units were authorized to wear yellow or white epaulettes in 1812.

Facing: the collar, cuffs, lapels, and turnbacks of a solider's coat, when a different colour from the rest of the uniform. The distinctive or facing colour is a means of identifying the unit. Facing is sometimes used to denote only the coat lapels.

Gorget: originally a piece of armour worn below the neck, the gorget became a crescent-shaped symbol of officer's rank worn in European armies by the mid-seventeenth century. By the mid-eighteenth century, the gorgets of the French service were usually gilt and bore the Royal Arms in silver. British gorgets were silver or gold, depending on the colour of the regimental lace, until 1796, when all gorgets were ordered to be gilt. The gorget was abolished in the British service in 1830. Used mainly as a symbol for the officer on duty, the gorget was adopted as a rank badge for militia officers during French regime in Canada.

Glengarry: Originally worn by Scottish regiments, the Glengarry cap was taken into general use by the British infantry in 1868, and by the Canadian militia during the 1870s.

Grenadiers: soldiers specially chosen and trained to throw grenades at the enemy. During the second half of the seventeenth century, soldiers were chosen from amongst the strongest and bravest men of a regiment, and were grouped into a separate grenadier company. The practice lasted long after grenades gradually became outmoded during the eighteenth century. Grenadiers usually wore caps rather than hats in order that they might more easily sling their muskets onto their backs, thus leaving both hands free for throwing grenades. In the British Army, bearskin caps were authorized for grenadiers in 1768.

Hussars: a type of light cavalry, of Hungarian origin, having particularly distinctive uniforms. Hussar-style uniforms patterned after that of the 13th Hussars of the British Army were adopted by several Canadian militia cavalry units during the 1860s and 1870s. Several of the hussar regiments still on the roll of the Canadian Forces were raised at that time. See, for example, The 8th Canadian Hussars (Princess Louise's).

Kilmarnock: a town in Scotland where the bonnets of the same name, used in the British service, have been made since at least 1800.

Kilt: Worn by Scottish highland units since the eighteenth century, the kilt of each corps was made up of a distinctive tartan. Derived from the ancient plaid, the kilt is worn today by several regiments of the Canadian Militia.

Lace: flat braid or tape used to trim uniforms. In the British service, lace also served as a regimental distinction. The lace worn by private soldiers was usually white interwoven with a pattern of coloured lines; that of officers was gold or silver. The lace was sewn onto the uniform in a set pattern. In 1855, lace was abolished from British infantry uniforms except to denote rank.

Lancers: a type of light cavalry, of Polish origin, armed with lances. Although lances were used by various Canadian cavalry units, there have never been Canadian lancer units as such.

Plaid (or Belted Plaid): traditional Scottish dress (*Breacan-an-fheilidh*) worn until the end of the eighteenth century. In the nineteenth century, the term came to denote a tartan scarf worn across the chest and over the left shoulder. It was worn by Scottish units throughout the British Empire.

Sabretache: a case or satchel used to carry documents. Worn by mounted officers and cavalrymen, it was especially popular in the early nineteenth century, but was no longer used by 1901. Officers' sabretaches were often lavishly decorated. Jacques Viger, an officer of The Provincial Corps of Light Infantry (Canadian Voltigeurs), entitled his diaries of the War of 1812 *Ma Saberdache*, an allusion to where he carried his notebooks.

Sash: a length of coloured material worn diagonally across the chest and over one shoulder or around the waist as a means of corps identification during the sixteenth and seventeenth centuries. As uniforms became simpler and less varied during the seventeenth century, the other ranks tended not to wear the sash, and in most armies it became an accessory only for officers. French officers wore white sashes until the beginning of the eighteenth century. British officers still wear their crimson sashes in full dress. British army sergeants wore a crimson sash with a centre stripe of regimental facing colour until 1845; since this date they have worn the plain crimson sash. Canada has no national sash; her soldiers wear British patterns.

Shako: headgear of Austro-Hungarian origin worn by British infantry units beginning in 1800. After many pattern changes, the shako was replaced by the spiked helmet in 1879. The various types of shako were adopted in Canada usually about one year after they appeared in Britain.

Sporran: a pouch or purse worn on the front of the kilt in Scottish regiments.

Sword-knot: a leather strap or cord fastened to the sword hilt and around the wrist of the wearer to prevent the loss of the sword during combat. During the eighteenth century, the sword-knot became more ornamental than practical. Officers in the British service have worn a gold and crimson sword-knot in full dress since 1768.

Touri: a small tuft or pom-pom worn on Scottish bonnets. The touri is usually red.

Voltigeurs: elite light infantry corps authorized by the French army on 19 September 1805. This corps inspired the name of The Provincial Corps of Light Infantry (Canadian Voltigeurs), raised in Canada during 1812. "Les Voltigeurs de Québec," raised in 1862, is still on the roll of the Canadian Militia.

Readers interested in a more detailed discussion of the terminology used in this book may wish to consult the following works:

Carman, William, Y. *Dictionary of Military Uniforms*. London: 1977.

Malibran, H. *Guide à l'usage des artistes et des costumiers contenant la description des uniformes de l'armée française de 1780 à 1848*. Paris: 1904.

Ross, David and René Chartrand. *Cataloguing Military Uniforms*. Saint John: 1977.

Bibliography

ARCHIVES AND MANUSCRIPT COLLECTIONS

CANADA

Archives nationales du Québec, Montreal: record books of notaries Foucher and J.-B. Adhemar.

Public Archives of Canada, Ottawa: Record Groups (RG) 8 and 9; Manuscript Groups (MG) 11 and 18. (The Public Archives of Canada also possess a large number of copies and microfilms of documents in French and British collections.)

Royal Canadian Mounted Police Museum, Regina: correspondence of superintendent J.M. Walsh.

Université de Montréal, Montreal: Collection Baby.

FRANCE

Archives de la Guerre, held in the château de Vincennes by the Service historique de l'armée française: series A1.

Archives nationales, Paris: series B, C11A, C11B, D26 and F1A of the Archives des Colonies; series B1 of the Archives de la Marine.

Bibliothèque du ministre des Armées, Paris: among the many manuscripts are *Les tiroirs de Louis XIV* and the superb volumes of plates, the *Collection des uniformes des troupes du roi, infanterie française et étrangère, 1757*, and the *Collection des drapeaux de l'infanterie française, 1741-1776*.

Bibliothèque nationale, Paris: Manuscript volume 4237 of the Fonds français and Collection Richelieu in the Cabinet des estampes.

GREAT BRITAIN

Army Museums Ogilby Trust, London: Benson-Freeman Papers.

National Library of Scotland, Edinburgh: manuscript acc. 406A.

Public Record Office, London: series War Office (WO) 1, 28 and 40.

BOOKS

Ainslie, Thomas.
Canada Preserved: The Journal of Captain Ainslie. Edited by Sheldon Cohen. Toronto: 1968.

Aleyrac, Jean-Baptiste d'.
Aventures militaires au XVIIIe siècle. Edited by Charles Coste. Paris: 1935.

Amherst, Jeffrey.
The Journal of Jeffrey Amherst. Edited by J.C. Webster. Chicago: 1931.

Anderson, E.J.; Dynes, R.J.; Gooding, S.J.; May, G.H.; Rowe, B.S.; Tweedie, G.A.
The Military Arms of Canada. West Hill, Ontario: 1963.

Aubert de Gaspé, Philippe.
Les anciens Canadiens. Québec: 1970. Originally published in 1863.

Barnes, R.M.
Military Uniforms of Britain and the Empire. London: 1960.

Baxter, John B.M.
Historical Records of the New Brunswick Regiment, Canadian Artillery. Saint John, New Brunswick: 1896.

Boss, William.
The Stormont, Dundas, and Glengarry Highlanders, 1783-1951. Ottawa: 1952.

A Brief History of the King's Royal Rifle Corps, 1755-1948. 3d ed. Aldershot, England: 1948.

Briquet, M. de.
Code militaire. Paris: 1761.

Butler, Lewis W.G.
The Annals of the King's Royal Rifle Corps. London: 1913-1932.

Campbell, D. Alastair.
The Dress of the Royal Artillery. London: 1971.

Canada, Army, Historical Section.
Introduction to the Study of Military History for Canadian Students. Edited by Charles P. Stacey. 3d ed. Ottawa: 1953.

Canada, Army, Royal Regiment of Canadian Artillery.
Standing Orders. 1963.

Canada, Army, The Royal Canadian Ordnance Corps.
Standing Orders. 1965.

Canada, Army, Royal 22e Regiment.
Standing Orders. 1963.

Canada, Department of Militia and Defence.
Dress Regulations for the Officers of the Canadian Militia. Ottawa: 4 March 1876.
Dress Regulations for the Officers of the Canadian Militia, 1907. Ottawa: 1907.
Dress Regulations for the Officers of the Canadian Militia, 1932. Ottawa: 1932.
Militia Circulars. Ottawa.
Militia General Orders and *General Orders.* Ottawa.
Regulations and Orders for the Militia of the Dominion of Canada, 1879. Ottawa: 1879.
Regulations and Orders for the Militia, Canada, 1883. Ottawa: 1883.
Regulations for the Clothing of the Canadian Militia. Ottawa: 1935.
Regulations Relating to the Issue of Uniform Clothing and Necessaries to the Volunteer Forces of Canada. Ottawa: 1866.

Canada, Department of Militia and Defence (continued).
Report, 1901. Sessional Papers, 35(a). Ottawa: 1902.
Report of the State of the Militia of the Dominion of Canada. Published annually in Ottawa.
Report upon the Suppression of the Rebellion in the North-West Territories by the Minister of Militia and Defence. Ottawa: 1886.
Supplementary Report, Organization, Equipment, Dispatch and Service of the Canadian Contingent During the War of South Africa, 1899-1900. Ottawa: 1901.
The Militia List of the Dominion of Canada. Published annually in Ottawa.

Canada, Department of National Defence.
Canadian Forces Dress Manual. PFC 265. Ottawa: 1973.
Provisional Dress Policy and Instructions; Introduction of the Canadian Forces Uniform. CFHQ Instruction CP 3/70. 3 April 1970.
Report for the Fiscal Year 1953-1954. Ottawa: 1954.
The Regiments and Corps of the Canadian Army. Ottawa: 1964.
White Paper on Defence. Ottawa: 1964.

Canada Gazette. Published daily in Ottawa.

Canada, Laws, Statutes, etc.
Acts of the Parliament of the Dominion of Canada, 1883. Ottawa: 1883.
Sessional Papers of the Dominion of Canada, 1911. Ottawa: 1911.
Statutes of Canada, 1922. Ottawa: 1922.
Statutes of Canada, 1966-1967. Ottawa: 1967.
Statutes of the Province of Canada. Quebec: 1855.

Canada, Militia Council.
Annual Report. Ottawa: 1910.

Canada (Province) Militia.
Standing Orders of the Provisional Brigade of Quebec Garrison Artillery, Volunteer Militia of Lower Canada. Montreal: 1866.

Canada, Royal North-West Mounted Police.
Report of the Commissioner. Ottawa: 1874-1881.

Canadian Cavalry Association.
Annual Report, no. 5. Ottawa: 1926.
Proceedings of the Canadian Cavalry Association, 1925.
Proceedings of the Canadian Cavalry Association, 1927.

Chambers, Ernest J.
The 5th Regiment, Royal Scots of Canada Highlanders. Toronto, (n.d.).
The Governor General's Body Guard. Toronto: 1902.
The Origin and Services of the 3rd (Montreal) Field Battery of Artillery. Montreal: 1898.
The Queen's Own Rifles of Canada. Toronto: 1901.
The Royal Grenadiers: a Regimental History of the 10th Infantry Regiment of the Active Militia of Canada. Toronto: 1904.
The Royal North-West Mounted Police: A Corps History. Montreal: 1906.

Champion, Thomas E.
History of the 10th Royals and of the Royal Grenadiers, from the Formation of the Regiment until 1896. Toronto: 1896.

Chichester, Henry M. and Burgess-Short, George.
The Records and Badges of Every Regiment and Corps in the British Army. London: 1970. (Facsimile of the 2d. ed. of 1900).

Chown, John D.
The 9-Pdr Muzzle Loading Rifle. Ottawa: 1967.

Christopher-Latham, R. and C.
Infantry Uniforms, 1855-1939. London: 1970.

Corrigall, David J.
The History of the Twentieth Canadian Battalion (Central Ontario Regiment) Canadian Expeditionary Force, in the Great War, 1914-1918. Toronto: 1935.

Crook, E.D. and Marteinson, J.K., eds.
A Pictorial History of the 8th Canadian Hussars (Princess Louise's). Petawawa, Ontario: 1973.

Daniel, Gabriel.
Histoire de la milice françoise. 2 vols. Paris: 1721.

Denison, Frederick. C.
Historical Records of the Governor-General's Body Guard, and its Standing Orders. Toronto: 1876.

Denison, George T.
Soldiering in Canada. Toronto: 1901.

Dollier de Casson.
Histoire du Montréal. Montreal: 1868. (Mémoires de la Société historique de Montréal, 4ᵉ livraison.)

Dornbusch, C.E.
The Canadian Army, 1855-1965. Cornwallville, New York: 1966.

Duguid, Archer Fortescue.
Official History of the Canadian Forces in the Great War, 1914-1919. Ottawa: 1947.

Eayrs, James G.
In Defence of Canada. Toronto: 1964.

Egan, Thomas J.
History of the Halifax Volunteer Battalion and Volunteer Companies, 1859-1887. Halifax: 1888.

État général des troupes françoises . . . sur pied en janvier 1753, n.p., n.d.

Fetherstonhaugh, R.C.
A Short History of the Royal Canadian Dragoons. Toronto: 1932.
The Royal Canadian Regiment, 1883-1933. Montreal: 1936.

Fortescue, John W.
A History of the British Army. London: 1899-1930.

Fraser, Alexander.
The 48th Highlanders of Toronto Canadian Militia. Toronto: 1900.

Goodspeed, Donald J.
Battle Royal: A History of the Royal Regiment of Canada, 1862-1962. Toronto: 1962.

Gould, L.M.
From B.C. to Baisieux: Being the Narrative History of the 102nd Canadian Infantry Battalion. Victoria: 1919.

Grierson, James M.
Records of the Scottish Volunteer Force 1859-1908. London: 1972. (Facsimile of the edition of 1909.)

Guignard, M. de.
L'école de Mars. Paris: 1725.

Hahn, J.E.
The Intelligence Service within the Canadian Corps, 1914-1918. Toronto: 1930.

Hamilton, Edward P., ed.
Adventure in the Wilderness: the American Journals of Louis-Antoine de Bougainville, 1756-1760. Norman, Oklahoma: 1964.

Haswell Miller, A.E. and Dawnay, N.P.
Military Drawings and Paintings in the Royal Collection. London: 1966-1970.

Hesketh, Christian.
Tartans. London: 1961.

Hitsman, J.M.
The Incredible War of 1812. Toronto: 1965.

Hodder-Williams, Ralph W.
Princess Patricia's Canadian Light Infantry, 1914-1919. Toronto: 1923.

Hutchinson, Paul P.
Canada's Black Watch: The First Hundred Years 1862-1962. Montreal: 1962.

How, Douglas.
The 8th Hussars. Sussex, New Brunswick: 1964.

Instruction sur la façon et traitement d'un justaucorps de soldat, du 29 janvier 1747. Paris: 1747.

Irving, L. Homfray.
Officers of the British Forces in Canada during the War 1812-15. Welland, Ontario: 1908.

J.C.B.
Voyage au Canada dans le nord de l'Amérique septentrionale fait depuis l'an 1751 à 1761. Quebec: 1887.

Kerry, A.J. and McDill, W.A.
The History of the Corps of Royal Canadian Engineers. Ottawa: 1962.

Knox, John.
An Historical Journal of the Campaigns in North America. Edited by Arthur G. Doughty. Toronto: 1914.

La Chesnaye-Desbois, François-Alexandre Aubert de.
Dictionnaire militaire. 2 vols. Dresden: 1751.

La Chesnaye-Desbois, François-Alexandre Aubert de and Badier.
Dictionnaire de la noblesse. Paris: 1863-1876.

La Hontan, Baron de.
New Voyages to North America. Edited and annotated by R.G. Twaites. Chicago: 1905.
Voyages du Baron de La Hontan dans l'Amérique septentrionale. Montreal: 1974. (Reprint of the edition of 1705.)

La Pause, Jean-Guillaume-Charles de Plantavit de Margon, chevalier de.
"Les 'Mémoires' du chevalier de La Pause." *Rapport de l'archiviste de la province de Québec pour 1932-1933.* pp. 305-91. Quebec: 1933.
"Les 'Papiers' La Pause." *Rapport de l'archiviste de la province de Québec pour 1933-1934.* pp. 65-231. Québec: 1934.
"Mémoire et observations sur mon voyage en Canada," dans *Rapport de l'archiviste de la province de Québec pour 1931-1932.* pp. 3-125. Quebec: 1932.

Lawson, Cecil C.P.
A History of the Uniforms of the British Army. London: 1940-1967.

Lelièpvre, Eugène.
Les troupes françaises au Canada, 1755-1760. 8 plates. Paris: 1961-1964.

Lettres et mémoires pour servir à l'histoire naturelle, civile et politique du Cap Breton depuis son établissement jusqu'à la reprise de cette isle par les Anglois en 1758. La Haye: 1966. (Reprint of the edition of 1760.)
A List of His Majesty's Land Forces in North America, with the Rank of the Officers in the Regiment and Army. New York: 1761.

McAvity, J.M.
Strathcona's 1939-'45: A record of Achievement. Toronto: 1947.

Macdonald, R.J.
The History of the Dress of the Royal Regiment of Artillery, 1625-1897. London: 1899.

MacPhail, Andrew.
Official history of the Canadian Forces in the Great War 1914-1919: The Medical Services. Ottawa: 1925.

Margerand, J.
Armement et équipement de l'infanterie française du XVIᵉ au XXᵉ siècle. Paris: 1945.

Marquis, Thomas G.
Canada's Sons on Kopje and Veldt. Toronto: 1900.

Massé, C.H.
The Predecessors of the Royal Army Service Corps. Aldershot, England: 1948.

Mercier, Francois Le.
"Relation de ce qui s'est passé en la Nouvelle-France ès années 1664 et 1665," in *Relations des Jésuites.* vol. 3, Relation 1665, p. 10. Quebec: 1858.
"Relation de ce qui s'est passé en la Nouvelle-France ès années 1665 et 1666," dans *Relations des Jésuites.* vol. 3. Relation 1666, pp. 7-9. Quebec: 1858.

Middleton, Frederick D.
Suppression of the Rebellion in the North West Territories of Canada, 1885. Edited by G.H. Needler. Toronto: 1948.

Milleville, Henry-J.-G. de.
Armorial historique de la noblesse de France. Paris: [1846?].

Moir, John S., ed.
History of the Royal Canadian Corps of Signals, 1903-1961. Ottawa: 1962.

Montandre-Lonchamps, de and de Montandre.
État militaire de France. Paris: 1758, 1759, 1760.

Nicholson, Gerald W.L.
The Canadian Expeditionary Force, 1914-1919. Ottawa: 1963.
The Fighting Newfoundlander. n.p., n.d.
The Gunners of Canada. Toronto: 1967.
The Official History of the Canadian Army in the Second World War. vol. 2. Ottawa: 1956.

O'Callaghan, E.B., ed.
Documents Relative to the Colonial History of the State of New York. Albany, New York: 1853-1887.

Pargelis, Stanley.
Lord Loudoun in North America, New Haven, Connecticut and London: 1933.
Military Affairs in North America, 1748-1765. New York: 1936.

Parkman, Francis.
Montcalm and Wolfe. New York: 1966. (paperback edition).

Peyrins, Étienne-Claude Beneton de Morange de.
Traité des marques nationales. Paris: 1739.

Phillips, R. and Kirby, S.J.
Small Arms of the Mounted Police. Ottawa: 1965.

Pouchot, Pierre.
Memoir Upon the Late War in North America, between the French and English, 1755-60. Translated and edited by Franklin B. Hough. Roxbury, Massachusetts: 1866.

Quebec Gazette. Published weekly in Quebec.

Récher, Jean-Félix.
Journal du siège de Québec en 1759. Quebec: 1759.

Regimental Executive Committee.
Princess Patricia's Canadian Light Infantry Recruit's Book.
Edmonton: 1957.

Reid, William S.
The Scottish Traditions in Canada. Toronto: 1976.

Robertson, Peter.
Relentless Verity: Canadian Military Photographers Since 1885.
Toronto: 1973.

Robson, J.O.
The Uniform of the London Scottish, 1859-1959. London: 1960.

Rogers, H.C.B.
Weapons of the British Soldier. London: 1960.

Rousselot, Lucien.
L'armée française, ses uniformes, son armement, son équipement. Plate
19. Paris: 1944.

Roy, Pierre-Georges, ed.
*Inventaire des testaments, donations et inventaires du régime français con-
servés aux Archives judiciaires de Québec.* 3 vols. Québec: 1941.

Roy, Régis and Malchelosse, Gérard.
Le régiment de Carignan. Montreal: 1925.

The Royal Welch Fusiliers, 23rd Foot. London: 1969.

Salone, Émile.
La colonisation de la Nouvelle-France. Paris: 1906.

Smith, Charles H.
Costumes of the Army of the British Empire. London: 1815.

Squires, W. Austin.
The 104th Regiment of Foot (The New Brunswick Regiment) 1803-1817.
Fredericton, New Brunswick: 1962.

Stacey, Charles P.
The Official History of the Canadian Army in the Second World War.
vols 1 and 3. Ottawa: 1955-1960.
Quebec, 1759: The Siege and the Battle. Toronto: 1959.

Stanley, George F.G.
Canada's Soldiers. 3d ed. Toronto: 1974.
Canada Invaded 1775-1776. Toronto: 1973.
New France, The Last Phase, 1744-1760. Toronto: 1968.

Stevens, G.R.
Princess Patricia's Canadian Light Infantry, 1919-1957. Griesbach,
Alberta: [1958].

Stewart, Charles H.
The Service of British Regiments in Canada and North America.
Ottawa: 1964.

Stewart, David.
*Sketches of the Character, Manners, and Present State of the
Highlanders in Scotland.* Edinburgh: 1822.

Strachan, Hew.
British Military Uniforms 1768-96. London: 1975.

Strange, Thomas B.
Gunner Jingo's Jubilee. 3d ed. London: 1896.

Susane, Louis.
Histoire de l'ancienne infanterie française. Paris: 1849-1853.

Swettenham, John A.
To Seize the Victory: the Canadian Corps in World War I. Toronto:
c. 1965.

Thompson, James.
*A Short Authentic Account of the Expedition Against Quebec in the
Year 1759, under Command of Major-General Wolfe by a Volunteer
upon that Expedition.* Québec: 1872.

**Upper Canada Historical Arms Society, Research
Committee.**
The Military Arms of Canada. West Hill, Ontario: 1963.

Wallace, Nesbit W.
*A Regimental Chronicle and List of Officers of the 60th, or the King's
Royal Rifle Corps, formerly the 62nd, or the Royal American Regiment of
Foot.* London: 1879.

Warren, A.
*Wait for the Waggon: The Story of the Royal Canadian Army Service
Corps.* Toronto: 1961.

Waugh, Nora.
The Cut of Men's Clothes 1600-1900. London: 1964.

Webber, David A.
Skinner's Fencibles: The Royal Newfoundland Regiment, 1795-1802.
St. John's, Newfoundland: 1964.

Williams, Jeffery.
Princess Patricia's Canadian Light Infantry. London: 1972.

Wood, Herbert F.
*Strange Battleground: The Operations in Korea and their Effects on the
Defence Policy of Canada.* Ottawa: 1966.

Worthington, Larry.
The Spur and the Sprocket. Gagetown, New Brunswick: 1968.

ARTICLES

Atkinson, C.T.
"British Forces in North America 1774-1781." *Journal of the Society for Army Historical Research*, vol. 16, no. 61 (1937), pp. 3-23.

Baxter, G.W.R.
"RCOC Diamond Jubilee, Sixty Glorious Years: 1903-1963." *Canadian Army Journal*, vol. 17, no. 1 (1963).

Boudriot, Jean.
"Le port d'Antibes peint par Joseph Vernet en 1756." *Neptunia*, 3d quarter, no. 111 (1973), pp. 8-20.

Cattley, A.R.
"The British Infantry Shako." *Journal of the Society for Army Historical Research*, vol. 15, no. 60 (1936), pp. 188-208.

Disher, Arthur L.
"The Long March of the Yukon Field Force." *The Beaver*, Fall 1962.

Edwards, Joseph P.
"The Militia of Nova Scotia, 1749-1867." *Collections of the Nova Scotia Historical Society*, vol. 17 (1913), pp. 63-109.

Gazette de France, no. 62, 15 May 1665, pp. 510-11.

"Gunner Centennial." *Canadian Army Journal*, vol. 9, no. 3 (1955).

Haarmann, Albert W. and Holst, Donald W.
"The Frederick von Germann Drawings of Troops in the American Revolution." *Military Collector and Historian*, vol. 16, no. 1 (1964), pp. 1-9.

"How to Fight Brother Jonathan." *The Museum of Foreign Literature, Science, and Art*, vol. 42, May-August 1841, pp. 210-14.

Howe, Jonas.
"The King's New Brunswick Regiment 1793-1802." *Collections of the New Brunswick Historical Society*, vol. 1 (1894), pp. 13-62.

Illustrated London News, 10 March 1860, supplement.

Le Couteur, John.
"A Winter March in Canada, in 1813." *United Service Journal and Naval and Military Magazine* (1831), pt. 3, pp. 177-87.

Lindsay, William.
"Narrative of the Invasion of Canada by the American Provincials." *The Canadian Review and Magazine* (1826), no. 5.

McBarron, H. Charles and Todd, Frederick P.
"British 84th Regiment of Foot (Royal Highland Emigrants), 1775-1783." *Military Collector and Historian*, vol. 11, no. 4 (1959), p. 109.

Manuel, T.C.
"Chart of Hereditary Descendancy, The Royal Canadian Ordnance Corps." *Canadian Army Journal*, vol. 18, no. 3 (1964).

Navy and Army Illustrated, vol. 6, no. 61, p. 48.

Pratt, F.W.
"Fifty Years of Canadian Military Communications." *Canadian Army Journal*, vol. 3, no. 3 (1953).

Rousselot, Lucien.
"Manuscrit de Tarascon." *Carnet de la Sabretache* (1972), no. 12, pp. 35-36.

The Springbok, Winter, 1968.

Stanley, George F.G.
"The New Brunswick Fencibles." *Canadian Defence Quarterly*, vol. 16, no. 1 (1935), p. 39.

Stewart, Charles H.
"Glengarry Light Infantry Regiment 1812-1816." *Military Collector and Historian*, vol. 16, no. 2 (1964), pp. 53-56.

Summer, Percy.
"Uniforms of the Rifle Brigade, circa 1804." *Journal of the Society for Army Historical Research*, vol. 20, no. 77 (1941), pp. 38-42.

Turcotte, Lucien.
"Le Royal 22ᵉ Régiment, 1914-1964." *Journal de l'Armée canadienne*, vol. 18, no. 2 (1964).

Index